FREE Test Taking Tips DVD Offer

To help us better serve you, we have developed a Test Taking Tips DVD that we would like to give you for <u>FREE</u>. **This DVD covers world-class test taking tips that you can use to be even more successful when you are taking your test.**

All that we ask is that you email us your feedback about your study guide. Please let us know what you thought about it – whether that is good, bad or indifferent.

To get your **FREE Test Taking Tips DVD**, email <u>freedvd@studyguideteam.com</u> with "FREE Test Taking Tips DVD" in the subject line and the following information in the body of the email:

    a.   The title of your study guide.

    b.   Your product rating on a scale of 1-5, with 5 being the highest rating.

    c.   Your feedback about the study guide. What did you think of it?

    d.   Your full name and shipping address to send your free DVD.

If you have any questions or concerns, please don't hesitate to contact us at <u>freedvd@studyguideteam.com</u>.

Thanks again!

AP World History
Study Guide 2016

Table of Contents

Quick Overview

As you draw closer to taking your exam, preparing becomes more and more important. Thankfully, you have this study guide to help you get ready. Use this guide to help keep your studying on track and refer to it often.

This study guide contains several key sections that will help you be successful on your exam. The guide contains tips for what you should do the night before and the day of the test. Also included are test-taking tips. Knowing the right information is not always enough. Many well-prepared test takers struggle with exams. These tips will help equip you to accurately read, assess, and answer test questions.

A large part of the guide is devoted to showing you what content to expect on the exam and to helping you better understand that content. Near the end of this guide is a practice test so that you can see how well you have grasped the content. Then, answers explanations are provided so that you can understand why you missed certain questions.

Don't try to cram the night before you take your exam. This is not a wise strategy for a few reasons. First, your retention of the information will be low. Your time would be better used by reviewing information you already know rather than trying to learn lots of new information. Second, you will likely become stressed as you try to gain large amount of knowledge in a short amount of time. Third, you will be depriving yourself of sleep. So be sure to go to bed at a reasonable time the night before. Being well-rested helps you focus and remain calm.

Be sure to eat a substantial breakfast the morning of the exam. If you are taking the exam in the afternoon, be sure to have a good lunch as well. Being hungry is distracting and can make it difficult to focus. You have hopefully spent lots of time preparing for the exam. Don't let an empty stomach get in the way of success!

When travelling to the testing center, leave earlier than needed. That way, you have a buffer in case you experience any delays. This will help you remain calm and will keep you from missing your appointment time at the testing center.

Be sure to pace yourself during the exam. Don't try to rush through the exam. There is no need to risk performing poorly on the exam just so you can leave the testing center early. Allow yourself to use all of the allotted time if needed.

Remain positive while taking the exam even if you feel like you are performing poorly. Thinking about the content you should have mastered will not help you perform better on the exam.

Once the exam is complete, take some time to relax. Even if you feel that you need to take the exam again, you will be well served by some down time before you begin studying again. It's often easier to convince yourself to study if you know that it will come with a reward!

Test-Taking Strategies

1. Predicting the Answer

When you feel confident in your preparation for a multiple-choice test, try predicting the answer before reading the answer choices. This is especially useful on questions that test objective factual knowledge or that ask you to fill in a blank. By predicting the answer before reading the available choices, you eliminate the possibility that you will be distracted or led astray by an incorrect answer choice. You will feel much more confident in your selection if you read the question, predict the answer, and then find your prediction among the answer choices. After using this strategy, be sure to still read all of the answer choices carefully and completely. If you feel unprepared, you should not attempt to predict the answers. This would be a waste of time and an opportunity for your mind to wander in the wrong direction.

2. Reading the Whole Question

Too often, test takers scan a multiple-choice question, recognize a few familiar words, and immediately jump to the answer choices. Test authors are aware of this common impatience, and they will sometimes prey upon it. For instance, a test author might subtly turn the question into a negative, or he or she might redirect the focus of the question right at the end. The only way to avoid falling into these traps is to read the entirety of the question carefully before reading the answer choices.

3. Looking for Wrong Answers

Long and complicated multiple-choice questions can be intimidating. One way to simplify a difficult multiple-choice question is to eliminate all of the answer choices that are clearly wrong. In most sets of answers, there will be at least one selection that can be dismissed right away. If the test is administered on paper, the test taker could draw a line through it to indicate that it may be ignored; otherwise, the test taker will have to perform this operation mentally or on scratch paper. In either case, once the obviously incorrect answers have been eliminated, the remaining choices may be considered. Sometimes identifying the clearly wrong answers will give the test taker some information about the correct answer. For instance, if one of the remaining answer choices is a direct opposite of one of the eliminated answer choices, it may well be the correct answer. The opposite of obviously wrong is obviously right! Of course, this is not always the case. Some answers are obviously incorrect simply because they are irrelevant to the question being asked. Still, identifying and eliminating some incorrect answer choices is a good way to simplify a multiple-choice question.

4. Don't Overanalyze

Anxious test takers often overanalyze questions. When you are nervous, your brain will often run wild causing you to make associations and discover clues that don't actually exist. If you feel that this may be a problem for you, do whatever you can to slow down during the test. Try taking a deep breath or counting to ten. As you read and consider the question, restrict yourself to the particular words used by the author. Avoid thought tangents about what the author *really* meant, or what he or she was *trying* to say. The only things that matter on a multiple-choice test are the words that are actually in the question. You must avoid reading too much into a multiple-choice question, or supposing that the writer meant something other than what he or she wrote.

5. No Need for Panic

It is wise to learn as many strategies as possible before taking a multiple-choice test, but it is likely that you will come across a few questions for which you simply don't know the answer. In this situation, avoid panicking. Because most multiple-choice tests include dozens of questions, the relative value of a single wrong answer is small. Moreover, your failure on one question has no effect on your success elsewhere on the test. As much as possible, you should compartmentalize each question on a multiple-choice test. In other words, you should not allow your feelings about one question to affect your success on the others. When you find a question that you either don't understand or don't know how to answer, just take a deep breath and do your best. Read the entire question slowly and carefully. Try rephrasing the question a couple of different ways. Then, read all of the answer choices carefully. After eliminating obviously wrong answers, make a selection and move on to the next question.

6. Confusing Answer Choices

When working on a difficult multiple-choice question, there may be a tendency to focus on the answer choices that are the easiest to understand. Many people, whether consciously or not, gravitate to the answer choices that require the least concentration, knowledge, and memory. This is a mistake. When you come across an answer choice that is confusing, you need to give it extra attention. A question might be confusing because you do not know the subject matter to which it refers. If this is the case, don't eliminate the answer before you have affirmatively settled on another. When you come across an answer choice of this type, set it aside as you look at the remaining choices. If you can confidently assert that one of the other choices is correct, you can leave the confusing answer aside. Otherwise, you will need to take a moment to try to better understand the confusing answer choice. Rephrasing is one way to tease out the sense of a confusing answer choice.

7. Your First Instinct

Many people struggle with multiple-choice tests because they overthink the questions. If you have studied sufficiently for the test, you should be prepared to trust your first instinct once you have carefully and completely read the question and all of the answer choices. There is a great deal of research to suggest that the mind can come to the correct conclusion very quickly once it has obtained all of the relevant information. At times, it may seem to you as if your intuition is working faster even than your reasoning mind. This may in fact be true. The knowledge you obtain while studying may be retrieved from your subconscious before you have a chance to work out the associations that support it. Verify your instinct by working out the reasons that it should be trusted.

8. Key Words

Many test takers struggle with multiple-choice questions because they have poor reading comprehension skills. Quickly reading and understanding a multiple-choice question requires a mixture of skill and experience. To help with this, try jotting down a few key words and phrases on a piece of scrap paper. Doing this concentrates the process of reading and forces the mind to weigh the relative importance of the question's parts. In selecting words and phrases to write down, the test taker thinks about the question more deeply and carefully. This is especially true for multiple-choice questions that are preceded by a long prompt.

9. Subtle Negatives

One of the oldest tricks in the multiple-choice test writer's book is to subtly reverse the meaning of a question with a word like *not* or *except*. If you are not paying attention to each word in the question, you can easily be led astray by this trick. For instance, a common question format is, "Which of the following is...?" Obviously, if the question instead is, "Which of the following is not....?," then the answer will be quite different. Even worse, the test makers are aware of the potential for this mistake and will include one answer choice that would be correct if the question were not negated or reversed. A test taker who misses the reversal will find what he or she believes to be a correct answer and will be so confident that he or she will fail to reread the question and discover the original error. The only way to avoid this is to practice a wide variety of multiple-choice questions and to pay close attention to each and every word.

10. Reading Every Answer Choice

It may seem obvious, but you should always read every one of the answer choices! Too many test takers fall into the habit of scanning the question and assuming that they understand the question because they recognize a few key words. From there, they pick the first answer choice that answers the question they believe they have read. Test takers who read all of the answer choices might discover that one of the latter answer choices is actually *more* correct. Moreover, reading all of the answer choices can remind you of facts related to the question that can help you arrive at the correct answer. Sometimes, a misstatement or incorrect detail in one of the latter answer choices will trigger your memory of the subject and will enable you to find the right answer. Failing to read all of the answer choices is like not reading all of the items on a restaurant menu. You might miss out on the perfect choice.

11. Spot the Hedges

One of the keys to success on multiple-choice tests is paying close attention to every word. This is never more true than with words like *almost, most, some,* and *sometimes.* These words are called "hedges", because they indicate that a statement is not totally true or not true in every place and time. An absolute statement will contain no hedges, but in many subjects, like literature and history, the answers are not always straightforward. There are always exceptions to the rules in these subjects. For this reason, you should favor those multiple-choice questions that contain hedging language. The presence of qualifying words indicates that the author is taking special care with his or her words, which is certainly important when composing the right answer. After all, there are many ways to be wrong, but there is only one way to be right! For this reason, it is wise when taking a multiple-choice test to avoid answers that are absolute. An absolute answer is one that says things are either all one way or all another. They often include words like *every, always, best,* and *never.* If you are taking a multiple-choice test in a subject that doesn't lend itself to absolute answers, be on your guard if you see any of these words.

12. Long Answers

In many subject areas, the answers are not simple. As already mentioned, the right answer often requires hedges. Another common feature of the answers to a complex or subjective question are qualifying clauses, which are groups of words that subtly modify the meaning of the sentence. If the question or answer choice describes a rule to which there are exceptions or the subject matter is complicated, ambiguous, or confusing, the correct answer will require many words in order to be expressed clearly and accurately. In essence, you should not be deterred by answer choices that seem excessively long. Oftentimes, the author of the text will not be able to write the correct answer without offering some qualifications and modifications. As a test taker, your job is to read the answer choices thoroughly and completely and to select the one that most accurately and precisely answers the question.

13. Restating to Understand

Sometimes, a question on a multiple-choice test is difficult not because of what it asks but because of how it is written. If this is the case, restate the question or answer choice in different words. This process serves a couple of important purposes. First, it forces you to concentrate on the core of the question. In order to rephrase the question accurately, you have to understand it well. Rephrasing the question will concentrate your mind on the key words and ideas. Second, it will present the information to your mind in a fresh way. This process may trigger your memory of some useful scrap of information picked up while studying.

14. True Statements

Sometimes an answer choice will be true in itself, but it does not answer the question. This is one of the main reasons why it is essential to read the question carefully and completely before proceeding to the answer choices. Too often, test takers skip ahead to the answer choices and look for true statements. Having found one of these, they are content to select it without reference to the question above. Obviously, this provides an easy way for test makers to play tricks. The savvy test taker will always read the entire question before turning to the answer choices. Then, having settled on a correct answer choice, he or she will refer to the original question and ensure that the selected answer is relevant. The mistake of choosing a correct-but-irrelevant answer choice is especially common on questions related to specific pieces of objective knowledge, like historical or scientific facts. A prepared test taker will have a wealth of factual knowledge at his or her disposal, but may be careless in its application.

15. No Patterns

One of the more dangerous ideas that circulate about multiple-choice tests is that the correct answers tend to fall into patterns. These erroneous ideas range from a belief that B and C are the most common right answers, to the idea that an unprepared test-taker should answer "A-B-A-C-A-D-A-B-A." It cannot be emphasized enough that pattern-seeking of this type is exactly the WRONG way to approach a multiple-choice test. To begin with, it is highly unlikely that the test maker will plot the correct answers according to some predetermined pattern. The questions are scrambled and delivered in a random order. Furthermore, even if the test maker was following a pattern in the assignation of correct answers, there is no reason why the test maker would know which pattern he or she was using. Any attempt to discern a pattern in the answer choices is a waste of time and a distraction from the real work of taking the test. A test taker would be much better served by extra preparation before the test than by reliance on a pattern in the answers.

World History

Prehistory to 1400

Prehistory

The Paleolithic period is the earliest period of human development, as well as the longest. It is also commonly referred to as the Old Stone Age. It lasted from about 2 million years ago until between 40,000 and 10,000 years ago. Development during this period was excruciatingly slow. The Paleolithic period is usually divided into three sections: the Lower, Middle, and Upper. The Lower Paleolithic period is characterized by the appearance of stone tools; the chopping tools found at the Olduvai Gorge in Tanzania are from this period, and date back over a million years. They were probably made by Australopithecus, an ancestor of modern humans. Anthropologists have also found stone tools believed to have been made by Homo erectus between 100,000 and 500,000 years ago.

The Middle Paleolithic period occurred between 100,000 and 40,000 years ago. During this time, the Mousterian culture of Neanderthal men was active in Europe, North Africa, Palestine, and Siberia. These ancestors of modern man lived in caves and had the use of fire. They hunted prehistoric mammals and had slightly more sophisticated tools than their forebears, including crude needles for sewing furs together. These people may have practiced some sort of religion. In the Upper Paleolithic period, Neanderthals were replaced by varieties of Homo sapiens, including Cro-Magnon man and Grimaldi man. A number of diverse cultures flourished during this period, and the first man-made shelters arose. This was also the period in which people first crafted jewelry and illustrated drawings on the walls of caves.

During the Upper Paleolithic period, hunters entered Europe from the east and conquered the more primitive cultures living there. These victorious hunters were known as the Solutreans. These people are noted for their fine spearheads which they used to hunt wild horses. The Solutreans were in turn replaced by the Magdelenians, the most advanced phase of the Paleolithic period. The Magdalenians subsisted mainly through fishing and reindeer hunting. They developed extremely precise tools and sophisticated weapons, such as the atlatl: a device that made it possible to throw a spear over a great distance. Most of all, though, the Magdalenians are known for their cave paintings in modern-day France.

The Mesolithic period, otherwise known as the Middle Stone Age, began roughly 10,000 years ago and ended with the introduction of farming (dates vary by culture). In some areas, the use of farming was already beginning at the end of the Paleolithic era, and therefore there may not be a true Mesolithic period. The most extense examples of this kind of culture are found in Northern Europe, where the end of the Ice Age created much greater changes in the ability to live off of the land. The remains of the Mesolithic period are mainly just middens (rubbish heaps), as well as some deforestation. The people of the Mesolithic period made small tools out of flint; fishing tackle, canoes, and bows have been found at some sites.

The Neolithic period, also known as the New Stone Age, refers to that stage of human cultural evolution in which man developed stone tools, settled in villages, and began making crafts. In order to begin living in towns, man had to learn how to domesticate animals and sustain agriculture; formerly, in the Paleolithic and Mesolithic periods, man had subsisted through hunting, fishing, and gathering. The Neolithic period is said to end when urban civilizations began, or when metal tools or writing began. Because the designation Neolithic depends on these factors, anthropologists date its occurrence differently for different regions and populations. At present, anthropologists believe that the earliest Neolithic culture was in southwest Asia between 8,000 and 6,000 B.C.

Most anthropologists date the beginning of Neolithic culture at somewhere between 8,000 and 6,000 B.C. It began with the domestication of plants (wheat, barley, and millet) and animals (cattle, sheep, and goats). The Neolithic culture in the valley between the Tigris and Euphrates Rivers gradually evolved into a more urban civilization by 3,500 B.C. Meanwhile, Neolithic cultural advances spread through Europe, the Nile Valley, the Indus Valley, and the Huang He Valley. In these regions, the innovations of the Neolithic period were intermixed with the particulars of the region; in the Huang He region, for instance, rice cultivation was a product of advances in agriculture. By 1,500 B.C., Neolithic culture had spread to Mexico and South America. In these areas, corn, beans, and squash were the major crops.

Early Mesopotamian Civilizations

Mesopotamia, the region between the Tigris and Euphrates Rivers in what is now considered the Middle East, contained several different early civilizations of which the Sumerians were one of the more prominent. They developed the system of writing known as cuneiform, by which they elaborated their theories on mathematics and astronomy. The Sumerians also had a detailed system of laws and traded widely with other groups throughout the region. They even traded with civilizations as far away as Egypt and India. There was no coin or currency system at this time, thus trade was conducted on the barter system, in which goods are exchanged for one another, directly.

The incredible engineering skills of the Egyptians are most famously displayed in the pyramids clustered along the Nile River. These were built roughly between 2,700 and 2,500 B.C. The largest of the structures, the Khufu pyramid at Giza, is estimated to have taken 20 years and 100,000 laborers to construct. Today, it stands at 450 feet; some of its height has been lost to erosion. These pyramids were built as burial sites for the pharaohs, who were believed to continue their rule in the after-life. Peasants worked on the pyramids in exchange for food and shelter. The shape of the pyramids was meant to symbolize the slanting rays of the sun, with sloping sides meant to help the ka (soul) of the pharaoh climb to the sky and join the gods.

After the Sumerian civilization declined, the next dominant civilization was Babylon. The Babylonians conquered the Sumerians and established a city on the Euphrates River in approximately 1,750 B.C. One of the most famous Babylonian rulers was Hammurabi, who established the famous Code, an extremely detailed set of laws. This marked the first time that a set of rules governing every aspect of social life was applied to an entire people. The Babylonians are also known for their construction of ziggurats, long pyramid-like structures that were used as religious temples. Over time, the Babylonians acquired a reputation as a sensuous and hedonistic people, and the name Babylon has come to stand for any debauched civilization.

Judaism was founded in the 20th century B.C. by a man named Abraham, who was chosen to enter into a covenant with God, whereby he would receive special treatment in exchange for obedience and worship. Abraham then moved to Canaan (present-day Lebanon). Later, his descendants would move to Egypt and be enslaved, before being eventually liberated by God through the leader Moses and reconquering Canaan. Moses received from God a set of strict laws, known as the Ten Commandments. All of this is described in the Torah, the essential Jewish Scripture. There are also several other important books, including the Talmud, and many important commentaries by learned Jewish theologians.

Around the year 1,020 B.C., the Hebrew leader Saul became the first king of the nation known as Israel. He was succeeded by King David, who conquered the important city of Jerusalem. In the 10th century B.C., King Solomon built the first Jewish Temple in Jerusalem, which was used to house the Ark of the Covenant which contained the twin tablets of commandments and other religious artifacts. Israel would be taken over by the Assyrians in the 8th century B.C., and later by the Babylonians. Finally, in 538 B.C., the Persian King Cyrus allowed the Jews to return to Jerusalem and rebuild the Temple. Israel would subsequently be taken over by the Greeks under Alexander, and later by the Romans under Pompey Magnus.

Hellenistic Age

Ancient Greece was dominated by two city-states, Athens and Sparta. These two had very distinct cultures. Athens was a coastal city with a democratic form of government which amassed wealth by trading overseas. Athens is also known as the city that gave life to philosophy and the arts. Socrates engaged in his famous dialogues in the streets of Athens, and though he was eventually executed by the Athenian government for supposedly corrupting the youth, his thoughts achieved immortality in the writings of his student Plato. In turn, Plato's student Aristotle developed a strict form of reasoning that has formed the basis of much subsequent Western thought. Athens is also renowned for the architectural marvel that is the Parthenon.

While Athens was known for its devotion to the arts and its democratic form of government, its rival city-state Sparta was devoted to agriculture and the military. Sparta was not located on the coast, and therefore the Spartans had little contact with distant peoples. Spartan society was governed by a strict class system. Most people (helots) worked the land of other people as virtual serfs. In the upper classes, participation in military training was compulsory. Indeed, Spartan youths left their families to begin military training at a young age. The Spartans did not produce any noteworthy philosophers, but as a culture they stressed the good of the group over that of the individual. This is in stark contrast to most Athenian thought, which celebrates the achievements of the individual.

The Periclean Age in Greece, so named because Pericles was the leader of Athens during the period, took place in the fifth century B.C. It was during this period that most of the great contributions to Western culture were made, including the philosophy of Socrates, the medical work of Hippocrates, and the great dramatic works of Aeschlyus, Sophocles, and Euripides. The Hellenistic Age (4th century B.C.), on the other hand, is more commonly known for the military conquests made by Alexander the Great. If it were not for the conquests of Alexander during the Hellenistic Age, many of the innovations and achievements of the Periclean Age may not have had such a great influence on the West. It should be noted that the Hellenistic Age was not without its own great thinkers; in fact, Alexander studied as a boy under Aristotle.

During the Age of Pericles, an alliance of Greek city-states was challenged by the mighty Persians. Miraculously, the outnumbered Greeks were able to defeat the Persians at Thermopylae and Marathon, and staved off conquest. The war with the Persians impoverished the Greeks, however, and increased rivalries among the city-states. In Athens, the requirements for citizenship were loosened, though slavery remained. Conflict between Sparta and Athens culminated in the Peloponnesian War, won by Sparta. Eventually, the whole of Greece would be conquered by Philip of Macedon, who allowed the Greeks to maintain their culture and traditions. Alexander the Great was the son of Philip and became the master of an empire larger than any the world had ever seen. During his reign, he united many disparate peoples through a common law and exchange policy. He died at the age of 33, and his empire was divided into three parts amongst his generals.

Roman Republic

Roman civilization dates from the founding of the city in 753 B.C. until the defeat of the last Emperor, Romulus Augustus, in A.D. 476. The republic itself lasted from the overthrow of the monarchy in 509 B.C. until the empowering of the first Emperor, Octavian Augustus, in 27 B.C. The area along the Tiber River where Rome would be built was previously inhabited by a group known as the Etruscans. Rome took its name from the legendary Romulus, who is said to have founded it after triumphing over his brother Remus. The basic structure of Roman society consisted of patricians at the top of the social hierarchy, who were descendants of the founders of the republic and often wealthy. Beneath the patricians were the plebeians, which consisted of all other freemen. Finally, at the bottom of the social hierarchy were slaves. Women were not included in most social or economic business, although a Roman woman's rights were often significantly preferable to her contemporaries in other civilizations. The Roman Republic, which was the first political arrangement of Rome, was led by two consuls who were chosen annually. The Consuls presided over the Senate, made up of a permanent group of those who had been previously elected to a high-ranking magistracy (originally primarily patrician in composition); and the Assembly, which was solely for the plebeians. Rome had extensive laws covering individual and property rights.

The first real challenge to the territorial expansion of Rome was the city of Carthage, located across the Mediterranean in North Africa. Carthage was founded by the Phoenicians. There were three major conflicts, known as the Punic Wars, fought between Rome and Carthage. Rome won the First Punic War, and acquired Sicily in the process. The Carthaginian effort in the Second Punic War was led by Hannibal and included his famous crossing of the Alps. Hannibal was quite successful in Italy, but a combination of a war of attrition throughout Italy and the counterattacks on Carthaginian holdings in Spain and the city of Carthage itself by the Romans forced Hannibal to retreat to North Africa to defend Carthage. In the Third Punic War, Rome finally destroyed Carthage; in fact, it is often rumored that the victorious Romans burned Carthage to the ground and then salted the fields of their vanquished foe, a tribute to the Senator Cato the Elder's repeated cry at the end of various speeches of "*Ceterum censeo Carthaginem esse delendam*" ("Moreover, I have determined that Carthage must be destroyed").

After defeating Carthage once and for all, Rome met little resistance as it continued to acquire more territory. This was partly due to the superiority of Roman weaponry, and in part because the Romans were good at bringing conquered peoples into the fold. Rome typically allowed conquered people to maintain their native cultures, so long as they paid tribute to Rome. Rome defeated the Macedonians and took Greece, then conquered large portions of Gaul (France) and Spain. The vastness of the Roman Empire necessitated some advances in infrastructure technology. Romans are justly famous or their solid and durable roads and aqueducts (systems for delivering water), many of which survive today.

As Rome continued to expand, class conflicts developed between the nobility and the poor. In this era of unrest, it became possible for individual leaders to claim more power than the law had allowed previously. In 60 B.C., the famous general Julius Caesar formed a three-person alliance (often mis-termed the "First Triumvirate") to govern Rome. The other two members were Gnaeus Pompey Magnus and Marcus Licinius Crassus. During this period, Caesar led a successful campaign against the Gauls (a people in modern-day France) and made himself richer than the entire Roman State on the proceeds from his conquest. After Crassus was killed in battle, Caesar pushed Pompey out and assumed total control of Rome, crowning himself dictator-for-life. Though Caesar was very popular with the mob, his decision to claim lifelong power alienated him from the nobility in the Senate. He was assassinated by a group of senators, led by Marcus Iunius Brutus, in 44 B.C.

After the assassination of Caesar in 44 B.C., Rome was mired in chaos. Those who had conspired to kill Caesar had hoped to return to the republican form of government, but instead another trio of leaders came to the fore, this time as a governmental commission of "three men for reconstituting the Republic," known as the Triumvirate. The Triumvirate was composed of Marc Antony, one of Caesar's greatest generals and a Consul at the time; Octavius, the nephew and testamentary heir of Caesar; and Marcus Aemilius Lepidus, a third wheel who was quickly made a non-entity. While Octavius stayed in Rome, Antony left for Egypt, where he stayed for a time as the guest and lover of Cleopatra. Eventually, infighting between Octavius and Antony led the former to mount a campaign against Egypt. When they realized that they were defeated, Antony and Cleopatra committed suicide to avoid the shame of being paraded in Octavian's triumph. Lepidus, having been marginalized, Octavius (now known as Augustus) became the first Emperor.

Roman Empire

After the ascension of Augustus, Rome entered a period of relative tranquility. Augustus dubbed this era, which lasted about forty years, the Pax Romana. Rome remained an empire, although the conquered peoples were able to obtain Roman citizenship without having to forfeit their native customs. It was at this period that Rome reached its greatest geographic proportions, stretching all the way from to present-day Scotland to the Middle East. This was also the greatest period for Roman artistic achievement; both Virgil and Ovid were active during the Pax Romana, and, indeed, the Aeneid of Virgil was written in part to glorify Augustus. It was at this time that the polytheist religion of Rome was challenged first by the Judaism of the conquered Hebrews, and later by the early Christians.

Early Christianity was a mass of competing doctrines, including various groups such as the Gnostics and Arians who all sought to have their view legitimized as the truth. Eventually, the orthodox church through an ecumenical council of bishops created in the fourth century A.D. the canon of New Testament texts which exists today. The apostles had created a hierarchy of bishops, priests, and deacons who stressed obedience to duly constituted church authority. By the middle of the second century, Christianity began to attract intellectuals in the Roman Empire. Although Christians were still liable to be persecuted in the farther reaches of the empire, many turned to the Church as the empire crumbled, as the Church was all that was left of civilization, and would rebuild Europe over the next millennium.

The Roman Emperor Constantine, in response to the inconvenient vastness of his dominion, established an eastern capital: Constantinople, in A.D. 330. Having received a sign in the heavens which promised him victory over his rivals for the office of Emperor should he convert to Christianity, Constantine famously issued the Edict of Milan, in which he called for the end of the persecution of Christians, after a sound victory as promised. After this act, Christianity flourished in the Roman Empire and became the official religion of the state. A movement called monasticism developed within the religion, advocating the renunciation of worldly goods in favor of contemplation and prayer. After the death of Constantine, the empire once again proved unwieldy for one man, and therefore it split as it had previously, with the western half being governed from Rome, and the eastern half from Constantinople. This arrangement would prove untenable, however; a Germanic tribe of barbarians eventually sacked Rome, and the western Roman capital fell in A.D. 476.

One of the major barbarian tribes to challenge the Roman Empire in its decline were the Huns. The Huns were a nomadic people who moved east across central Asia during the 4th century A.D. The Huns were divided into several branches: the White Huns overran the Sasanian Empire and conquered many cities in the northern part of the Indian subcontinent; another group roamed eastern Europe and established a strong empire on the Hungarian Plain around A.D. 400. The Huns were known for their amazing horsemanship and for being aggressive on the battlefield. It was under the guidance of Attila (440s) that the Huns reached their highest level of prominence. During this period, they collected tribute from many of the areas within the Roman Empire. Soon after the death of Attila, however, the Huns became complacent and lost most of their territory.

The eastern half of the Roman Empire became known as the Byzantine Empire. After the fall of Rome and the western Roman Empire, a series of Emperors, including the Emperor Justinian, led the Byzantine Empire from Constantinople and even managed to successfully reconquer large parts of the former western empire for a number of years. The Justinian era is especially remembered for the contributions to law and religious art work, in particular the development of mosaics. In the years after the fall of Rome, the Catholic Christian Church gradually rose to fill the power vacuum. In what had been the western Roman Empire, the Church acted completely independent of any political body, while even in the Byzantine Empire the Church was increasing in power. Only the influence of the Byzantine Emperor kept the Church from being the most powerful group in all of Europe.

Islam

The religion of Islam was founded by the prophet Muhammad in A.D. 610. Islam is a monotheistic religion based on the Koran, a book of scripture according to the muslim god, Allah. The practice of Islam is based on "Five Pillars": faith in Allah, a pilgrimage to the city of Mecca; a yearly fast during the month of Ramadan; the giving of alms; and prayer five times a day. Muhammad also asserted that Islam should be spread throughout the world. Indeed, as the Christian Church was becoming the dominant factor in Europe, Islam was spreading throughout North Africa, the Middle East, parts of Asia, and even Spain. The simultaneous ascensions of Christianity and Islam inevitably led to conflict, most notably in the Crusades.

After the formation of Islam in the 7th century A.D., it took 3 or 4 centuries to develop the institutional structures of the religion. Islamic law was created, and a new class of Muslim religious leaders and scholars emerged who took a prominent place in society. The Islamic civilization drew elements from its surroundings, namely the culture of the Greeks, Iranians, Christians, Jews, and Zoroastrians. At first, the Islamic Empire was ruled by a single caliph and a small Arab elite. As the empire expanded, however, this became untenable and the lands were divided into a number of independent political entities. Also, factions began to emerge among Muslims, most notably between the Sunnis and Shiites, who rivaled over the true successor to Muhammad, among other issues. Because the entire Islamic world operated with a common system of trade, it quickly became very wealthy.

Between the years A.D. 1,000 and 1,450, invaders from the steppes conquered parts of Asia, the Middle East, and Europe. These people had originally been nomads, but in this period they began to settle and become tradesmen. The clans that made up this group were loosely based on family ties; once they became stationary, they began to appoint powerful chiefs for leadership support. Near A.D. 1,000, the Seljuk Turks moved from Central Asia into the Middle East after converting to Islam. This group then controlled the trade routes between Asia, Africa, and Europe, and charged tolls on these routes, building an empire with their wealth. In 1071, the Seljuk Turks defeated the Byzantines at the Battle of Manzikert; a Christian defeat which would be part of the motivation for the First Crusade. The Seljuk Turks were known as excellent fighters and mediocre rulers; local leaders frequently ignored the central government and fought one another for control of land. This infighting weakened the group until they became prey to new nomadic invaders from Central Asia.

European Middle Ages

In the Middle Ages, Russia had a complicated and inefficient system of succession, which meant that the various lands were constantly being fought over and authority was often dubious. For a long time, Russia was dominated by the Mongols (Tatars), who kept the local governments weak in order to continue receiving tributes. Moscow as able to parlay loyalty to the Tatars and colonization of other feudal estates into a great deal of power during this period. Supported by their Tatar overlords, the Muscovite princes were able to partition off their new lands in such a way that it became very difficult for nobles to consolidate their land holdings, which prevented any wealthy lords from ever challenging the princes of Moscow. This made the Grand Duchy of Moscow the most powerful political unit in the area and planted the seed of what would become the empire of Russia centuries later.

Feudalism was the system of social and economic organization that developed in Europe in the Middle Ages: roughly A.D. 750 to 1300. Feudalism is characterized by rigid hierarchies among the various classes. At the top of the hierarchy was the king, and below him lords, who oversaw a smaller area of land. Below the lords were noblemen who had been granted control over farmland in exchange for their pledge of allegiance to the king. These noblemen were known as vassals and subvassals. The land managed by each vassal was known as a fief, and the home of the vassal was known as the manor. Each manor and the community surrounding it comprised a self-sufficient unit. The laws of primogeniture were enforced at this time, meaning that the ownership of the fief would descend to the firstborn son of the lord. Finally, the land was actually cultivated either by peasants or serfs; peasants were free farmers, while serfs were basically slaves who were forced to work for the lord and were bound to their lands.

The emergence of the feudal system in western Europe meant that instead of a centralized power, there were many local authorities. Charlemagne (A.D. 742-814) was a Germanic leader who tried to unify the former western Roman Empire. In A.D. 800, Pope St. Leo III crowned Charlemagne Emperor of Rome during Christmas Mass at St. Peter's Basilica in Rome, establishing a political relationship with the Church that would last throughout the Middle Ages. Charlemagne allocated a great deal of power to regional leaders, and did not tax his subjects. For this reason, he was unable to make many internal improvements during his reign. Nevertheless, Charlemagne is credited with promoting the arts, especially within the thriving monasteries, without which much of antiquity would not have been transcribed and thus preserved. After the death of Charlemagne, his lands were divided up among his three grandsons according to the Treaty of Verdun.

The Holy Roman Empire was the name given to the holdings of Otto the Great in 962, who had unified the central area of Charlemagne's empire. As in Charlemagne's day, this was a disparate group of territories, and proved difficult to govern. Otto incorporated the Church into his government, though he continually sought to minimize its power. One of the legacies of Otto's reign would be the rivalry between the Church and state. Gradually, the Church leaders acquired power, until they were exercising great control over the day-to-day activities of most citizens. Perhaps inevitably, this great power began to corrupt many of the Church's leaders. Indicative of the state of the Church was the often unpunished offense of simony, in which prestigious and important offices were bought and sold.

During the 13th century, France was transformed from a group of disparate fiefs into a centralized monarchy by Philip Augustus (Philip II). His heir, Philip IV, would establish the Estates General, a governing body composed of representatives from each province. The Estates General contained noblemen as well as wealthy commoners. Meanwhile, Germany endured an interregnum, or period between kings, after the ruler died without a clear successor. Italy, as well, spent this period as a collection of strong and independent townships. In a decentralized state, it became easier for wealthy merchants to wield power. In Germany and the Baltic coast, the Hanseatic League, an association of merchants, set regional trade policy.

England, unlike many of the other regions of Western Europe, had been accustomed to a strong monarchy. This tradition was challenged in A.D. 1215, when noblemen forced King John to sign the Magna Carta, a document which gave feudal rights back to the nobles and extended the rule of law to the middle-class burghers. The Magna Carta made the formation of the Houses of Parliament possible. Over time, Parliament would evolve into a two-house structure: the House of Lords which contained nobles and clergy and the House of Commons which contained knights and burghers. The House of Lords was mainly occupied with legal questions, while the House of Commons dealt mainly in economic issues.

During the Middle Ages, a number of different leaders tried to unite the various lands of Poland. These attempts were always defeated by the nobility, who preferred the country to be an oligarchy rather than a monarchy. Poland was also much involved during this period in a battle with the Teutonic knights over the Baltic coastline. Hungary was a feudal state by the beginning of the 14th century, and the various patches of land which constituted the country were ruled as if they were independent. Bishops in the Eastern Orthodox Church were among the largest landholders. Ostensibly, the nobility was in charge of the defense of the Hungarian people, though they rarely supplied the money and material for war.

In the 12th century A.D., the various fiefs in Western Europe increasingly came into contact with one another. As advances in transportation technology made trade with distant neighbors possible, there developed more necessity for specialization. Rather than be entirely self-sufficient, lords found it was more economically advantageous to perfect the cultivation of one crop and exchange that for everything else. As trade became more important, so did the merchants in towns, known as burghers, who wielded considerable political power. Trade arrangements led to alliances between various towns, and the whole of Western Europe became more homogenous. The distinction between classes also became much less pronounced during this period. There were drawbacks, however: the increasing number of people in towns as well as the more frequent travel between towns contributed, no doubt, to the bubonic plague epidemic of the mid-14th century.

In the late 13th century, increased contact between regions and greater representation in government culminated in a number of peasant revolts and serf uprisings. During this period, members of the clergy became even more secular and open in their greed for fame and power. This alienated many common citizens from the Church. The invention of gunpowder also changed the social arrangements in Western Europe; fewer noblemen were willing to participate in combat, and so the code of chivalry gave way to mercenary soldiers. Noblemen largely turned their attention to acquiring some of the fantastic wealth available in trade. The quality that men strived for in these days was called virtue, meaning a solemn dedication to the arts and sciences.

Surprising though it may seem, one of the best things that happened to Christian thought during the Middle Ages was its contact with Islam. The complex philosophies of Muslim scholars helped spur the evolution of Christian theology. These in addition to the rediscovery of ancient philosophers such as Aristotle led Christians to begin to glorify reason as the God-given tool for investigating religious faith. Many assertions made by the new rational theologians, however, were dubbed heresy by many Church leaders, as more and more Christian thinkers were bemoaning the materialistic ways of the Church leaders. One of the leading Christian thinkers of the Middle Ages was St. Thomas Aquinas, whose Summa Theologica outlined rational explanations for the belief in God and in the miracles of Christianity.

The rapid evolution in Christian thought that took place during the Middle Ages gave rise to the formation of the first universities. For the first time in Western Europe, young men would move to large cities to study theology, law, and medicine at formal institutions. In addition to this trend, the academic method known as scholasticism was developed, in which scholars would use logic and deductive reasoning in order to analyze a work or determine something of an abstract nature. Among the so-called scholastics, two schools of thought developed: those scholars who adhered to the ideas of Plato were known as realists, and those who followed Aristotle were known as nominalists. The word "realist" is somewhat confusing when used to refer to the work of Plato, who believed that our perceptions of objects were merely perceptions of the barest shadows of their reality. Another development of Christianity in this period was mysticism; Christian mystics believed that they could achieve union with God through self-denial, contemplative prayer, and alms-giving.

Around the year 1300, the power of the Pope in political affairs was weakening because of the rise of strong monarchs and a spirit of nationalism. Pope Boniface VIII attempted to force kings to obey him, but was unsuccessful. In response, Boniface issued a papal bull in 1296 that instructed King Philip IV of France to not tax the church; Philip ignored this command. Boniface would not relent, and issued the bull "Unam Sanctam," in which he declared that there are two powers on the earth, the temporal and the spiritual, with the latter always superior, and that there is no salvation outside of loyalty to the Roman Pontiff. Once again, Philip refused the claims of the Pope, and decided to silence him by having him kidnapped and brought to France. Boniface was able to escape captivity, but died soon afterward. This significantly weakened the political authority of the papacy.

After the death of Pope Boniface VIII, King Philip IV of France persuaded the College of Cardinals to select a French archbishop as the next pope. This pope, Clement V, moved the papacy to Avignon, France, where it would remain for 67 years. Debate raged during this period as to whether a pope could be legitimate in any city other than Rome. Also, Clement's court became notorious for its extravagance. In 1378, a new pope was chosen; an Italian, who chose the name Urban VI to indicate that he planned on keeping the papacy in Rome. Upset with Urban's policy, 13 French cardinals selected a new pope, the French-speaking Clement VII. Now, there were two popes, and each one declared the other illegitimate. This confusion lasted from 1378 until 1417, with the Pope in Rome and an antipope in Avignon.

England made a claim on the French throne in 1337, and the result was a war (or series of wars) that lasted for 116 years. France was angry, in return, that England had not upheld its feudal obligations to the French throne, to whom the English king was technically a distant vassal. France had the support of the Pope, but England used the innovation of the longbow to score some significant victories. It was during this war that the charismatic figure Joan of Arc emerged. Joan was a French peasant who led troops to several unlikely victories after being visited by God. Her deeds rallied the spirits of the French, and France eventually won. The catastrophic losses suffered by both sides had major consequences: England withdrew from contention as a land power, electing instead to develop a navy; in France, Louis IX—St. Louis—took advantage of the chaos to consolidate power in the monarchy.

Towards the end of the Middle Ages, two events greatly shaped future events. The bubonic plague, also known as the Black Death, killed between 30 and 60% of the European population. The influx of people to squalid cities made the rapid spread of this disease possible. The seemingly random devastation caused by the disease caused many people to question their faith, and the power of the Church suffered as a result. The other monumental event was the invention of the printing press by Johannes Gutenberg in about 1436. This invention was used first to produce a cheap copy of the Bible. Soon, though, printing presses with movable type were being used to print all sorts of things, and the literacy rate in Europe rose dramatically. It immediately became possible to disseminate ideas quickly.

African Kingdoms

For most of its history, much of Sub-Saharan Africa was composed of disparate tribes. Most of Africa practiced animistic religion, in which it is believed that deities are embodied in the animals that people depend upon for food and service. Ritual and participatory worship was important; common activities include drumming, dancing, divination, and sacrifices. These religions typically had well-developed concepts of good and evil; they believed that some evil, disasters and illnesses were produced by witchcraft, and that specialists (known as diviners) were required to combat the power of these malevolent beings. Many African peoples shared an underlying belief in a creator deity, whose power was expressed through the ancestors who founded the tribe. These deceased ancestors were a link between the living and the deities. African tribal religions showed a remarkable resilience when they began to come into contact with monotheistic religions.

One of the most successful cultures of the African Iron Age was the Nok culture. The Nok developed ironworking technology before anyone else, and also created a rich artistic culture that spread throughout the West African forest region. The Nok were mainly active between the 5th and the 1st centuries B.C. Their creation of iron farm implements made it possible for farmers to develop surplus crops, and thus urban centers could develop. This increase in agricultural productivity also made it possible for there to be more specialization of labor. Therefore, not only were civilizations more stable, but they were also better able to protect themselves, as they now had both better weapons made of iron and more time to train warriors.

Kush was a powerful African kingdom that lasted in some form from 2,000 B.C. until A.D. 350. For a long time, Kush was based around the city of Kerma, in what is now the Sudan. Kushites became wealthy because of their mineral resources and because of their advantageous location in the northwest corner of Africa where they were at the crossroads of several intercontinental trade routes. There was a great deal of contact between Kush and Egypt in this period. In 767 B.C., King Kashta of Kush defeated the Egyptians, and the Kushites had control of the entire Nile Valley. Kush would soon be weakened by the Assyrians, however, and would eventually fall prey to the Romans; in A.D. 350, the new capital of Kush, Meroe, was sacked.

Aksum, a town in what is now northern Ethiopia, was the capital city of one of Africa's most powerful kingdoms between the first and sixth centuries A.D. The kings of Aksum were said to have descended from Menelik, one of the sons of the famous King Solomon. These people controlled almost all of the trade on the Red Sea and made tremendous profit on the exchange of ivory. In the 4th century A.D., Aksum eliminated the kingdom of Kush and became the predominant power in Africa. It was also during this century that Aksum was Christianized; it remains a hub of Ethiopian Christianity to this day. In its later stages, Aksum's control extended into southern Arabia, and would eventually give way to the Persians and the Arabs.

Beginning in the 7th century A.D., Ghana was a major trading power in west Africa. It was mainly located in the areas that are now known as Mali and Mauritania. The people of Ghana grew rich by exchanging ivory and gold from the south and salt from the north. Eventually, Ghana would become an empire, and would collect lavish tributes from all of the lands within its control. In the 11th century, the capital of Ghana was Kumbi. In 1076, however, Kumbi fell to the Almoravids, a Muslim tribe. The whole of Ghana would eventually be subsumed into the burgeoning empire of Mali.

Today, Mali is the largest nation in west Africa. Indeed, throughout African history Mali has been a major power. Until the 11th century, it was a part of the empire of Ghana, a wealthy trading nation. Mali would eventually rise to prominence in its own right. The economy of Mali was based upon the rich mineral resources (especially gold) of the region. Mali reached its highest prominence during the reign of Mansa Musa (A.D. 1312-7). This ruler introduced Islam to his people, which at this time lived as far north as Morocco. The city of Timbuktu became a cultural center for the region, as well as a crossroads for trade routes that stretched across the Sahara. Over time, internal disputes would divide Mali into several smaller kingdoms.

The Songhai empire flourished in west Africa between the 14th and 16th centuries. Centered in the valley of the Niger River, the Songhai were first organized by Christian Berbers in the 7th century. Four hundred years later, they established their capital at Gao and became an Islamic nation. Except for a brief period in which they were ruled by the empire of Mali, the Songhai controlled over a thousand miles along the Niger. Like most of the African powers, the Songhai made their money through trade. Muhammad I, who ruled from 1493 to 1528, expanded the empire to its greatest area. One of the weaknesses of the Songhai, however, was that they did not have a traditional means of succession, and thus frequent infighting among the powerful eventually led to the empire's demise.

American Civilizations

Mesoamerica, which is now known as Central and South America, were both host to developed civilizations 3,000 years before the arrival of Columbus. These civilizations were largely dependent upon water-supported agriculture. The most important crop in the region was maize. The first dominant group in this region, the Olmecs, was based in what is now the gulf coast of eastern Mexico. The Olmecs were known for making large and elaborate stone carvings. There were also major civilizations at this time in what is now Peru. In the Andes Mountains of that region, the Chavin culture developed intricate stone temples and pyramids. These sites have been explored carefully by archaeologists.

The Mayas were based in the Mexico's Yucatan Peninsula, Tabasco, and Chiapas, as well as in what is now Guatemala and Honduras. Between the years A.D. 200 and 950, they developed a sophisticated civilization, with complex religions, architecture, arts, engineering, and astronomy. The Mayas did have a form of hieroglyphic writing, but most of their history and folklore was preserved orally. The Mayas are responsible for creating an extremely accurate calendar and for first conceiving of the number zero. The Mayan civilization was supported by agriculture, but it was run by a class of priests and warriors. In the 9th century, the Mayans were overrun by Toltecs from the north, who created the legend of the feathered serpent Quetzalcoatl.

The Mayans conceived of the universe as a flat, square earth, whose four corners and center were dominated by a god. Above the sky, there were 13 levels, and below were 9 underworlds, each dominated by a god. The sun and moon, deities in their own right, passed through all of these levels every day. Each male god had a female goddess counterpart. The Mayans also had patron gods and goddesses for various occupations and classes. Mayan rulers had religious powers. Religious ritual often entailed human sacrifice and self-mutilation. The Mayans also played a ritual ball game that had religious importance; the losers of this game stood to lose their lives. Mayans developed their cities as tributes to the gods.

When the Toltec empire had been eradicated around the year 1150, the power in Mesoamerica shifted to the valley of Mexico, around three lakes. By about 1325, the Aztecs had seized control of this area. The Aztec civilization was organized into city-states, much like early medieval Europe; political intrigue and state marriages were as common among the Aztecs as among the French. The Aztecs were known as fierce warriors and were hated by their neighbors because of their brutality. According to legend, the Aztecs settled in Tenochtitlan after a scout saw an eagle with a serpent in its beak perched on a cactus there. The Aztecs formed alliances based on threats and forced tributes.

The Incas inhabited a huge area, from present-day Ecuador to central Chile to the eastern side of the Andes Mountains. The Incas territory expanded especially after the 14th century A.D. The Incas were engaged in frequent conflicts with rival groups, and they frequently enslaved the groups that they defeated. They eventually formed a permanent underclass of serfs in order to ensure that the lands of the military leaders would be cultivated. Incas typically dispersed rival groups in order to prevent being attacked. The Incan religion contained a god in heaven, a cult of ancestors, and a number of sacred objects and places. The Incas called themselves the children of the Sun.

Eastern Civilizations

The Indus River Valley is an area bordered by the Himalayan Mountains in what is now Pakistan. The two great cities of this civilization were Harappa and Mohenjo-Daro, though there were also a large number of smaller communities in the area. The people of this region developed a system of writing, as well as systems of weight and measurement which were useful in trade. They exchanged goods with the people of Mesopotamia in the west as well as with the people of Tibet in the east. The Aryans invaded this region and brought with them iron technology and the Sanskrit language. The introduction of iron tools made it possible to cultivate the forests of the Ganges River Valley in what is now India.

Both the Indus Valley and Egyptian civilizations featured extremely well-planned cities. In the Indus Valley, the cities of Mohenjo-Daro and Harrapa were located along the Indus River, in what is now Pakistan. Each of these cities was built around 2,500 B.C. and housed approximately 30,000 citizens. They were each designed in a grid-like pattern, with streets running east-west and north-south. Both Mohenjo-Daro and Harrapa had bath houses, sewer systems, and organized garbage collection. The structures in these cities were built with oven-fired bricks which made them durable. Unlike in Egypt, where technological advances were used to enhance religious practice, the people of the Indus Valley used their technology to improve sanitation.

The Vedic Age is the period recounted in the Indian Vedas, the earliest known records of Indian history. The dates of the Vedic age are considered by most to be between 2,000 and 1,000 B.C. The oldest Vedic text is the Rig-Veda, which bears many Indo-Iranian elements. It is a collection of religious hymns and stories and describes a nomadic people who were ruled by a king who depended on their consent. His main duty was to protect the people. Religion in this period primarily consisted of chanting and the performing of sacrifices. During this period, elaborate rules concerning marriage were created, and the rigid social stratification that would become known as the caste system evolved.

The Hindu caste system is a means of organizing society. It divides the populace into four groups, each associated with a part of the body of the Hindu god Parusha. The highest class is the brahmins, associated with the mouth of the god. In the original system, the brahmin class was made up of priests. The second caste is the kshatriyas, made up of rulers and soldiers; this caste is associated with the arms of Parusha. Next are the vaishyas, associated with the legs of the god. This caste was composed of landowners, merchants, and artisans. The last group is the shudras, associated with the feet of the god. This caste was composed of servants and slaves. Women do not have a place in the traditional Hindu caste system.

Hinduism is the traditional religion of India. It is expressed in an individual's philosophy and behavior, rather than in the performance of any specific rituals. Hinduism does not claim a founder, but has evolved slowly over thousands of years; the first Hindu writings date back to the third millennium B.C. There are a few concepts that are common to all permutations of Hinduism, such as the Vedas, which are considered to be the sacred texts of the religion. The chief aim in life for a Hindu is to liberate himself from the cycle of suffering and rebirth. Hindus believe in reincarnation and that a person's conduct in this life will affect his or her position in the next (karma). Although Hinduism is frequently associated with the caste system, the two are actually unrelated.

The earliest civilizations in what would become China flourished along the banks of the Huang He (Yellow) River before the year 2,000 B.C. The first Chinese dynasty was the Xia (Hsia), succeeded by the Shang dynasty. In this period, the rulers established an intricate system of government and a comprehensive judiciary. The basic components of this system would be preserved in Chinese civilization for centuries. The distinctive Chinese style of writing also developed during this period. Like Egyptian hieroglyphs, the Chinese pictographs are meant to resemble their definition. Over time, though, the Chinese characters have come to resemble their definitions less and less.

The Zhou dynasty, which ran from roughly 1,030 to 221 B.C., is generally considered to be the third Chinese dynasty, after the Shang. The Zhou were brought into power by the commander Wu, who declared that the decadent Shang monarchs had forfeited the mandate of heaven (in other words, God's approval of their reign). The Zhou dynasty is generally divided into two parts; the Western Zhou ran a feudal-type state in the central plain and the area around the Yellow River. The later Eastern Zhou had a more difficult time maintaining control of rival states within its control. The Zhou dynasty was the period in which Chinese civilization spread to most parts of Asia. Both Confucius and Lao Tzu were active during this period. China became the preeminent state during this period.

Next to Confucianism, Daoism (also Taoism) is the most important philosophy to have emerged out of China. Taoist thought is based on the 6th century B.C. writings of Lao Tzu, specifically on the Tao Te Ching. Lao Tzu was a student of Confucius and taught that individuals should discover the essential nature of things and of themselves, and should not seek to challenge the natural harmony of life. A proper Taoist should be patient and austere. Unlike Confucianism, Daoism contains an element of mysticism and so may be called a religion. Taoism introduced the concept of the yin and yang, the contrasting male and female elements that make up every thing in existence, and which must be harmonized in order to achieve self-realization.

Persia is the European name for the region that is now Iran. This area has been the site of a number of vibrant cultures. The Medes were the first to develop there, lasting from approximately 700 to 549 B.C., when they were expelled by the army of Cyrus. This great king then established the Achaemenid dynasty, which itself was destroyed by Alexander the Great in 330 B.C. After this, a succession of peoples including the Parthians—rivals to Rome—inhabited the region, until a durable Sasanian dynasty was established in A.D. 224. Persia was in constant conflict with the Byzantine Empire, and would eventually be overtaken by the Arabs in the seventh century A.D.

Zoroastrianism was the state religion of Persia during the Sasanian dynasty between the years A.D. 224 and 651. It is based upon the prophecies of Zoroaster (also known as Zarathustra, c. 628-551 B.C.), a Persian who claimed to have encountered the divine being Ahura Mazdah. Zoroastrians believed that the world was composed of good and evil spirits, who are in constant conflict. Fire was sacred to the Zoroastrians. Many of the concepts of Zoroastrianism would be included in Christianity, especially by the Manichean sect, who also saw the world as a struggle between absolute good and absolute evil. Zoroastrianism receded in popularity with the rise of Islam.

The Mauryan Empire lasted approximately between the years 321 and 185 B.C. in India. It was established by the powerful leader Chandragupta Maurya, and featured a strong military and an efficient bureaucracy. The Mauryan empire eventually spread as far west as the Indus River as present-day Afghanistan. At its greatest expansion, the Mauryan empire comprised almost the entirety of what is now India. The leader Ashoka (c. 272-232 B.C.) converted to Buddhism, and his rule was prosperous for rich and poor alike. After the death of Ashoka, however, the Mauryan Empire splintered, as the southern lands sought autonomy and the northern lands were subject to constant foreign invasions.

Buddhism was created by Gautama Siddhartha (otherwise known as Buddha) in about 528 B.C. It was in part a response to Hinduism, which Buddha felt had become bloated with worldliness and politics. Traditional Buddhism is based upon the Four Noble Truths: existence is suffering, suffering is caused by desire, an end of suffering will come with Nirvana, and Nirvana will come with the practice of the Eightfold Path. The steps of the Eightfold Path are: right views; right resolve; right speech; right action; right livelihood; right effort; right mindfulness; and right concentration. Buddhism has no deities. Buddhism did not receive any official sanction for a long time, but eventually spread and took hold in India, China, Japan, and elsewhere.

The Han dynasty ran from approximately 206 B.C. to A.D. 220. It began when a peasant, Liu Pang, led a successful insurrection against the Qin dynasty leaders. The Han shifted the capital of China to Changan (Xian). This was the period in which Confucianism became the dominant political and social ideology in China. The Han developed a code of laws and a form of government based upon the proper Confucian relations between king and subject, husband and wife, and father and son. The Han dynasty saw China accrue fantastic wealth, and become one of the most sophisticated and resplendent countries the world has seen. Eventually, though, peasant revolts weakened the Han and made them susceptible to overthrow.

The Mongols, who descended from the Huns, were a nomadic group that roamed east central Asia. Around the year A.D. 1206, the various Mongol tribes were united under Genghis Khan, whose empire then stretched from the Black Sea to the Pacific Ocean, and from Tibet to Siberia. After the death of Genghis, the Mongol lands were divided up. This did not, however, slow expansion; Mongols eventually controlled parts of Iran as well. Kublai Khan was another prominent Mongol leader; he destroyed the Song dynasty in China and replaced it with the Yuan. By the 14th century, the Mongol Empire was beginning to disintegrate. Like many of its kind, it proved too large to govern. The Ming and subsequently the Qing dynasties put the remaining Mongols under Chinese control.

The Ming dynasty lasted in China from A.D. 1368 to 1644. This dynasty was established by a Buddhist monk, Zhu Yuanzhang, who quickly became obsessed with consolidating power in the central government and was known for the brutality with which he achieved his ends. It was during the Ming dynasty that China developed and introduced its famous civil service examinations, rigorous tests on the Confucian classics. The future of an ambitious Chinese youth depended on his performance on this exam. The capital was transferred from Nanjing to Beijing during this period, and the Forbidden City was constructed inside the new capital. The Ming period, despite its constant expansionary wars, also continued China's artistic resurgence; the porcelain of this period is especially admired.

1400-1914

Renaissance

In the 14th century, the turmoil caused by war and plague weakened the power of Christian theology. In its place came the philosophy of humanism, in which the emphasis is placed on individual potential and determination while detracting from one's attention to the realm of the divine. Humanist thought contributed to a resurgence in the arts and sciences, which eventually came to be known as the Renaissance. In the 14th and 15th centuries, the center of this resurgence was in Northern Italy, in large part because this was the crossroads of several important trade routes. Specifically, the city-states of Milan, Florence, and Venice cultivated excellent artists. Talented youths typically studied in these cities with their expenses paid by a wealthy patron; the most famous patrons were the Medici family in Florence.

The early part of the Renaissance was dominated by the artists congregated in Northern Italy. Among them were several immortal talents. Donatello (1386-1466) sculpted a marvelous David, and was the first artist in this period to depict the naked human body (religious concerns had kept recent artists from doing so). Botticelli (1444-1510) is the painter of the famous Birth of Venus. Leonardo da Vinci (1452-1519) excelled in a number of different fields, but he is perhaps best known for painting the Mona Lisa and the Last Supper. Michelangelo (1475-1563), though, was probably the most famous painter and sculptor of the time; he painted the ceiling in the Sistine Chapel and sculpted the most famous David.

Although the Renaissance is typically associated with achievements in visual art, the period also saw a magnificent outpouring of literary and scientific talent. One of the most significant works to emerge from this period was The Prince, by the Florentine Niccolo Macchiavelli. This book outlined a practical plan for political management, one that would be emulated by ruthless leaders in the future. Some of the other noteworthy authors were Erasmus (In Praise of Folly), Sir Thomas More (Utopia), Montaigne, Cervantes (Don Quixote), Ben Johnson, Christopher Marlowe, and, of course, William Shakespeare. At the same time, remarkable advances were being made in the sciences. Copernicus incited controversy by suggesting that the Earth revolved around the Sun; Kepler and Galileo would acquire hard data to support this claim.

Age of Exploration

At the same time that the Renaissance was reinvigorating European cultural life, a desire to explore the world abroad was growing. Indeed, the ability to make long voyages was facilitated by the advances in navigational technology made around this time. The main reason for exploration, though, was economic. Europeans had first been introduced to eastern goods during the Crusades, and the exploits of Marco Polo in the 13th century had further whetted the western appetite for contact with distant lands. This increasing focus on exploration and trade caused a general shift in the balance of power in Europe. Land-locked countries, like Germany, found that they were excluded from participating in the lucrative new economy. On the other hand, those countries which bordered the Atlantic (England, France, Spain, and Portugal) were the most powerful players.

Before 1400, few Europeans knew anything about the world. When Christopher Columbus read of the exploits of the Italian Marco Polo, however, he was inspired to seek out new trade routes. Also, Prince Henry of Portugal established a navigation institute that encouraged sailors to explore. For a long time, extended sea voyages were restricted by a lack of navigational and seafaring technology; the inventions of the compass, astrolabe, and caravel remedied this situation. There was also a high cost associated with long travels; around 1400, however, new monarchs in France, England, Spain, and Portugal decided that they were willing to pay a high price to get a piece of the spice trade. Finally, the question of a motive for exploration was answered by the increasing fervor for missionary work, as well as the economic necessity of developing new trade routes.

As exploration created new opportunities for amassing wealth, Portugal enjoyed special favor because of its excellent location and cordial relations with many of the Muslim nations of North Africa. The ruler of Portugal at this time was even known as Prince Henry "the Navigator" (1394-1460). In order to solidify trade arrangements, European rulers began to think about colonizing foreign lands. In order to fund these expensive trips, a new kind of business known as the joint-stock company was developed. In a joint-stock company, a group of merchants would combine their resources to pay for the passage of a vessel. These groups would later be influential in securing colonial charters for many of their agents. One of the most powerful examples was the Muscovy Company of England, which controlled almost all trade with Russia.

Vasco da Gama was the first European to sail around the Cape of Good Hope, on the southern tip of what is now South Africa. This made it possible to reach Asia by boat. Balboa explored Central America, and was the first European to view the Pacific Ocean. Magellan is remembered as the first to circumnavigate the globe. Cortes was a powerful commander who subjugated the Aztecs in what is now Mexico; he used great brutality to achieve his ends. Pizarro, like Cortes, was a conquistador; he conquered the Incas in what is now Peru. Amerigo Vespucci, from whose name the word "America" was derived, mapped the Atlantic coast of South America and was able to convince stubborn Europeans that these lands were not a part of India.

Hernán Cortez (1485-1547) was a Spanish conquistador. He assisted in the conquest of Cuba, and lived there until 1518, when he was assigned to lead an expedition into Mexico. He and 700 men landed on the Mexican shore and he promptly had his ships burnt, in order to indicate his sincerity about establishing a foothold in the country. Cortez then led his troops into Tenochtitlan, the capital of the Aztec Empire. They were received graciously by the Aztec ruler, Montezuma, whom they immediately enslaved. The Aztecs tried to revolt against the Spanish influence, but Cortez formed a coalition with other anti-Aztec groups and brutally eliminated the Aztec uprising. Cortez went on to rule "New Spain" for a number of years.

Francisco Pizarro (c. 1478- 1541) was a Spanish explorer. He lived for a time in what is now Panama, where he heard tales of the fabulous wealth enjoyed by the Incas in the Andes Mountains. Pizarro determined to conquer this empire, and with 168 men he reached the Incan city of Tumbez in 1532. At this time, the Incas were in the middle of a civil war. Pizarro used this to his advantage: he massacred one side and took their leader prisoner. In order to free himself, the leader arranged a huge ransom, which Pizarro collected and then ignored, killing the leader anyway. Soon, Spaniards conquered the Incan city of Cuzco, and installed a puppet regime. After some turmoil, Pizarro took over the leadership of Peru until his assassination in 1541.

As foreign trade became the most important part of every nation's economy, the economic theory of mercantilism became popular. According to mercantilism, a nation should never import more than it exports. Of course, it is impossible for every country to achieve this goal at the same time, and so European countries were in fierce competition at all times. The solution that most nations pursued was to establish colonies, because these could supply resources for export by the mother country without really being considered imports. This rush to colonize had disastrous consequences for the indigenous peoples of the Americas and Africa. Europeans often looted the Native Americans for anything of value, and their need for cheap labor to cultivate the land there spawned the African slave trade.

Reformation

A response to corruption in the Catholic Church and lapses in enforcement of the basic tenets of the faith, such as those against simony, the Reformation was a movement that called for a return to what many believed to be a simpler message of salvation that they felt to be more scripturally accurate. Many people in this time were outraged by the vast land holdings and stuffed coffers of the Church, which they felt should be concerned with tending to the spiritual health of its members. The invention of the printing press had made it possible for ideas to be disseminated more widely, and authors of the Renaissance had sharply criticized the greed of the clergy. People were also angered by the selling of ecclesial offices and especially the selling of indulgences, in which a person would pay money to have one's time in Purgatory shortened. Selling salvation was indeed against the tenets of the Church, but was often largely unenforced. The general distrust of the Church in this period is known as anticlericalism.

Martin Luther was a German friar who first became famous for criticizing the Catholic Church's sale of indulgences. In accordance with the tradition of theological debate, Luther posted his critique of this practice on the door of his local church; the document known as the "Ninety-five Theses" won him immediate fame. Luther then set about undermining the institution of the Church, arguing that individuals did not need the help of clergy to establish a strong relationship with God. Luther went even further, stating that faith, rather than obedience to arbitrary Church rules, would be what got individuals into heaven. The final straw for the Church came when Luther directly challenged the Pope, declaring that no one man could be the perfect interpreter of Scripture. Luther was excommunicated, but continued to spread his message. Germany was then wracked by a war between the Lutherans of the north and the Catholics of the south. The Peace of Augsburg in 1555 was the resolution to this conflict, in which the subjects of a prince would follow that prince's faith, a practice referred to as "cuius regio, cuius religio"—literally, "whose jurisdiction, whose religion".

Inspired by Luther, many other critics of Catholic excess joined together throughout Europe. These groups were known collectively as Protestants. One of the largest sects of Protestants were the Calvinists, named after founder John Calvin. This group believed in the idea of predestination, or that God had already fixed each person's eternal destiny, and that only the Elect would join Him in heaven. Naturally, most people believed themselves to be among the Elect. In England, King Henry VIII split from the Catholic Church after his request for a marriage annulment from Catherine of Aragon was denied by the Pope. Henry established the Church of England with himself as leader, and had five more wives before his death.

After being bombarded by Protestant attacks for years, the Catholic Church finally began to make some positive changes. This program was known as the Counter-Reformation, and it was aimed at stopping the spread of Protestantism. For instance, the sale of indulgences was halted, and more authority was given to local bishops. The Church reaffirmed many of its core teachings (such as the earning of indulgences, transubstantiation, veneration of the Virgin Mary, the necessity of works, et cetera) yet admitted its errors with regard to simony and abuses of clerical power, which were quickly remedied. One of the most influential men of this movement was Sir Ignatius Loyola, a Spaniard who founded the Society of Jesus (the Jesuits) to promote the Catholic interpretation of Scripture. The Council of Trent was a 20-year meeting that determined the official Catholic interpretation on all matters of theology. The Counter-Reformation also saw the reemergence of the Inquisition, in which heretics were sought out and punished.

Absolute Monarchs and Religious Wars

Between the years 1500 and 1650, most of the major European powers were led by absolute monarchs, who claimed a divine right to rule. These European monarchies often consolidated their power by marrying into one another. The strength of the monarchies fostered a resurgent spirit of nationalism, and consequently led to more frequent conflicts between nations. In 1500, Spain was probably the most powerful nation in Europe, because of her lucrative colonies and impressive Armada. Over the next century and a half, however, France and England would emerge as the dominant powers in the region. German states and Russia, though largely excluded from shipping, were still powerful during this period.

As the nations of Western Europe were beginning to rely on foreign trade almost exclusively to support themselves, Russia remained a feudal nation. After the Mongols were overthrown, Russia was ruled by a succession of Czars, and Russia was largely excluded from the cultural rejuvenation of the Renaissance period. Instead, Russians suffered through the reign of Ivan the Terrible (1530-1584), a fierce ruler who pushed the borders out in the east with horrible brutality, and suffocated any rivals or critics. Ivan's reign was so oppressive that Russia could not develop a merchant class to match those of the Western European powers, despite having some impressive natural resources.

The height of Spanish power began with the reign of King Ferdinand and Queen Isabella; these monarchs promoted exploration and became fantastically rich as a result. The Hapsburg King Charles V would increase Spain's prominence and territory, because he had acquired lands in France, Austria, and Germany through inheritance. Spain was drawn into a number of conflicts over these new possessions, however: France disputed his claim to parts of Italy, and the Ottoman Turks challenged his Armada in the Mediterranean. Charles V would finally be forced to abdicate the throne, leaving his brother Ferdinand I in control of Austria and Germany, and his son Philip II in control of Spain and some western lands. During Philip's reign, most of these possessions would be lost; particularly bitter was the loss of the Netherlands, which quickly became a trading power in their own right.

For many years, England was ruled by the Tudor family. Henry VIII, the founder of the Anglican Church, had been a Tudor, and his daughter Elizabeth continued his policies. During the Elizabethan age in England, trading and exploration increased and the Spanish Armada, sent to overthrow Elizabeth as a protestant heretic, was defeated. After Elizabeth died in 1603, the Stuart family ascended to the throne. The Stuart period would be marked by conflict. Both James I and Charles I butted heads with Parliament over the issue of taxation, and there were also continual conflicts between Puritans (followers of John Calvin) and Anglicans (adherents of the Church of England). The Puritans joined with Parliament in opposition to the monarchy.

The alliance of Parliament and the Puritans was led by Oliver Cromwell. His army was successful in deposing and executing King Charles I, and Cromwell was subsequently installed as Protector of England. Cromwell's rule was undermined by Anglican nobles and clergy who disliked his Puritanism. After the death of Cromwell, England was ruled by the two sons of Charles I, Charles II and James II, the latter of which was forced to abdicate by Parliament. After this period of relative chaos, William and Mary of the Netherlands were asked to rule England in a limited monarchy. This shift in power was known as the Glorious Revolution. The Declaration of Rights that limited the power of the monarchy gave Parliament more power, and made possible a long period of tranquility.

While England was undergoing a turbulent transition from an absolute to a limited monarchy, France was governed by a succession of powerful and talented Bourbon monarchs. The Estates General, the French counterpart to the British Parliament, was not especially powerful. During a period in which the Bourbon heir was too young to govern himself, the charismatic Cardinal Richelieu governed France. Cardinal Richelieu was a Catholic, of course, but he did not persecute the French protestant Huguenot sect. Rather, he compromised with his enemies in an attempt to consolidate the power of the French crown. Cardinal Richelieu also established a strong bureaucracy, known as the noblesse de la robe.

Unlike many of the other Western European powers in 1500, Germany was still essentially just a collection of disjointed city-states. The Hapsburg family was powerful there, but the lands they called their Holy Roman Empire were not well organized, and the Hapsburgs were weak compared to other European leaders. The Peace of Augsburg, which had quelled disputes between Lutherans and Catholics, was destroyed by the Thirty Years' War (1618-48), which began when Protestants challenged the authority of the Hapsburg emperor. Germany would become so chaotic and disjointed during this period that other nations would step in, whether to seize some land or to help out one side or the other. The brutality of this war left Germany in a state of turmoil.

The monarchs of the Enlightenment period found themselves under increasing pressure to be tolerant and benevolent. In Western Europe, so-called "enlightened despots" governed in order to promote the best interests of their subjects; this was probably done more to retain power than to express any profound solidarity with the commoners. France had become the central power on the European continent after the Peace of Westphalia (1648), which ended the Thirty Years' War and weakened Germany. The long reign of Louis XIV of France was characterized by grandiosity and the cultivation of the arts. Louis spent considerable effort trying to acquire new territories for France and glory for himself, and so alarmed the other European powers with his swiftness from victory to victory that many former enemies allied against France.

Enlightenment

The rapid advance in learning known as the Scientific Revolution was a product of the systematic form of inquiry known as the scientific method. With the scientific method, learning is incremental: a question is posed, a hypothetical solution is offered, observations are made, and the hypothesis is either supported or refuted. The consistency of the method made it easy for scientific discoveries to be transferred from one country to another. Along with a standardized form of measurement, the development of the scientific method gave scientists a common language. Scientists also benefited from the development of powerful telescopes and microscopes.

After Copernicus startled the world by challenging the geocentric (that is, earth-centered) model for the universe, the Italian Galileo Galilei supplied scientific experiments that proved the accuracy of Copernicus' theory. One of the philosophical heroes of the Scientific Revolution was the Frenchman Rene Descartes, who attempted to base his beliefs about the world upon empirical and provable facts: most famously, "I think, therefore I am." Francis Bacon was an English intellectual who wrote copiously on the possibilities for science to improve the human condition. Sir Isaac Newton excelled in many fields, but is best known for his theories of motion and gravitation. Newton helped create the general idea that objects in the world behave in regular and predictable ways.

Between the years 1600 and 1770, political and social philosophy in Europe underwent a tremendous change, known collectively as the Enlightenment. Just as Northern Italy had been the center of the Renaissance, so now Paris was the hub of progressive thought. The collection of philosophes, who sought to bring every subject under the authority of reason, included both deists (those who believed in God) and atheists (those who did not). The study known as political science first emerged during this period. Intellectuals began to question the divine right that had been claimed by absolute monarchs in the past; they sought to determine which was the best form of government for all the citizens of the country.

One of the most sparkling wits of the Enlightenment period belonged to the Frenchman Voltaire (1694-1778). He challenged the authority of the Church, declaring that people should tolerate the views of others and that no one man or group had a monopoly on absolute truth. Thomas Hobbes (1598-1679) was one of the most influential political theorists of the period. In his masterpiece "Leviathan," he declared that the base impulses of the people had to be restrained by a powerful and just monarch. John Locke (1632-1704), on the other hand, declared that men were born with natural rights which could not be justly denied them. Rousseau (1712-78), a Swiss philosopher, asserted that the government only ruled so long as it did so to the satisfaction of the General Will of the people.

Peter the Great (1672-1725) was responsible for the transformation of Russia from an impoverished agricultural nation to a strong commercial nation. Peter was enamored of the ways of the western European nations, and made several trips to other capitals to learn the intricacies of Enlightenment politics and trade. St. Petersburg was intended to be a Russian city in the style of Paris or Berlin. Peter's innovations revitalized the economy, but they also set a standard for decadence that would be carried on by future czars. Catherine II, otherwise known as Catherine the Great, ruled from 1762 to 1796 and implemented many Enlightenment policies in education and the arts. Nevertheless, in the remote provinces of Russia the feudal system endured, and the economy remained stunted.

The Peace of Westphalia (1648) established the independence of several small sections of Germany; chief among these new states was Prussia. Frederick the Great (1712-86) became the ruler of Prussia in 1740 and displayed marvelous efficiency and benevolence. He made a genuine effort to allow for the coexistence of all the religious groups in Prussia, and also worked to improve the lives of the serfs. Frederick also encouraged immigration to Prussia, which brought in new ideas and technological advances. Prussia, which had long suffered economically because of the German religious wars, now became a producer of luxury goods like porcelain and silk and commerical power with the acquisition of more territory along the Baltic coast.

French Revolution

Before the revolution, France was governed by an absolute monarch and with regard to matters of taxation, the Estates General, which had been formed in order to represent the common people. The Estates general was composed of three estates: the clergy (First Estate), nobility (Second Estate), and everyone else (Third Estate). Unfortunately, this body had been marginalized by a series of powerful monarchs, and it was arranged such that the largest group by far, the Third Estate, only had one-third of the vote. In any case, the Third Estate usually found its desires opposed by the other estates. Another source of anger for the middle class and peasants was the tax structure; the nobles and clergy were not forced to pay taxes, and thus the burden of France's depressed economy fell upon the Third Estate.

Aware of the injustice of the French tax policy, King Louis XVI tried to pass some reforms but was repeatedly thwarted by the greedy nobles and clergy. The Third Estate was infuriated, and refused to vote in the Estates General anymore. Instead, prominent members of the middle class banded together to form the National Assembly, which purported to represent the interests of common Frenchmen. At the same time, the peasants were in full revolt. On July 14, 1789, they stormed the Parisian prison known as the Bastille. The success of this riot inspired more peasants to clamor for representation, and the diversion it caused kept the government from dealing with the National Assembly.

After the storming of the Bastille and the formation of the National Assembly in 1789, the French middle and lower classes joined together and established a new government with the slogan "Liberty, Equality, Fraternity." This government quickly reformed the tax code and declared that government offices would henceforth be filled on the basis of merit. The National Assembly also eliminated serfdom and drafted a Declaration of the Rights of Man, which was similar to the American Bill of Rights. The National Assembly then seized the lands that belonged to the

Church, and eliminated the feudal rights of the aristocracy. However soon, there was dissension within the Third Estate, and the revolution became more radical and violent.

As the government established by the Third Estate descended into chaos, the radical Jacobin leader Robespierre took charge. He had an idealistic vision of what France could become, and he was willing to kill thousands in order to see it realized. The guillotine provided a swift way to execute scores of opponents, a group that included anyone who dared challenge the Jacobin party line or was suspected of retaining their Catholic faith in the new culture of state-mandated atheism. Among those executed were King Louis XVI and his wife, Marie Antoinette. After a while, the French tired of the violence and turmoil of the Reign of Terror, and Robespierre himself fell victim to the guillotine. A group of five prominent men, known as the Directory, was established to restore calm. This group would last until 1799, when it was overthrown in a coup that would eventually bring Napoleon Bonaparte to power.

Napoleon Bonaparte

Napoleon Bonaparte (1769-1821) began his career as a French military commander, scoring major victories in Austria and England. Upon his return to the chaos of France, he led a coup and was installed as the leader of France. He was subsequently elected by a popular vote. Almost immediately, Napoleon reformed French education, agriculture, and infrastructure. The main object of Napoleon's rule, however, was the acquisition of territory both in Europe and in the New World. Napoleon's troops quickly conquered Austria, Portugal, Spain, and Prussia. Napoleon, who modeled himself after Charlemagne in many ways, then crowned himself emperor. The French empire proved too large to manage, however, and Napoleon further weakened himself with a disastrous campaign against Russia.

After Napoleon's debacle in Russia debilitated his military, revolts sprung up in many of the nations that he had conquered, and Napoleon was overthrown. The leaders of the countries that had overthrown Napoleon met in Vienna to decide how to respond to him. These three men, Prince von Metternich of Austria, the English Duke of Wellington, and Alexander I of Russia, were constantly in disagreement, however, and Napoleon used this opportunity to return from his exile on the Isle of Elba in the Mediterranean and reclaim power. Finally, Napoleon was defeated at Waterloo and sent into permanent exile. The allies met again at the Congress of Vienna in 1815 where France was not treated too harshly, and it was determined that a balance of power should be maintained in Europe to ensure that no one in the future tried to dominate the Continent.

Industrial Revolution

The Industrial Revolution in Europe in the nineteenth century produced immediate and far-reaching changes in the social structure. England was perhaps the first to feel the effects of rapid industrialization; the factory system for manufacturing textiles was implemented, meaning that individuals were only required to do one in the series of tasks required to prepare a piece of cloth. This division of labor increased productivity. New energy sources, such as the steam engine, also made fabulous increases in productivity possible. Coal was introduced as an aid to the iron-smelting process, and the mass production of cotton textiles was soon propelling the English economy.

With the success of the textile industry, more and more workers were needed in the European cities, and therefore people began to abandon their country lives and take factory jobs in town. This rapid urbanization created a new middle class in Europe, and it also created a number of problems. Most cities did not have the infrastructure to support such an explosion in population, and as such disease, crime, and poverty were common. The booming success of industry made many people rich as investors and merchants, and therefore the middle class assumed even more political power in Europe. Social mobility was infinitely more possible in this economic environment, encouraging many people to stick with jobs that were demeaning and not especially lucrative.

As people flooded the cities to work in the booming factories, large landowners consolidated the farmlands they left behind. Working class individuals were probably not pleased with their new lives: 18-hour days, low wages, and dangerous machinery were among the problems faced by this new underclass. Oftentimes, women and children were employed for the most menial jobs, and they were paid less than men. A small rebellion, led by a group called the Luddites, tried to resist the tide of industrialization and were known for vandalizing factory equipment. Still, most individuals were enticed by the prospect of upward mobility that the new, fluid class system offered, and were willing to endure hardship in exchange for hope.

Anti-Colonial Struggles

When Spain fell to Napoleon's forces in 1809, the provinces of Chile and Buenos Aires both declared themselves independent. At this time, Peru was the stronghold of Spanish power in the New World, and therefore the rebels attacked the government there. Led by the Argentinean Jose San Martin, rebels entered Lima and declared Peru an independent state in 1821. The greatest military leader of the independence movement, however, was Simon Bolivar. He had traveled extensively in Europe, and used his knowledge of the enemy to run the Spaniards out of Colombia, Venezuela, and Central America. Bolivar eventually seized control of Peru, and hoped to form a great union of South American nations, but this alliance was eventually torn asunder by internal feuds.

The Opium War lasted between the years 1839 and 1842. It began because the British kept trafficking opium from India into China because they wanted to trade with the Chinese, and opium was the only product that China could not produce for itself. The Chinese government, however, was appalled by the effect that the drug had on its citizens, and mounted a serious anti-opium campaign. When British merchants appealed to their leaders, the British navy was sent in order to force the Chinese to accept the opium. The British ended up seizing several Chinese cities, including Shanghai and Nanking. The war ended with the Treaty of Nanking in 1842; China was forced to cede Hong Kong to the British, and several Chinese ports had to be left open for trade.

The Taiping Rebellion lasted in China between the years 1850 and 1864. It was a religious and political rebellion against the government of the Manchus, led by the Christian Hung Hsiu-chuan. The rebels advocated the public ownership of land and a self-sufficient economy. They wanted to rid China of the encroaching influences of foreign merchants. Hung's troops were able to conquer Nanking and make it the capital of their "Great Peaceful Heavenly Dynasty." Internal feuds weakened the Taiping, however, and the western powers (concerned that they would lose the Chinese market) helped to oust them in 1864. The Taiping Rebellion was by far the bloodiest war of the nineteenth century.

In 1854, an American group led by Commodore Matthew Perry forced Japan to open its ports to foreign merchants. Japan had been closed to the West for 200 years. The Japanese people were not pleased with this development, and they blamed the Tokugawa shogun (the military leader of the period). In 1867, the shogun resigned and Emperor Matsuhito declared that he was now in charge. The Japanese capital was moved from Kyoto to Edo (which was renamed Tokyo). The ensuing period in Japanese history is known as the Meiji Period. During it, the feudal system was abolished, and Western ideas became popular. The samurai had their land right revoked and were eventually eliminated altogether. In the late nineteenth century, Japanese leaders began to turn their attentions to expansion onto the Asian continent; in the Sino-Japanese war, they conquered parts of China and Korea.

The Boxer Rebellion was a peasant uprising in China around the turn of the twentieth century. The aims of the rebels were to overthrow the Manchu government and to cast all foreigners out of China. The rebels were known as the Boxers because they practiced certain mystical boxing rituals. After Japan had defeated China in 1895, the Japanese had exercised a great deal of influence on the Chinese economy. Around 1900, Boxers began to kill foreign merchants and diplomats. An international force was assembled to defeat the Boxers. During the ensuing fight the city of Peking was almost entirely destroyed. Eventually, the western powers prevailed and forced the Boxer leaders to sign an incredibly unfavorable treaty.

19th Century Politics

The political and economic philosophies of the Enlightenment gave rise in the nineteenth century to classical liberalism. Adam Smith summarized the classical liberal view of economics in his book "The Wealth of Nations"; there Smith invoked the idea of the "invisible hand" to suggest that markets, if left alone, would regulate themselves. Smith endorsed the changes brought on by the Industrial Revolution as part of the natural evolution of the capitalist economy. Thomas Malthus is another intellectual associated with classical liberalism; he declared that the world was in danger of becoming overpopulated, and that the natural solution would be for the poor to die of disease and starvation. Malthus, too, tacitly supported the Industrial Revolution by suggesting that the plight of the poor was in the best interest of humanity.

Social liberalism developed in the late nineteenth century as an alternative to classical liberalism. Social liberalism declares that political problems can be solved by the work of liberal institutions in the government. Unlike the classical liberals, social liberals believe that the government should exercise some influence on the economy, and should extend some basic welfare services to the people. The aim of social liberalism was to improve life for the poor and disadvantaged. Social liberals were also very outspoken on issues of civil rights and individual liberties. Some of the most famous social liberals are Jeremy Bentham, John Stuart Mill, and John Dewey.

Socialism is a political philosophy which declares that the economic means of production should be owned by the workers. This control may either be exercised directly by the workers through local councils, or by the state with the consent of the workers. Socialists hope thereby to create a state of social equality and an even distribution of wealth. Not surprisingly, this movement was most popular among the working classes in nineteenth-century Europe. Socialists at this time declared that capitalism served only the interests of the very wealthy, and exploited everyone else. In their view, a socialist society would provide a greater reward for hard work, and would create harmonious societies.

The political theories of socialism and communism both take their inspiration from the works of Karl Marx (1818-83). Marx declared that economics have been the primary determinant in history, and that the history of society is nothing more than a "history of class struggle." Marx asserts that problems have been created in situations where the material that a worker produces is worth more than the compensation he receives for his work. The surplus goes to the capitalist owner, and the worker is caught in a situation where he can never get ahead. The inevitable result, according to Marx, is a revolution of the working class (which he called the proletariat), and the installation of an economic system similar to socialism or communism.

In the nineteenth century, the spirit of nationalism that had been building in Europe since the Middle Ages reached a critical mass. Nationalism refers to pride in the traditions, culture, language, and past of a certain nation of people, and not necessarily to pride in one's country. This is important to note, because in the 19th century there were many nations of people thrown together as parts of a larger kingdom. The rising tide of nationalism, then, was a concern to the ruling monarchs, who hoped to hold together disparate nations under their control. Russia, for instance, contained a wide variety of cultures and languages under one leadership.

During the nineteenth century, the memory of Napoleon and the balance of power established by the Congress of Vienna prevented any large conflicts. The Industrial Revolution had made Britain the wealthiest and most powerful nation in Europe. The rise of a rich middle class caused the British Parliament to alter voting laws so that more of the wealthy would have influence. This was done with the Reform Act of 1832; in 1833, Britain abolished slavery in its colonies. This was not enough for the many working-class Britons, however, and they lobbied long and hard for universal suffrage, until it was finally granted in the 1880's. The British movement for universal suffrage was known as Chartism.

Internal turmoil caused France to miss out on much of the wealth of the Industrial Revolution. After the demise of Napoleon, Louis XVII had been restored to the throne by the Congress of Vienna. He was succeeded by the arch-conservative Charles X, who was quite unpopular and was chased off the throne in the July Revolution of 1830. In his place came Louis Philippe, who administered over a fairly stable country for eighteen years until he was deposed in the revolution of 1848. Next came Napoleon III: elected the emperor of France in 1851, he remained in power until the French defeat in the Franco-Prussian War of 1870. From 1870 until 1940, France would be governed by a constitutional and democratic government which was for the most part conservative.

Ever since the end of Charlemagne's empire, Austria and Germany had not been unified as a single nation. This was finally achieved by the Prussian Otto von Bismarck after a long period of suppression of German nationalists. Bismarck's unification of Prussia was mainly aimed at defeating the rival Hapsburgs, who controlled Austria. When Prussia won the Austro-Prussian and Franco-Prussian wars in quick succession, Bismarck declared that he had achieved his ends and unified the German empire. He oversaw the creation of the Reichstag, a legislative body that would provide representation to the middle and lower classes. Germany threw itself into the project of industrialization.

Italy, like Germany, had really been more of a disjointed collection of independent city-states than a nation in its own right. In the nineteenth century, however, there was a drive to unify the region. A leader from the Piedmont region, Camillo Cavour, tried to bring the various city-states together through diplomacy rather than combat. This process took a very long time, but was eventually completed in the 1870s. Northern Italy, which had intimate contact with Germany, became industrialized during this period, and the city of Milan enjoyed immense growth. Southern Italy, on the other hand, remained largely rural. This distinction between the two halves of Italy would be a source of conflict in the future.

At the beginning of the nineteenth century, much of Russia was still mired in an impoverished, quasi-feudal state. After the death of Alexander in 1825, the Decembrists tried to force the incoming Czar to adopt a constitution allocating some power to the people. This next Czar was Nicholas I, who used a secret police to try and eliminate the roots of the popular insurrection. This policy of suppression only further isolated Russia from the rest of Europe, which was at that time reducing the power of the monarch. Russia later lost the Crimean War to Britain, France, and the Ottoman Empire, and many Russians bemoaned the backward state of their country. Finally, a new czar, Alexander II, freed the serfs and tried to industrialize. This happened slowly.

At the turn of the twentieth century, Russia was torn by the trends of industrialism and imperialism. Russia, despite still being an absolute monarchy, was trying to modernize its cities. In other words, Russia was attempting to create all of the economic changes of Western Europe without allowing any of the accompanying social changes. Russians were also disheartened by the defeat of their navy in the Russo-Japanese War. The socialist party in Russia, known as the Bolsheviks, began to lead revolts against the Mensheviks. When a peaceful demonstration against the Czar was brutally suppressed, the rebels became energized. The Russian Revolution of 1905, as this was known, continued with revolts by peasants and soldiers, until the czar promised to create a constitutional monarchy with a powerful legislative body, known as the Duma.

1914-Present

World War I

In the early years of the twentieth century, relations among the various European powers were complex. Ever since the Franco-Prussian War, won by Prussia, the two sides had been enemies. At the center of their conflict was the territory of Alsace-Lorraine, which each side claimed as its own. In order to bolster their position in the region, each side entered into networks of alliances. After years of negotiations, two main alliances contained the major European powers: the Triple Alliance (Germany, Austria, Italy) and the Triple Entente (France, Britain, Russia). These two alliances would end up being the opposing sides in the great war of the ensuing years.

In the years before the First World War, the Balkans were attempting to gain independence from the Hapsburg empire of Austria. This insurrection culminated in the assassination of Austrian Archduke Franz Ferdinand in 1914 by Gavrilo Princip, a member of a Serbian nationalist group. At this point, a chain reaction of war declarations (spurred by the comprehensive alliances of the time) ensued. Austria declared war against Serbia; Germany and Turkey joined with the Austrians; Russia declared war on these countries in support of Serbia; France joined with Russia; and Britain and Italy joined forces with France, even though Italy had been a member of the Triple Alliance.

Despite the fact that almost every nation in Europe had entered into World War I, most Europeans thought the conflict would be brief. Instead, advances in weapons technology made the war bloody and excruciatingly slow. Much of the fighting was done from trenches, and some battles would see the deaths of thousands of soldiers at a time. The war was also slow because the sides were very evenly matched; that is, until 1917, when the United States entered on the side of Britain. Also in 1917, the Russians exited the war via the Brest-Litovsk Treaty. Russia was basically exhausted after suffering through a Revolution in 1917 in which the Bolsheviks came to power. The entry of the US provided the British and French with supplies and troops, and Germany was soon forced to call for a truce.

As the First World War wound down, a disgruntled German populace ousted the emperor and installed a moderate socialist government. This government, known as the Weimar Republic, would last until 1933. At the Paris Peace Conference, the victors of the war (the US, Britain, France, and Italy) exacted some revenge on Germany. The Treaty of Versailles penalized Germany economically and territorially: Alsace-Lorraine became independent, and the German military was dismantled. The Treaty of Versailles would need to be modified by two subsequent agreements: the Treaty of Locarno which outlined a more reasonable reparations plan for Germany, and the Kellogg-Briand Pact which asserted that diplomacy rather than force would be used to resolve conflicts.

Interwar Years

After the Revolution of 1905, Russia had enjoyed a few years of relative peace. After a while, however, the peasants became dissatisfied with the weakness of the Duma, and after strikes and protests Czar Nicholas II was forced to abdicate the throne. In place of the monarchy, a Provisional Government was set up to work alongside more progressive local councils, known as Soviets. These two groups were constantly at odds, however, especially during Russia's participation in the First World War (the Soviets wanted to withdraw and focus on national issues, while the Provisional Government felt obliged to fight). During this period, Vladimir Lenin rose to prominence as the Marxist leader of the Bolshevik Party. In the Russian Revolution of 1917, Lenin and his supporters ousted the Provisional Government and exited the War. Lenin then began the immense project of nationalizing the Soviet economy.

After his success in the Revolution of 1917, Lenin began to advocate the revolt of the working class in other nations. Naturally, this did not endear the new Russian government to the leaders of other nations. Russia became increasingly isolated both economically and politically from the rest of the world. Domestically, Lenin established the New Economic Policy, which blended capitalism and communism. This plan worked well enough in agriculture, but it never achieved much success in industry. After Lenin's death, Joseph Stalin came to power and began an ambitious plan of collectivizing farms and nationalizing factories (known as the Five Year Plans). Stalin was ruthless in the pursuit of his goals; he established labor camps to house his opponents. It is estimated that 20 million people were killed by Stalin's regime during the period now known as the Great Terror.

In 1911, the Manchu dynasty, which had been significantly weakened by the Boxer Rebellion, was finally overthrown. A period of instability followed, in which Sun Yat-sen declared the creation of a republic with its headquarters in Nanking. Sun Yat-sen began a political party aimed at improving life for the common people; it was known as the Kuomintang. During this period, both Mongolia and Tibet declared their independence from China. The Chinese people became disenchanted with the Kuomintang government after what they saw as unfavorable agreements following World War I. After the death of Sun Yat-sen in 1925, a national government was established at Canton; the communist party was a major participant in this government.

In 1926, the military leader Chiang Kai-shek led campaigns in central and northern China, in the hopes of unifying the country. During this period, Chiang broke with the communist party, and Communists were persecuted in Shanghai. In 1927, a national government led by the Kuomintang, who had previously fallen out of favor, was established in Nanking. The peasants were not pleased with this leadership, and they were organized as the Red Army under Mao Tse-tung in the south. In what is known as the Long March, Mao led his army north to Yenan, where they would gather strength. The situation in China was made even more volatile by the Japanese invasion in 1937. In what is known as the "Rape of Nanking," Japanese troops killed over 200,000 Chinese. The people were outraged, and the partisan splits between Mao's communists and Chiang's government only widened.

In 1926, amid growing nationalism, Hirohito became the Emperor of Japan. The next year, the Japanese prime minister declared that Japan should dominate Asia, and four years later Japanese forces invaded Manchuria. Some historians consider this to be the beginning of the Second World War. After establishing a puppet regime in Manchuria, the Japanese withdrew from the League of Nations and attacked China. The Sino-Japanese War ensued. In 1938, Japan outlined its new vision of Co-prosperity Spheres: Japan would be the industrial center of Asia, and would acquire its raw materials from its colonies in the rest of Asia. Japan promoted this idea as an opportunity to break from European imperialism, but it was really just the substitution of one master for another. In 1940, Japan would complete its transformation into a fascist state by dissolving all political parties.

In the years after the First World War, the general mood in Europe was one of wariness. Most nations were exhausted by the conflict, and few felt that the signing of the Treaty of Versailles and the formation of the League of Nations had created a permanent peace. In the 1920s, Britain, Germany, France, and the United States were all liberal democracies without a strong executive. Unlike the United States, however, even the victorious European nations suffered a profound economic depression. One nation that saw no diminution in nationalism was Italy. In part out of a fear of communism, Italians supported the rise of the fascist dictator Benito Mussolini. Fascism was a political philosophy that promised Italians a return to the glory days of Rome, when they were a mighty power ruled by a dominating executive. Of course, in order to maintain his authority Mussolini had to brutally suppress any opposition.

After the abdication of the emperor, Germany was ruled by a legislative body known as the Weimar Republic. Most Germans felt that this group had been too willing to accept punishment in the treaties that followed the war. Germans also thought that this government was responsible for the inflation which crippled the German economy in the post-war period. Germany, then, was vulnerable to the charms of a leader who told them they had nothing about which to be ashamed. This leader was Adolf Hitler (1889-1945). A failed artist, Hitler became the head of the National Socialist, or Nazi, party. His speeches were expressions of ardent nationalism, although often Hitler seemed to be calling for a return to an ideal German state that had never actually existed.

Led by Adolf Hitler, the Nazi party championed the Aryan race as superior to all others, especially the "insidious" Jews. Hitler suggested that the noble ambitions of the true German people required lebensraum, or living space. In other words, Germany needed more territory. In its early days, the Nazi party was part of the German republican system; Nazi candidates ran for office and served in the Reichstag (German parliament). As Germany suffered through a terrible economic depression in the early 1930s, however, the people became impatient. In 1933, the Reichstag "accidentally" caught on fire and the Nazis used the opportunity to claim total control of the government. Hitler was named Chancellor of Germany. He was able to quickly improve the German economy, mostly through the expansion of the weapon-building industry. At the same time, the new government began to quietly round up Jews, Gypsies, and homosexuals.

Still shell-shocked from the First World War, the nations of western Europe were slow to respond to the growing menace of Nazi Germany. In general, they pursued a policy of appeasement and isolation. The British prime minister Neville Chamberlain was especially committed to using diplomacy over war. Then, in 1936, Hitler sent troops to occupy the Rhineland, a strip of territory on the German border. At around the same time, Mussolini invaded Ethiopia; the two aggressors, Germany and Italy, entered into an agreement making them the Axis Powers. In 1938, Germany annexed Austria and indicated that it was about to attack Czechoslovakia. In response to these actions, Chamberlain brought together Mussolini and Hitler for the Munich Conference of 1938. These talks would only briefly suspend German aggression.

World War II

After Chamberlain had tried to forestall German aggression at the Munich Conference of 1938, Germany nevertheless invaded Czechoslovakia in 1939. It was also during this year that Hitler signed a secret agreement with Stalin pledging not to attack Russia so long as Russia stayed out of German affairs. Hitler then declared war on and conquered Poland. At this step, Great Britain and France were finally forced to declare war upon Germany. Germany at this point was a dominating military adversary. New advances in motorized military vehicles made it possible for Germany to conquer large areas of land quickly in a new form of warfare called Blitzkrieg (lightning-war). The Axis powers conquered almost the entire European continent, including France, over the course of 1940. Only Great Britain remained in opposition, and the Nazis undertook a ferocious aerial assault on the British, who were by then led by Winston Churchill, but failed to do enough damage to make an invasion of the island country practical. Instead, Hitler turned East and decided to violate his truce with Stalin, invading Russia in 1941 and overwhelming much of the Soviet military and advancing deep into Russian territory in a huge surprise offensive.

The tide turned against Hitler once the United States entered the war. The harsh Russian winter halted the German advance into Russia short of Moscow in 1941. The Germans made further gains in the summer of 1942, but were decisively beaten at the battle of Stalingrad and were slowly pushed back out of Russia from then on. American and British troops landed in North Africa in 1942 and used that as a springboard to invade Italy in 1943. In 1944, the Americans and British opened yet another front with a massive invasion of northern France in the D-Day landings. Fighting numerically superior forces on multiple fronts, the Germans steadily lost ground and the Allies pushed into Germany from both East and West in 1945. Surrounded and with the war lost, Hitler commited suicide in his bunker in Berlin in April, 1945 and the remaining German forces surrendered shortly afterwards.

The Japanese, like the Germans, became seduced by the notion of their own racial superiority during the 1930s. As in Germany, this inevitably led to a lust for territorial expansion. By 1941, Japan had conquered Korea, Manchuria, and parts of China. Japan was also threatening to invade American interests in the Philipines. The United States imposed economic sanctions on Japan making it difficult for the Japanese war industry to function. In response, the Japanese launched a surprise attack on the United States by bombing the US naval base of Pearl Harbor. After the attack on Pearl Harbor, the United States would declare war upon Japan (and Germany would in turn declare war on the United States). The Japanese made huge territorial gains before the US turned the tide at the Battles of Midway and Guadalcanal. The war in the Pacific would take much longer than the war in Europe due to the island hopping nature of the fight. The Japanese unwillingness to surrender made it almost impossible for America to entirely vanquish them without enormous lose of life. So the United States decided to drop atomic bombs on Hiroshima and Nagasaki to force Japan to surrender and finally end the war in the Pacific in August 1945.

The Holocaust

The Holocaust is the name given to the systematic killing of Jews, gypsies, homosexuals, and others by the Nazis. Anti-Semitism had existed in Europe for millennia, but the Nazis gave it renewed emphasis, and after making numerous false claims about Jews, began persecuting them upon Hitler's rise to power in 1933. Jews were disenfranchised, forced into ghettos, had their property taken, and were finally sent to work and be killed in concentration camps. Approximately 6 million Jews were killed during the Holocaust. As the situation for the Germans became more dire in the Second World War, Hitler sought to implement what he called the "final solution," in which hundreds of thousands were killed just before the fall of Nazi Germany.

Many of the Nazi leaders were tried and convicted at the Nuremberg trials for their roles in the Holocaust. West Germany would later issue a Federal Compensation Law, through which billions of dollars were paid to survivors. During and after the Holocaust, Zionist Jews fled to Palestine. Public sympathy with their plight would be a main reason for the creation of Israel in 1948. The total destruction of the Jewish community in Europe caused many Jews to question their faith, and those that remained in Europe are markedly more secular than their ancestors. The shock of the Holocaust has also caused many institutions, including the Roman Catholic Church, to consider their own latent anti-Semitism. Unfortunately, the anti-genocide legislation created in response to the Holocaust was not strict enough to rally international support against the Rwandans (who slaughtered hundred of thousands of Tutsis in 1994), or the Bosnian Serbs and Croats (who killed thousands of Muslims in the early 1990s).

Cold War

After the defeat of the Axis powers in WWII, the United States and Russia entered into a long and often secret conflict, in which each side used diplomatic, economic, and occasionally military forces to try and assert itself as the dominant world power. The first issue on which these nations butted heads was the rebuilding of Europe. Germany was divided into an eastern and western section; the western half was democratic and looked to the US for guidance, while Eastern Germany became a communist nation in the USSR's sphere of influence. Russia worked to bring all of its neighbors (including Poland, Czechoslovakia, Hungary, Romania, and Bulgaria) under its control. The western borders of these nations formed what Churchill referred to as the iron curtain, dividing communist Eastern Europe from democratic Western Europe.

China was torn by civil strife all throughout the Second World War. At one point, the American government had to renounce its trade rights in China in order to persuade China not to sign a peace treaty with Japan while the US still needed Chinese support. Once Japan had been defeated, the Red Army under Mao moved into Manchuria (which had recently been vacated by the Soviets). The major cities were still occupied by Nationalist forces, supported by the Americans. In 1946, fighting resumed between the opposing factions, and the Nationalists under Chiang were eventually forced to abandon central China. In 1949, the Red Army forced Chiang Kai-shek to leave the mainland and find refuge on Taiwan. On October 1, 1949, the communists declared the official creation of the People's Republic of China.

In order to stop the spread of communism in Europe and elsewhere, the President Truman asserted his policy of "containment" in the so-called Truman Doctrine. This meant that the US would support the anticommunist governments throughout the world. The Marshall Plan advanced this policy by supplying aid to war-ravaged countries in Western Europe. When the Eastern Bloc countries prevented aid from reaching West Berlin, the US , England, and France organized the Berlin Airlift to overcome this obstacle. In 1949, the Western European and North American nations entered into a mutual defense treaty, NATO (North Atlantic Treaty Organization). As a response, the eastern Bloc nations joined with the Soviet Union in the Warsaw Pact.

During the Cold War, the United States and the Soviet Union each tried to deter an attack by the other by building up fantastic arsenals of nuclear missiles. The two nations would also expend considerable effort trying to be the first in space. Finally, in the late 60s and early 70s, the two nations would begin talks aimed at mutual disarmament. This occurred in part because relations between China and the USSR had cooled. Before this period of détente, however, there had been a couple of serious threats to global peace. In 1961, the US had financed an unsuccessful invasion of Cuba at the Bay of Pigs. This led the Soviet Union to establish missile bases on communist Cuba; the US and USSR almost declared war on one another during the Cuban Missile Crisis of 1962.

Over time, the leaders of the Soviet Union and United States began to realize the total annihilation that would ensue if nuclear war was declared, and it was agreed that both sides would disarm. The two treaties that were signed during the 1970s are known as the Strategic Arms Limitation Talks (SALT) I and II. When Mikhail Gorbachev came into power in the USSR in 1985, he established a policy of glasnost, or "openness." In response to US President Ronald Reagan's military build-up using the might of the US economy, Gorbachev understood that the Soviet Union could not economically compete militarily under a communist system and overcome the military might of the United States. He thus advocated perestroika, a gradual metamorphosis of the Soviet economy. In 1991, these reforms culminated in the disintegration of the ruling Communist party, and the disbanding of the Soviet Union. This occurred two years after the Berlin Wall, which for more than forty years had separated communist and anticommunist Germany, was finally torn down.

Post-Colonialism

In 1947, after years of peaceful protests led by Mahatma Gandhi, India was given its independence and partitioned into three states, India and Pakistan. The following year, Gandhi would be assassinated in India. In 1965, border disputes would flare into the Indo-Pakistani War. In 1971, Pakistan would fend off attacks from Bengali rebels, who sought to achieve independence. The next year, however, Bangladesh would be established as an independent state. In 1984, India had its own internal problems: after the Indian army occupied the Golden Temple sacred to the Sikhs, the Indian leader Indira Gandhi was assassinated by her Sikh bodyguards. Anti-Sikh riots resulted, and much blood was shed.

After WWII, the United Nations announced that Palestine would be partitioned in order to make room for a new Jewish state. Israel was created in 1948. In 1951, the Iranian leader Mossadegh nationalized the oil interests, making his government extremely wealthy and powerful. This move would be emulated by future leaders. In 1967, in the Six Day War, Israel routed a coalition of Arab nations, seizing the West Bank, Sinai, and Jerusalem. In 1972, Palestinian terrorists murdered 12 Israeli athletes at the Olympics in Munich. In 1973, the oil-producing Arab nations placed an embargo on shipments to the West, causing major energy crises in the US and Europe. Also in 1973, Israelis and Arabs battled again in the Yom Kippur War. In 1977, Egyptian leader Anwar Sadat became the first Arab leader to visit Israel.

In 1978, American President Jimmy Carter hosted successful peace talks between Egypt and Israel at Camp David. The next year, however, a fundamentalist Islamist regime would take power in Iran, and many Americans would be taken hostage, only released upon the election of Ronald Reagan. Between 1980 and 1988, Iran and Iraq engaged in a bloody and brutal war, begun when the Iraqi leader Saddam Hussein seized territory in western Iran. Also during this period, Afghan rebels were engaged in a prolonged, ultimately successful fight for independence from the Soviets. In 1982, Israel attacked Lebanon, which was harboring the Palestinian leader Yasser Arafat. Lebanon would be forced to oust Arafat the next year. Israel would continue attacking Arafat and the Palestinian Liberation Organization, and the PLO would continue to sponsor terrorist activities against Israel.

Globalization

In 1987, Syrian troops entered Lebanon and stopped the civil war. Also during this year, 402 pilgrims died during riots in the Saudi Arabian sacred city of Mecca. In 1988, the Palestinian resistance (known as the Intifada) began in earnest against Israel. Iraq invaded Kuwait in 1990, and after UN sanctions were levied, the US invaded in 1991. The Iraqi soldiers set fire to thousands of Kuwaiti oil wells while retreating. In 1992, Arafat and Israeli PM Yitzhak Rabin shook hands in Washington and Arafat would soon return to Gaza after years of exile. In 1995, the Israelis and Palestinians signed an agreement giving the Palestinians autonomy in the West Bank and Gaza areas. Despite continuing violence, another agreement was reached in 1998, this one stating that the Palestinians would be granted land in exchange for keeping the peace. Violence continued, however, and in 2003 Israel began construction of a barrier between itself and the Palestinian territories.

In 1991, Gorbachev resigned as the last president of the USSR, and a number of the Soviet provinces, including Lithuania and Latvia, declared independence. The Maastricht Treaty, formally announcing the creation of the European Union, was signed in 1992, and the next year a unified European stock market opened. In the "Velvet" Revolution of 1993, Slovakia separated from Czechoslovakia, which became the Czech Republic. Meanwhile, the former USSR was enduring civil strife until Boris Yeltsin seized power in 1993. In 1994, Russian troops attacked Chechnya, which was trying to achieve independence. In 1998, President Clinton helped broker a peace agreement between the British and North Irish rebels.

In 1999, the Czech Republic, Poland, and Hungary all joined NATO, further eliminating the old divides between western and eastern Europe. The conflict in Chechnya increased during this year, and Yeltsin was succeeded as Russian leader by the former KGB agent Vladimir Putin. An International Criminal Court was created in the Hague (Netherlands) in 2002, despite the vehement opposition of the United States. In the late nineties, many of the western European governments had become quasi-socialist, and they spent much of their time debating the immense increase in immigration. Meanwhile, the former Soviet states have had a rough transition from command to market economies, and are still somewhat economically depressed.

First World nations are those that have advanced capitalist economies and are fully industrialized. The former Soviet states, which are slowly developing capitalist economies after having inefficient socialist economies for so long, are classified as Second World nations. This term has fallen out of general use, as these nations have slowly become more similar to First World nations. The relatively poor and nonindustrialised nations of Latin America, Africa, and Asia, most of which were colonized or involved in other exploitative trade arrangements with the Western empires at one time, are known as the Third World nations. Although these nations are far more numerous than those of the First or Second World, they wield much less political power.

In the 1990's and early years of the 21st century, Japan and China have emerged as two major economic powers. Despite suffering a prolonged recession, Japan continued to be one of the world's manufacturing leaders. However, several internal scandals have shaken Japanese confidence and caused many to question the close relations between corporations and government. In China, the suffocating communist regime has relaxed its economic strictures somewhat, and the result has been an economic boom. China created several Special Economic Zones along its eastern coast to lure foreign business; at present, however, Chinese firms are beginning to control a sizable portion of the market in their own right.

In 1993, the first web browser was developed, beginning the era of internet communications that has revolutionized every area of human life. The Internet did not become widely used, however, until 1997 and 1998. In 1997, a Scottish lab successfully cloned a lamb from adult sheep DNA, opening the door to the cloning of other animals, or human organs for medical purposes, and even for the cloning of entire human beings. This last possibility was strengthened in 2001, when the work of sequencing the DNA of the human genome was finally finished. Although embryonic stem-cell research has been limited in the US (other sources than embryos remain legal), other countries are using cells from human embryos to search for cures for disease.

Renaissance

During the Medieval period, the Christian church dominanted much of life; however the Renaissance saw the growth of a number of ideologies which sought to minimize or eliminate the church's influence. Humanism refers to a Renaissance movement that was based on the philosophical idea that the actions and problems of mankind are more important than other issues. This movement primarily used literature and art to encourage individuals to participate in society, but there were numerous humanist writers and artists who also attempted to imitate or discuss the literature and art of the ancient Greeks and Romans. Individualism refers to the philosophical idea that an individual is defined by his own actions. Individualism primarily focuses on an individual's ability to reach his full potential rather than on an individual's ability to prove his faith or religious beliefs. Secularism refers to the philosophical belief that an individual's life has value regardless of his religious beliefs. According to secularists, it is important for society to focus on more than just an individual's religion. Secularism primarily focuses on the separation of religion from other areas of life.

In response to this, a number of religious ideas rose to compete with the new secular ideologies. Christian humanism refers to a Renaissance movement that was based on the philosophical idea that the actions and problems of mankind are more important than other issues. Christian humanism, like standard Humanism, used literature and art to encourage individuals to participate in society. However, the writers and artists of the Christian humanist movement attempted to imitate or discuss the Bible instead of the literature or art of Greek and Roman mythology that the standard humanists attempted to write about and paint. Mysticism refers to the religious belief that the average person can explore his own spirituality and communicate with God without a priest or any other religious individual, structure, or artifact. The term pagan is used to describe any individual, text, or belief that is related to a non-monotheistic religion (i.e., which is not Christian, Jewish, or Muslim). The term is frequently used to describe the literature and belief system of the ancient Greeks and Romans.

The Renaissance brought about several important changes in the artwork that was being created in Europe. First, most paintings up until the Renaissance depicted religious themes for the Church. This changed during the Renaissance, however, as a number of painters began to depict other aspects of society as well as the mythology of the ancient Romans and Greeks. There were still numerous painters painting religious themes for the Church, but there were also several individuals painting other themes as well. Second, there were many new art techniques that were invented or mastered during the Renaissance, including the mastery of oil painting, the use of different perspectives, and the ability to create a sense of depth in a piece of art. Finally, there was a movement in art during the Renaissance to create more accurate depictions of the people portrayed in art, which led to the creation of artwork that was anatomically correct.

The Renaissance saw a flourishing of the arts and new artistic ideas and concepts. The term fresco refers to a painting that is painted on the wall or ceiling of a structure. Frescoes were extremely common during the Renaissance, and they were typically used to depict religious themes. Some famous frescoes include Leonardo da Vinci's The Last Supper, Raphael's School of Athens, and Michelangelo's Creation of Adam. The term Madonna refers to a painting of the Virgin Mary. Madonnas were extremely common during the Renaissance, and they would often depict the Virgin Mary holding the baby Jesus. Some famous Madonnas include Leonardo da Vinci's Virgin of the Rocks, Raphael's Madonna of the Meadow, and Raphael's Sistine Madonna. The term pietà refers to a painting or a sculpture of the Virgin Mary holding Jesus after his death. Numerous artists and sculptors created pietàs during the Renaissance, but Madonnas were actually more common. Some famous pietàs include Giovanni Bellini's Pietà and Michelangelo's Pietà.

The Renaissance brought about several important changes in both southern and northern Europe. However, it is important to note that the changes that occurred in each section of Europe were different, namely because southern Europe had access to several major ports that traded with the Middle East, which allowed Italy and the rest of southern Europe to become major hubs for banking, manufacturing, and the spice trade. The merchants of southern Europe had more money, which made it easier for individuals outside the Church to become patrons of the arts. Northern Europe, on the other hand, didn't have access to the financial resources that southern Europe had at the time, so the changes that occurred there were more practical. In fact, most of the changes that occurred in northern Europe were related to scientific discoveries such as Copernicus's assertion that the sun is at the center of the universe, inventions such as Johann Gutenberg's moveable type for the printing press, and other scientific or technological advancements.

Renaissance in Italy

Northern Italy was the birthplace of the Renaissance and thus many Italian words were used for Renaissance concepts. The Italian term condottiero literally means "contractor." The term was used during the Renaissance to refer to the commander of a group of mercenaries. The Latin term virtu literally means "virtue" or "the quality of a man." The term is used to describe a state of being in which an individual or an organization is able to accomplish everything that the individual or organization could possibly accomplish. However, it is important to note that an individual or an organization can only achieve this state if the individual or organization has the ability to effectively perform a variety of different tasks. The Italian term quattrocento literally means "400." The term is used to refer to the artwork, literature, and cultural accomplishments of Italy in the fifteenth century.

The three major city-states that existed in northern Italy during the Renaissance were the Republic of Florence (which became the Duchy of Florence and then the Grand Duchy of Tuscany in 1569), the Duchy of Milan, and the Venetian Republic. The Republic of Florence, which was located on the northwestern side of Italy in the region now known as Tuscany, housed a number of important ports that regularly traded with cities throughout Asia and the Middle East. The Republic of Florence was also well-known for its banking and textile industries. The Duchy of Milan, which was located in the center of northern Italy in the region now known as Lombardy, was a major outpost for caravans transporting goods throughout Italy and Europe. The Duchy of Milan was also known for its armor, banking, farming, and silk industries. The Venetian Republic, which was located on the northeastern side of Italy in the region now known as Veneto, was well-known for the control that the area exercised over the spice trade.

The **Medici family** played an important role in the politics of the Republic of Florence because their wealth granted them the ability to exert a great amount of influence over the democratic voting process that existed in Florence at the time. However, the family's true influence did not begin in the area until Giovanni de' Medici formed the Medici bank, which was one of the first banks to offer loans that had to be paid back with interest. This lending practice allowed the family to amass a great deal of wealth. This wealth helped Giovanni's son, Cosimo de' Medici, encourage the people of Florence to vote in the manner that Cosimo saw fit. In this way, Cosimo could effectively rule the Republic even though he was not officially a member of the Republic's government because he could use his wealth to bribe officials and manipulate the laws and actions of the government. In fact, these tactics were also used by Cosimo's son, Piero di Cosimo de' Medici, and eventually his grandson, Lorenzo de' Medici, to control the Republic of Florence long after Cosimo's death.

The **Sforza family** was originally a peasant family known as the Attendolo family, but the family earned the name Sforza because of the tactics it used to seize control of Milan. The name Sforza comes from the Italian word sforzare, which literally means "to force." The Sforza family, as the name implies, took control of the Duchy through the use of military force. Muzio Attendolo and his son, Francesco I Sforza, were condottieri who fought for the King of Naples. They commanded a mercenary army that they could use to establish themselves as the official rulers of Milan. However, this not only allowed the family to take control, but also allowed the family to maintain its control, as the family could use the threat of force to encourage the other noblemen and officials of the area to comply with the family's orders.

Both the Medici family and the Sforza family were strong supporters of the arts during the Renaissance. In fact, both families are known for their support of a number of different artists during the Renaissance, including the famous Raphael Santi (supported by the Medici family) and the even more famous Leonardo da Vinci (supported by the Sforza family). This support had an essential role in the artwork of the time because the artists, architects, inventors, sculptors, writers, and other artistic individuals of the Renaissance relied on the money they received from wealthy patrons like the Medici family and the Sforza family to pay for their day-to-day living expenses. As a result, artists like Raphael Santi or Leonardo da Vinci may not have been able to create the artwork, inventions, and other masterpieces that they created without the support of individuals or groups like the Medici family, the Sforza family, and other wealthy families.

Countless artists, painters, philosphers, writers, and inventors participated in the Renaissance in Italy, here are some of the most famous and important ones:

Giotto di Bondone was an artist and architect who lived in the city of Florence and the surrounding area during the late thirteenth to early fourteenth centuries. Giotto is primarily known for the religious landscapes and frescos he painted. He used a combination of light and shadow to depict a sense of depth in his frescoes. He is also known for the bell tower he designed for the Florence Cathedral. It is important to note that Giotto is sometimes considered to be one of the first Renaissance artists, but he is not a Renaissance artist in the strictest sense because his artwork was created nearly a hundred years before most of the other Renaissance artists.

Tommaso di Ser Giovanni di Simone, who is more commonly known as Masaccio, was an Italian artist who lived in the city of Florence during the early fifteenth century. Masaccio is primarily known for his frescoes, which use a combination of light and shadow to create different perspectives.

Sandro Botticelli was an artist who lived in the city of Florence during the mid fifteenth century to early sixteenth centuries. He is primarily known for paintings that depict mythological figures, but he is also known for his frescoes, Madonnas, and portraits. Botticelli's artwork includes works such as Adoration of the Magi, Primavera, Venus and Mars, Painting of a Young Man, and The Birth of Venus.

Domenico Ghirlandaio was an artist who lived in the city of Florence during the mid to late fifteenth century. He is primarily known for the role he played in teaching Michelangelo the techniques that Michelangelo needed to develop his masterpieces later in life. Ghirlandaio is also known for his frescoes, Madonnas, and portraits. Ghirlandaio's artwork includes works such as Adoration of the Shepherds, Birth of John the Baptist, and Portrait of Giovanna Tornabuoni.

Raphael Santi was an artist and architect who lived in the city of Florence and then, in his later life, in Rome during the late fifteenth and early sixteenth centuries. Raphael is known for the frescos, Madonnas, and portraits that he painted. His artwork includes works such as Wedding of the Virgin, Madonna of the Meadow, Saint Catherine of Alexandria, School of Athens, Portrait of Pope Julius II, and Sistine Madonna.

Michelangelo Buonarotti was an artist, architect, and sculptor who lived and worked in the city of Florence and, for a short time, in Rome during the late fifteenth to mid sixteenth centuries. Michelangelo is primarily known for the statues that he sculpted, including sculptures such as the statue of Bacchus, the Pietà, the statue of David, the statue of Moses, and Genius of Victory. He is also known for his paintings and frescoes, including paintings such as The Torment of Saint Anthony and Creation of Adam, that he painted on the ceiling of the Sistine Chapel.

Francesco Petrarca, who is more commonly known as Petrarch, was a poet who lived in the city of Florence during the 1300s. He is primarily known for the sonnets that he wrote. (In fact, he actually invented the Italian sonnet.) He is also known for the essays and books that he wrote promoting humanist ideals. These essays and books had a significant impact on the writers of the Renaissance because a number of writers attempted to expand on Petrarch's writings. As a result, Petrarch's writings ultimately encouraged the humanist movement that took place during the Renaissance.

Giovanni Boccaccio was a writer who lived in the city of Florence during the 1300s. He is primarily known for his collection of novellas, The Decameron, but he is also known for the essays and books that he researched and wrote to expand on the humanist ideals that Petrarch initially discussed.

Nicollò Machiavelli was a diplomat, musician, philosopher, and writer who lived in Florence during the late fifteenth to early sixteenth centuries. He is primarily known for his treatise (in other words, his long essay), The Prince, which discussed his belief that the true purpose of any politician or government is to protect his, her, or its own power by any means necessary. It is important to note, however, that Machiavelli never actually said that maintaining power by any means was right or wrong, but instead said that it was necessary for a government to stay in power.

Baldassare Castiglione was a diplomat and writer who lived in a variety of places throughout northern Italy during the late fifteenth to early sixteenth centuries. He is primarily known for his book, The Book of the Courtier, which describes the characteristics that Castiglione believed a man must have to be considered a gentleman as well as the rules that a man must follow to maintain his status as a true gentleman.

Laura Cereta was a philosopher and writer who lived in the Duchy of Milan during the late fifteenth century. She is primarily known for the letters that she wrote to a number of prominent individuals to discuss a variety of topics ranging from insomnia to war. Cereta, however, is best known for the letters she published in her collection, The Epistolae Familiars, which literally means Familiar Letters, in which she discusses women's rights.

Artemesia Gentileschi was an artist who lived in Rome, Florence, and eventually in Naples during the late sixteenth to mid seventeenth centuries. She is primarily known for her religious paintings that depict the story of Judith from the book of Judith as it appears in the Old Testament. These paintings include works such as Judith Beheading Holofernes, Judith and Her Maidservant, and Judith and Her Maidservant with the Head of Holofernes.

Major Contributors to the Renaissance

The printing press had several effects on the people of Europe during the Renaissance primarily because the only way to copy a text, up until the invention of the printing press, was to do so by hand. This meant that an individual would have to rewrite an entire book, word for word, to obtain a single copy. The printing press changed this, as it allowed individuals to mass-produce books, which in turn made it easier and cheaper for individuals to obtain books. This allowed average European citizens to access information and religious texts that they had never been able to access before. It also encouraged the citizens of Europe to not only read, but also to convey new information that other individuals could use to reevaluate their social, political, and religious beliefs.

The role that the average woman played in society during the Renaissance remained much the same as it had been during the Middle Ages, as the average woman was expected to tend the home and care for the children. In addition, a woman was ultimately considered to be the property of her father or her husband. The role that the noblewoman played in society during the Renaissance, however, changed drastically from the role that the noblewoman played during the Middle Ages. This is because the codes of chivalry that existed during the Middle Ages required a man to treat a noblewoman with a certain level of respect. Unfortunately, this expectation disappeared during the Renaissance, as the codes of chivalry began to become less and less important. Consequently, the women of wealthy and noble families began to see the rights, the power, and the influence that they had been granted during the Middle Ages disappear during the Renaissance.

While the Renaissance was born in Italy, it soon spread throughout all of western and central Europe. Here are some of the important non-Italian contributors to the Renaissance:

Nicolaus Copernicus was an artist, astronomer, mathematician, and physician who lived in Prussia during the late fifteenth to mid sixteenth centuries and who played an important role in changing the way that not only the people of Europe, but also the people of the rest of the world looked at the Earth. Copernicus suggested that the Earth and the other planets of the solar system actually revolved around the sun, which was a major change from the standard view of the universe that existed at the time. In fact, the scientists of the world, up until this point, had primarily agreed with the Roman Catholic Church in its assessment that the Earth was located at the center of the universe and that the sun, moon, and planets actually revolved around the Earth. Copernicus, however, helped to change the minds of not only scientists, but the rest of the world as well through his book De Revolutionibus Orbium Coelestium, which literally translates to On the Revolutions of the Heavenly Spheres.

Gerard Groote was a traveling priest who preached throughout Holland during the mid to late fourteenth century. He is primarily known for his role as the founder of the Brethren of the Common Life, which was a religious society that encouraged individuals to imitate the behavior of Jesus Christ by putting the lessons that each individual learned from the stories of Christ into practice. The society primarily focused on the actions that Christ took during his life and encouraged individuals to act toward their fellow man in the same way that Christ would. This idea was later put into writing in Thomas A. Kempis's book, The Imitation of Christ. This book and the ideas it contained ultimately played an important role in defining the basic ideals on which Christian humanism was founded. This is because both the Brethren of the Common Life and the Christian humanism movement believed that the Bible could help the average person to be more kind, more tolerant, and ultimately better than he had been before.

Desiderius Erasmus was a priest who lived in southern Holland during the late fifteenth to early sixteenth centuries. However, he is not typically known for his contributions to the Church; he is instead primarily known for the books that he wrote discussing the ideals of Christian humanism. In fact, Erasmus's contributions to the Christian humanist movement are so great that he is sometimes known as "The Christian Gentleman," "The Prince of Humanists," and "The Crowning Glory of the Christian humanists." Erasmus's most influential contribution to the Christian humanist movement, however, was his book, The Praise of Folly, in which he poked fun at a number of superstitions, social issues, and religious beliefs that he believed prevented the average citizen from assuming a meaningful role in society or discouraged the average citizen from thinking independently. Some of Erasmus's other works include Adages, Handbook of a Christian Knight (or, as it is sometimes translated, Handbook of a Christian Soldier), and The Gospel Preacher.

Albrecht Dürer was an artist who lived in Nuremberg, Germany, during the late fifteenth to early sixteenth centuries. He is primarily known for his portraits and religious woodcuts, but he also painted numerous landscapes as well. Some of his more famous works include The Four Horseman of the Apocalypse; Adam and Eve; The Knight, Death, and the Devil; and his Self-Portrait.

Jan van Eyck was an artist who lived in Belgium during the late fourteenth to mid fifteenth centuries. He is primarily known for his oil paintings, and the invention of oil painting is, in fact, often incorrectly attributed to Jan van Eyck because of the skill he demonstrated with oil paints. Some of Jan van Eyck's more famous paintings include Madonna in the Church, Stigmata of St. Francis, Portrait of a Man in a Turban, and Virgin of Chancellor Rolin.

François Rabelais was a doctor, a priest, and a writer who lived and worked throughout France during the late fifteenth to mid sixteenth centuries. He is primarily known for the books that he wrote in which he discusses his views on politics, religion, the actions of the Church, and French society as a whole. These books are all part of a famous series of books known as Gargantua and Pantagruel.

Michel de Montaigne was a writer who lived in the southeastern part of France during the mid to late fifteenth century. He is primarily known for the role he played in creating the essay, as he was the first writer to ever publish a collection of essays. His collection of essays, entitled Essais (a French term that literally translates as To Test), discussed numerous issues related to religion, religious tolerance, politics, society, and other similar topics.

Miguel de Cervantes was a writer who lived in Madrid during the mid sixteenth to early seventeenth centuries. He is primarily known for his novel, Don Quixote (which is also known as The Man of La Mancha), in which he pokes fun at the way people viewed the knights of the Middle Ages. However, he is also known for a series of short stories and plays he wrote in which he addresses a variety of topics related to the political and social issues of the time. Some of his more famous works include The Gypsy Girl, The Novel of Lady Cornelia, El Trato de Argel, and La Numancia.

Lope de Vega was a writer who lived in Madrid and then, later in his life, in Valencia during the mid sixteenth to early seventeenth centuries. He is primarily known for the plays he wrote, but he is also known for his sonnets, novels, and epic poems. Some of his more famous works are The Dancing Master and Fuenteovejuna.

Christopher Marlowe was a writer who lived in Canterbury during the mid to late sixteenth century. He is primarily known for his plays, but he also wrote several poems. Some of his more famous works include The Jew of Malta, Doctor Faustus, The Massacre at Paris, and The Passionate Shepherd to His Love.

Edmund Spenser was a poet who lived in London during the mid to late sixteenth century. He is primarily known for his epic poem, the Faerie Queene, but he also wrote several other poems, including The Shepheardes Calendar, The Ruines of Time, and Prothalamion.

William Shakespeare was a writer who lived in various places throughout England during the mid sixteenth to early seventeenth centuries. He is primarily known for the plays he wrote; in fact, he is often considered to be one of the greatest playwrights of all time. Some of his most famous works include Romeo and Juliet, Macbeth, and Hamlet. It is important to note, however, that he is also known for his poetry.

Martin Luther and the Beginning of the Reformation

Despite the growing secularism accompanying the Renaissance, Christianity and the Catholic Church remained a powerful force. Over the centuries a huge religious tradition had been built and formalized by the Catholic Church. A decretal is a formal letter from the pope that identifies the Roman Catholic Church's position on a specific matter. Decretals are typically used to respond to an issue that a priest has asked the Church to review, so the Church can identify the appropriate course of action. However, it is important to note that the Church can issue a decretal for any issue even if the Church was not specifically asked to address it. An encyclical is a formal letter that is, in effect, a religious newsletter for the Church. Encyclicals are typically issued by the pope, and they may be sent to all the priests and churches of the Roman Catholic Church or to only certain priests and churches, depending on the circumstances. Encyclicals are typically used to inform the priests and churches of the Church's position on important issues.

A diet is a meeting in which the leadership of an organization or the leadership of a nation makes decisions regarding actions or new regulations that the organization or nation must take or adopt. A diet, in terms of the Holy Roman Empire, was specifically a meeting in which the emperor, the noblemen, members of the clergy, and other officials discussed the issues that the empire needed to address. Excommunication refers to the process by which an individual is cast out of the Church. It is typically reserved for individuals who might interfere with the ability of the Church's members to understand or follow the Church's doctrines. A papal bull is a formal letter from the pope in which the Church makes an official decree. Papal bulls may be used to issue virtually any type of decree, but they are typically used for issues that the Church considers to be serious in nature such as excommunications.

There were several practices in the Roman Catholic Church that the Reformation attempted to eliminate, but there were three major practices of the Church that the average supporter of the Reformation considered to be outright corrupt. These three practices were nepotism, simony, and indulgences. Nepotism, in terms of the Roman Catholic Church, refers to a common practice of the time in which a church official would place a friend or a relative into a position of power within the Church even if the individual didn't have any formal training or didn't have enough formal training as a priest to assume the position. Simony refers to a common practice of the time in which a church official would allow an individual to purchase a position of power within the Church. Indulgences, in terms of the Roman Catholic Church, refer to a common practice of the time in which a priest would sell an individual the right to enter heaven before the individual had actually paid for all of his sins in purgatory.

The way that society viewed the Roman Catholic Church changed drastically during the Renaissance and the period immediately before the Reformation because the average person began to look at religion in a new way. The humanists of the Renaissance had begun to shift society's focus away from the afterlife, which meant that people were quickly becoming more interested in their current status rather than their status after death. This change in the importance that people placed on their mortal lives greatly diminished the power of the Church because the Church, up until this point, had relied on the idea that a person could only be saved if he complied with the Church's doctrines. The Renaissance changed this idea, however, as it introduced the notion that an individual could find his own path to salvation. This change in the societal view of the time ultimately led to the Reformation, as more people gained faith in their own ability to find salvation and lost faith in the Church's ability to grant salvation.

The Protestant Reformation refers to a religious movement that took place shortly after the Renaissance in which several individuals attempted to bring about reform in the doctrines of the Roman Catholic Church. The movement ultimately succeeded in bringing about reform in the Church, but it also led to the creation of numerous smaller Christian sects.

Johann Tetzel was a traveling friar who preached throughout the Holy Roman Empire during the mid fifteenth to early sixteenth centuries. He was a member of an order of preachers known as the Dominican Order, which spent a great deal of time at the beginning of the Reformation promoting the doctrines of the Roman Catholic Church and discouraging the pagan beliefs and philosophies that people had developed during the Renaissance. However, his true role in the Reformation had very little to do with his order and significantly more to do with the tactics he used to gather money. Tetzel attempted to gather funds for the reconstruction of the rapidly deteriorating St. Peter's Basilica by selling indulgences. Indulgences, of course, were a major issue with the reformers who brought about the Reformation, but Tetzel's influence on the Reformation was only made worse by the fact that Tetzel had actually received permission from the Church (specifically from Pope Leo X himself) to sell the indulgences.

Martin Luther was a priest and professor who lived in Germany during the late fifteenth to early sixteenth centuries. He originally attended a law school at the University of Erfurt to become a lawyer, but he dropped out of the school after a series of misfortunes and strange events to become a monk instead. During his early years as a monk, he taught theology at the University of Wittenberg, but it was actually at the church in Wittenberg and not at the university where Luther played his role in the Reformation. This is because Luther set the foundation for the Reformation when he attached his religious pamphlet, Ninety-Five Theses, to the door of the Castle Church. This pamphlet was Luther's response to the Church's decision to allow Tetzel to sell indulgences, and it is here that Luther described the reasons why he felt indulgences were inappropriate.

Johann Maier von Eck was a theologian who lived in Germany during the late fifteenth to mid sixteenth centuries. He is primarily known for the role that he played in the Leipzig Debate where he attempted to support the position of the Roman Catholic Church against Martin Luther and Andreas Karlstadt. Eck had difficulty defending the Church's position, however, as Luther and Karlstadt made a strong argument against the views of the Church. This caused Eck to become frustrated with the fact that he could not prove his point. As a result, Eck attempted to shift the focus of the debate from the abuses of the Church to the issue of whether Luther actually agreed with the doctrines of the Church. This allowed Eck to portray Luther as a heretic, which led Pope Leo X to later issue a papal bull threatening to excommunicate Luther if he did not recant his position. Luther burned the papal bull in response, which led the Church to excommunicate him.

Charles V was a Spanish prince, and later a king and emperor, who lived in Spain during the early to mid sixteenth century. He was the rightful heir to the Holy Roman Empire, and he assumed the throne in 1519. This made Charles V the Holy Roman Emperor, which had historically been a figurehead for the empire rather than an actual leader; the actual leaders of the empire were the princes of the lands that Charles V ruled. Charles V, however, wanted to change this fact, and he made it very clear that he was going to solidify his power over the lands of the empire. This fact was not well-received by the princes who ruled the lands of the empire, however, and the princes set out to prevent Charles V from solidifying his power as a result. To do this, some of the princes decided to undermine the largest supporter of Charles V's power, the Roman Catholic Church, by supporting the Protestant Reformation.

The Diet of Worms was a meeting in which the leadership of the Holy Roman Empire met in Worms, Germany to discuss some of the issues that the empire needed to address in 1521. During the Diet of Worms, the leadership of the empire discussed Martin Luther's actions to determine his fate after his excommunication. Charles V, Emperor of the Holy Roman Empire, summoned Luther to Worms to recant some of the claims he had made. Luther, however, refused to recant, stating that he was "neither able nor willing to recant, since it is neither right nor safe to act against conscience." Charles V, as a result, declared Luther to be an outlaw, which was a crime punishable by death (specifically by burning at the stake). Prince Frederick the Wise, elector of Saxony, rescued Luther from his fate, however, by having Luther "kidnapped" by supposed bandits and taken to the prince's castle in Wittenberg.

Martin Luther was forced into hiding after Charles V issued the Edict of Worms at the Diet of Worms in 1521. This did not stop Luther from his attempts to further the Reformation, however, as Luther continued to write and work toward his reforms even though he was a wanted fugitive. In fact, Luther spent most of his time at Wittenberg Castle translating the Bible into German so that the average peasant could read the Bible and understand it. Luther also spent a great deal of time working with Frederick the Wise to implement his reforms in the local churches. Once implemented, these reforms began to spread throughout the other churches of Germany and the churches of other countries as well. This quickly led to the creation of a new Christian religion, which was eventually called Lutheranism.

The Peasants' War refers to a revolution that started in Germany in 1524 and ended in 1525. The peasants of Germany, who were starving at the time, petitioned the Holy Roman Emperor Charles V to make several changes to the laws of the empire. These changes were primarily related to the taxes the Holy Roman Empire demanded, the way the various lands of the empire could be used, and the way that the churches within the empire could be operated. Charles V ignored the petition and refused to implement any of the changes. This caused the peasants to revolt, and a series of conflicts began to erupt between the peasants and the wealthy landowners throughout Germany. As the war waged on, the peasants continued to fight under the hope that they might receive reinforcements from Martin Luther and his supporters. However, Martin Luther disagreed with the peasants' decision to revolt, and the revolt ultimately failed because the peasants never received reinforcements.

Foundation of the Reformation

The Five Solas refer to a series of Latin phrases that the members of the Reformation used to describe the religious truths on which the Reformation was founded. Each of these truths refers to a specific religious concept that is different from the religious concepts the Roman Catholic Church considered to be true at the time of the Reformation. In other words, the Five Solas were the five major religious beliefs that the reformers were attempting to implement in the Church. These concepts, as a result, were an extremely important part of the Reformation because they were the specific religious issues on which the reformers and the Church disagreed. The Five Solas include Sola Fide (by faith alone), Sola Scriptura (by scripture alone), Soli Deo Gloria (by the glory of God alone), Solus Christus (by Christ alone), and Sola Gratia (by grace alone).

The Latin phrase sola fide literally means "by faith alone." Sola Fide refers to the belief that an individual's salvation is the result of his faith and not a result of the individual's actions on Earth. In other words, the religious concept of Sola Fide suggests that an individual will be saved through faith, rather than through good works. This concept demonstrates a major shift in the beliefs of the time because the Roman Catholic Church at the time of the Reformation asserted that an individual could only be saved if he demonstrated his faith through penance, sacraments, righteous action, and other similar activities.

The Latin phrase sola scriptura literally means "by scripture alone." Sola Scriptura refers to the belief that the Bible is the only place an individual can find the truth of God. In other words, Sola Scriptura suggests that the doctrines an individual follows must come from the Bible and not from any other religious text or from any priest, scholar, or even the pope himself. This religious concept demonstrates a major shift in the beliefs of the time because the Roman Catholic Church, at the time of the Reformation, asserted that the pope and other high-ranking members of the Church could make doctrine as long as those doctrines were based on the traditions of the Church. It is important to note that the religious concept of Sola Scriptura suggested that the pope and other members of the Church could interpret the doctrines of the Bible and help others understand those doctrines as long as they didn't actually create doctrine.

46

The Latin phrase soli deo gloria literally means "for the glory of god alone." Soli Deo Gloria refers to the belief that an individual must honor God in every aspect of his life and that an individual cannot honor God simply by performing a specific action (such as going to church). In other words, soli deo gloria suggests that an individual must demonstrate his faith in all the things he does to honor God and that an individual cannot honor God by honoring something other than God. This religious concept demonstrates a major shift in the beliefs of the time because the Roman Catholic Church, at the time of the Reformation, asserted that an individual could honor God by honoring the Church.

The Latin phrase Solus Christus literally means "by Christ alone." Solus Christus refers to the belief that Jesus Christ is man's only mediator to God and that an individual needs no other mediation to achieve salvation. In other words, Solus Christus suggests that the priesthood of the Roman Church are not necessary to attain eternal life, and especially that nothing needs to be added to Christ's sacrifice to make it efficacious unto salvation. This religious concept demonstrates a major shift in the beliefs of the time because the Roman Catholic Church, at the time of the Reformation, believed that the Church and all its priests were representatives of God, and they, therefore, were necessary for an individual to achieve salvation.

The Latin phrase sola gratia literally means "by grace alone." Sola Gratia refers to the belief that an individual can only receive absolution through God. In other words, Sola Gratia suggests that an individual can only be forgiven for his sins through God's grace and that an individual cannot relieve himself of his sins through any other means. This religious concept demonstrates a major shift in the beliefs of the time because the Roman Catholic Church, at the time of the Reformation, asserted that an individual's sins could be absolved if the individual confessed his sins to a priest, purchased indulgences, took part in a pilgrimage, touched a holy relic, or took part in any of a number of other similar activities.

Martin Luther wasn't the only major reformer. Huldrych Zwingli, who was also known as Ulrich Zwingli or Hyldreich Zwingli, was a priest who lived in Zurich, Switzerland, during the late fifteenth to early sixteenth centuries. He is primarily known for the opinions, sermons, and other works that he wrote in which he discussed the abuses of the Roman Catholic Church and the need for religious reform. In fact, Zwingli is often considered to be the founder of the Swiss Reformation movement because his works ultimately led to the rise of Protestantism in Switzerland. It is important to note that Zwingli's works also played a role in his death, as he was killed by the army of the Five Catholic States during the Second Kappel War. John Calvin was a priest who lived in France, and later in Switzerland, during the early to mid sixteenth century. He is primarily known for his book, Institutes of the Christian Religion, in which he set forth the religious tenets that would later form the basis for Calvinism.

The basic foundational beliefs of the Lutheran and Calvinist faiths are closely related, and there are a number of similarities between the two religions. However, there are two major differences that are important to note. First, each religion has a different view of the role of the church in politics. Lutherans believe that the church should stay out of politics because it is the church's responsibility to interpret the Bible and lead the faithful, but it is not the church's responsibility or the church's right to lead a town, city, or country. Calvinists, however, believe that the church has a duty to ensure that the politics of the land is conducted in a fashion consistent with the morals of the church. Second, each religion has a different view of the role that an individual plays in his own salvation. Lutherans believe that an individual may attain salvation as long as the individual is faithful, but Calvinists believe that God has already chosen the individuals who will be saved.

The Reformation Spreads

The First Diet of Speyer was a meeting of the Holy Roman Empire that took place in Speyer, Germany, in 1526. This meeting played an important role in the Reformation because the leadership of the Holy Roman Empire voted to suspend the sanctions enacted against the Protestant movement in the Edict of Worms until a formal council could be called to discuss the matter. The Second Diet of Speyer was a meeting of the Holy Roman Empire that took place in Speyer, Germany, in 1529. This meeting is significant because the leadership of the Holy Roman Empire reversed the decision it had made at the First Diet of Speyer, which meant that the Edict of Worms would be carried out. The Diet of Augsburg was a meeting of the Holy Roman Empire that took place in 1530. This meeting is significant because it was the location where Martin Luther delivered the Confessio Augustana, which literally means Confession of Augsburg, in which he proclaimed the major tenets of Lutheranism.

The Schmalkaldic League was a military alliance formed by the Lutheran princes of Germany in 1531. The alliance was primarily designed to help the princes protect their lands if the Holy Roman Emperor Charles V decided to attack them and put an end to the Protestant Reformation. The princes, however, began to use the alliance as a means to expand their power by taking the land that they converted. Charles V was eventually forced to intervene, which led to a yearlong conflict known as the Schmalkaldic War that lasted from the summer of 1546 to the late spring of 1547.

The Peace of Augsburg refers to a treaty that was signed at the end of the Schmalkaldic War in which the Holy Roman Empire agreed to recognize the right of the Lutherans to worship as they deemed fit. This treaty, which was signed in Augsburg, Germany, in 1555, stated that the prince of each Imperial State had the right to determine the religion of his people based on his own religion. In other words, the religion of the people within a particular state would be the same as the religion of the prince who ruled that state. This right was expressed in the Latin concept cuius regio, eius religio, which literally means "whose region, his religion." It is important to note, however, that the Peace of Augsburg only recognized the right of the Lutherans to worship within the empire. This meant that a prince could choose to practice Catholicism or Lutheranism, but he could not choose to practice Calvinism, Anabaptism, or any other religion.

Counter-Reformation

Ignatius Loyola was a priest and a knight who lived in Spain during the late fifteenth to mid sixteenth centuries. He is primarily known as the founder of the Society of Jesus, which he designed and organized to help the Roman Catholic Church resist the Reformation. The Society of Jesus is known for its loyalty to the Church, its willingness to enforce the doctrines of the Church, and its desire to teach and convert individuals to the Catholic faith. However, Loyola is also known for his religious work, Spiritual Exercises, in which he set forth a series of prayers and other religious activities that are still used in a number of churches to this day.

The Index of Prohibited Books, which is also known as the List of Prohibited Books or the Index Librorum Prohibitorum, was a list of books and other documents that were banned by the Catholic Church. The Index of Prohibited Books was first issued by the leaders of the Catholic Church in Holland in 1529, but other countries began to issue similar lists in 1542 after the leaders of the Church in Venice issued their own version of the list. The first official Index of the Roman Catholic Church, however, was not issued until 1559 when Pope Paul IV ordered any book written by an author considered to be inappropriate by the Church to be banned. This meant that the Church could ban everything an author wrote if he wrote a single work that the Church considered to be inappropriate, which made it significantly more difficult for Catholics to read the works of Protestant authors such as Martin Luther, Huldrych Zwingli, or John Calvin.

The Council of Trent was a religious conference in which the leaders of the Roman Catholic Church discussed the doctrines that the Protestants disagreed with and the alleged abuses within the Church that the Protestants had already identified. This conference, which actually consisted of a series of meetings that took place in Trent, Italy, from 1545 to 1563, was designed to help the Church identify the specific areas in which abuses were actually occurring. The Council of Trent ultimately identified a number of issues that needed to be addressed and suggested reforms for each of these issues, which included reforms such as banning simony, banning the sale of indulgences (although they could still be issued in exchange for an individual's service to the religious community), establishing additional seminaries to train priests, and other similar reforms. Despite these reforms, the Council of Trent ultimately determined that the doctrines of the Church were sound and made it clear that the Protestants were indeed heretics.

The Counter Reformation, which is also known as the Catholic Reformation, refers to a religious movement that took place within the Roman Catholic Church after the Council of Trent in which the Church attempted to address some of the issues that the Protestant Reformation had identified. It is important to note that the Counter Reformation typically refers to the period when the Church actually implemented some of the reforms that the Protestant Reformation had demanded. The Inquisition refers to a religious movement in which the Roman Catholic Church attempted to enforce the doctrines of the Church and protect its religious authority by punishing anyone who violated the Church's doctrines.

Pope Paul III was a priest, and later a pope, who lived in Rome during the late fifteenth to mid sixteenth centuries. He is primarily known for the role he played in the Counter-Reformation because he ordered the Council of Trent to take place. However, Pope Paul III is also known for a variety of Church reforms that he implemented outside the Council of Trent as well as for his papal bull, Sublimus Dei, in which he described the basic human rights of the Native Americans and the need to protect those rights.

Thirty Years' War

The uneasy Peace of Augsburg was shattered by the Thirty Years' War. The Bohemian Phase, which is also known as the Bohemian Period or the Bohemian Revolt, refers to the first stage of the Thirty Years' War in which the peasants of the Bohemian States, which now make up the nation of Czechoslovakia, revolted in 1618. This occurred because the peasants were primarily Calvinists, and they were concerned that a king with strong ties to the Roman Catholic Church might prevent them from worshipping in the way that they deemed fit. These fears were strengthened when King Mathias of Bohemia declared Ferdinand II, heir to the throne of the Holy Roman Empire, to be the rightful heir to the Bohemian throne. Ferdinand II was well-known at the time for his support of the Catholic Church, and the peasants, as a result, began to throw Bohemian officials out of windows to demonstrate their discontent. The situation only escalated from there, however, as the peasants took control of the city of Prague and declared Frederick V to be the rightful King of Bohemia. This led Ferdinand II to send troops into Bohemia to crush the rebellion.

The Danish Phase, which is also known as the Danish Period or the Danish Intervention, refers to the second stage of the Thirty Years' War in which the King of Denmark Christian IV attempted to help the Protestants maintain their control of northwest Germany. This occurred because the Protestants began to find it more and more difficult to practice their religious beliefs after Ferdinand II crushed the Bohemian Rebellion. Christian IV, however, was a strong supporter of the Protestant movement, and he sent forces into Germany in 1625 to ensure that Ferdinand II would not be able to remove the leaders of the Protestant movement from power. As a result, Ferdinand II sought the aid of Duke Albrecht von Wallenstein of Bohemia, who gathered over 50,000 mercenaries to fight the Danish Army. This ultimately allowed Ferdinand II to defeat the Danish forces and issue a decree known as the Edict of Restitution. In the Edict of Restitution, Ferdinand II declared all the German states that were converted to Protestantism after the Peace of Augsburg to be Catholic.

The Swedish Phase, which is also known as the Swedish Period or the Swedish Intervention, refers to the third stage of the Thirty Years' War in which Cardinal Richelieu of France offered to support the King of Sweden Gustavus Adolphus if King Adolphus attacked the Holy Roman Empire in exchange. This deal occurred because the Holy Roman Empire was beginning to gain more and more power throughout the world, as Ferdinand II continued to achieve victory after victory. Cardinal Richelieu wanted to stop the empire from gaining any more power than it already had, so he offered his financial resources to anyone who would attack the empire. The Swedish Army attacked the Holy Roman Empire in 1630, so they could accept Richelieu's offer and preserve the power of the Protestants. The Swedish Army was ultimately defeated by the Holy Roman Empire, however, and King Adolphus was killed during the conflict.

The French Phase, which is also known as the French Period or the French Intervention, refers to the final stage of the Thirty Years' War in which Cardinal Richelieu of France encouraged King Louis XIII to form an alliance with the Dutch and the Swedes to put an end to the Holy Roman Empire's expansion once and for all. Armand Jean du Plessis de Richelieu, who is more commonly known simply as Cardinal Richelieu, was the Prime Minister of France during the early to mid seventeenth century. The Holy Roman Empire was beginning to expand its influence into France, and Richelieu wanted to stop the empire from further expanding its power at any cost. Richelieu, as a result, pushed for an alliance between France and the other countries interested in preventing the Holy Roman Empire's expansion, which ultimately led France and its allies to attack the Holy Roman Empire and its ally, Spain in 1635. The French and its allies succeeded in defeating the Holy Roman Empire and forced the empire to engage in peace talks. Richelieu is primarily known for the role he played in bringing France and a number of other nations into the Thirty Years' War, but he also played an important role in granting the king absolute power by strengthening the king's army and removing the strongholds of the king's nobles and the king's enemies.

The Peace of Westphalia refers to a treaty that was signed at the end of the Thirty Years' War in which the Holy Roman Empire agreed to recognize the right of the Calvinists to worship as they deemed fit. Some of the countries involved in the conflict signed this treaty in Osnabrück in 1648, and the rest of the countries involved signed it later in Münster. Both of these cities are located in the Westphalia region of Germany. According to this treaty, the agreement that the Holy Roman Empire had made in the Peace of Augsburg would be enforced, and the princes could choose to practice Catholicism, Lutheranism, or Calvinism. The treaty also stated that the Holy Roman Empire would surrender some of its land to France and its allies as well as recognize the independence of Holland and Switzerland.

Age of Exploration

At the same time that the Renaissance was reinvigorating European cultural life and the Reformation was shaking the political and relgious order in Europe, a desire to explore the world abroad was growing. Indeed, the ability to make long voyages was facilitated by the advances in navigational technology made around this time. The main reason for exploration, though, was economic. Europeans had first been introduced to eastern goods during the Crusades, and the exploits of Marco Polo in the 13th century had further whetted the western appetite for contact with distant lands. This increasing focus on exploration and trade caused a general shift in the balance of power in Europe. Land-locked countries, like Germany, found that they were excluded from participating in the lucrative new economy. On the other hand, those countries which bordered the Atlantic (England, France, Spain, and Portugal) were the most powerful players.

Prince Henry the Navigator was a prince who lived in Portugal during the late fourteenth to early fifteenth centuries. He is primarily known for the navigation school that he established and the vast number of expeditions to Africa and the surrounding area that he sponsored. In fact, Prince Henry's ships explored most of the Atlantic coast of Africa, and they were the first European ships to actually reach the equator. It is important to note, however, that Prince Henry never actually took part in any of his expeditions because these expeditions would have required the prince to potentially put his life at risk.

Bartolomeu Dias was a nobleman and an explorer who lived in Portugal during the mid to late fifteenth century. He was the first European to discover and sail around the Cape of Good Hope south of Africa.

Christopher Columbus was a sailor and an explorer who realized that the journey east to India was a difficult one by land or sea, and he wanted to find an easier route for the Europeans to travel to India. To do this, Columbus tried to calculate the distance that a ship would have to travel to sail west from Europe to Japan. Columbus incorrectly estimated the distance, but he did determine a route that he thought would bring him to Japan and eventually India by sailing west. Columbus then designed a proposal for a voyage to India via the west that he brought to the King of Portugal. The king rejected the proposal, however, and Columbus was forced to seek funding from Spain. The Spanish Queen Isabella agreed to fund the expedition, and Columbus ultimately set sail for India in August 1492.

However he never actually reached his intended destination. Columbus incorrectly estimated the distance that he would need to travel to sail around the world, which meant that his journey to India would have taken significantly longer than he expected. Columbus, as a result, thought he had reached India when he reached a stretch of land that was further than the distance he had calculated, but the land he had reached was actually an island in the Bahamas. Columbus hadn't discovered a route to India, but he had discovered a route that thousands of colonists, explorers, and other individuals would eventually use to reach the Americas and the surrounding islands. It is important to note, however, that Columbus's discovery, and the colonization it later brought, ultimately led to the decline and the downfall of the Aztecs, Incas, and other natives of the Americas, as the Europeans attempted to seize their lands.

Vasco da Gama was a sailor and an explorer who lived in Portugal during the late fifteenth to early sixteenth centuries. He was the first European to actually reach India without traveling by land. It is important to note, however, that da Gama is also known for the trading post that he established in India as well as the violent tactics that he used to protect the trading post and Portugal's other assets from the Arabs.

Pedro Cabral was a sailor and an explorer who lived in Portugal during the late fifteenth to early sixteenth centuries. He was the first European to discover Brazil. He discovered the nation after his ship was accidently thrown off course. It is important to note, however, that Cabral is also known for the role he played in expanding the Portuguese trading posts located in India.

Ferdinand Magellan was a sailor and an explorer who sailed from Portugal during the late fifteenth to early sixteenth centuries. He was the first person to circumnavigate, or sail all the way around, the world. Magellan was also the first European to discover a route to sail from the Pacific Ocean to the Atlantic Ocean, which he accomplished through the use a waterway that would later be known as the Strait of Magellan.

The discovery of the new world by Columbus and other explorers prompted Spain to quickly dispatch military adventurers to claim the new territory for the Spanish Empire.

Hernán Cortés was an explorer and a conquistador (a Spanish term that literally means "conqueror") who sailed from Spain during the late fifteenth to mid sixteenth centuries. He is primarily known as the conqueror of the Aztecs because he formed an alliance with the enemies of the Aztecs to create a single unified army that he could lead into Mexico. This army ultimately allowed Cortés to defeat the Aztecs of Mexico and bring the Aztec Empire under Spanish rule.

Francisco Pizarro was an explorer and a conquistador who sailed from Spain during the late fifteenth to mid sixteenth centuries. Pizarro, who was actually a cousin of Hernán Cortés, is primarily known as the conqueror of the Incas because he led a Spanish expeditionary force into Peru to kill the leaders of the Incan Empire. This ultimately allowed Pizarro to seize control of the lands of the Incas for Spain.

Vasco de Balboa was an explorer and a conquistador who sailed from Spain during the late fifteenth to early sixteenth centuries. He was the first European to reach the Pacific Ocean by crossing Panama.

European Monarchs

The sixteenth through eighteenth centuries was marked by the rule of absolute monarchies in Europe. Absolutism refers to a state in which a king or queen has the ability to rule over his land without internal interference. In other words, absolutism refers to a type of government in which a monarch can rule as he deems fit despite the objections of his nobles, the objections of the Church, or the objections of any other entity. This was often based on the Theory of Divine Right which refers to the idea that a king or queen is actually chosen by God, and he, therefore, has the God-given right to rule in whatever way he deems fit. In contrast, Constitutionalism refers to a state in which a series of laws form the foundation for the country's government, and the leaders of that country receive their powers from those laws. It is important to note that the laws that form the foundation for a constitutional government may be part of a written constitution, but they do not necessarily have to be part of a single, written document.

There were three main ruling dynasties in central and eastern Europe during this time period. The czars, which is also sometimes spelled tsar, was the title used by the Russian emperors derived from the term "caesar." Some examples of the more well-known czars include Ivan the Terrible and Peter the Great. Hapsburg, which is also known as the House of Hapsburg or the House of Austria, actually refers to the noble family that ruled over the Holy Roman Empire and several other European countries throughout most of the fifteenth, sixteenth, and seventeenth centuries. Some examples of the more well-known members of the Hapsburgs include Charles V and Ferdinand II. Hohenzollern, which is also known as the House of Hohenzollern or the Zollern Family, actually refers to the noble family that ruled over Prussia and Germany throughout most of the eighteenth and nineteenth centuries. Some examples of the more well-known members of the Hohenzollerns include Frederick William I and Frederick II.

There were many notable absolute monarchs, here are some of the most important and famous ones:

Ivan Vasilyevich, who is more commonly known as Ivan the Terrible, was the Czar of Russia during the mid to late sixteenth century. He is primarily known for the brutal tactics that he used to maintain his control over the nobles of Russia (especially later in life) and expand the lands that Russia controlled. Ivan the Terrible also implemented a number of reforms. These reforms included the creation of the first Russian Parliament, significant modifications to the Russian justice system, and other similar changes.

Pyotr Alexeyevich Romanov, who is more commonly known as Peter the Great, was the Czar of Russia from the mid seventeenth to early eighteenth centuries. He is primarily known for the role that he played in expanding the influence and the lands of Russia through the powerful Russian Navy, which he established. Peter the Great also made several reforms to the Russian education system, the Russian Army, and other parts of the Russian government as well.

Suleiman I, who is more commonly known as Suleiman the Magnificent was the Sultan of the Ottoman Empire, or the ruler of the area that is now modern-day Turkey, during the early to late sixteenth century. He expanded the lands of the Ottoman Empire by seizing control of Belgrade, Hungary; most of northern Africa; and several areas throughout the Middle East. Suleiman I is also known for the Siege of Vienna in which he attempted to capture the city of Vienna, Austria, but he was ultimately defeated by the armies of the Holy Roman Empire.

Frederick William I was the King of Prussia during the early to mid eighteenth century. He is primarily known for the reforms that he instituted in Prussia to increase the efficiency and influence of the Prussian government. Frederick William's reforms included reforms to the Prussian Army, the Prussian education system, the Prussian government's spending, and a variety of other similar reforms.

Francis I was the King of France during the early to mid sixteenth century. He is primarily known for the repeated attempts that he made to eliminate Charles V and his allies. Although Francis ultimately failed to eliminate Charles V, he did manage to support several famous artists including Leonardo da Vinci, commission the construction of numerous castles throughout France, and support multiple French expeditions to the New World.

Francis II was the King of France for a short time during the mid sixteenth century. He allowed his mother, Catherine de Medici, to rule the country even though he was officially old enough to rule the kingdom himself. His willingness to allow his mother to rule in his stead may have been partially because Francis was always ill. In fact, he died when he was only sixteen years old.

Henry II was the King of France during the mid sixteenth century. He is primarily known for the series of harsh actions that he took against the Calvinists of France. The French Calvinists were known as the Huguenots. Henry II's actions included seizing the land that belonged to Huguenots as well as imprisoning, torturing, and executing Huguenots. He also implemented a variety of other similar actions designed to discourage individuals from taking part in Calvinist activities. It is important to note, however, that Henry II is also known as the inventor of the patent.

Henry IV was the King of France during the late sixteenth to early seventeenth centuries. He is primarily known for a decree that he issued called the Edict of Nantes, which granted several different rights to the Huguenots. He is also known for the structures that he commissioned including the Pont Neuf, which is a French phrase that literally means "New Bridge." He made improvements to the government's spending, and he supported French expeditions to Canada.

Louis XIII was the King of France during the early to mid seventeenth century. Because he was crowned before he reached adulthood, his mother, Marie de Medici, was granted the powers of the crown until Louis was old enough to rule the kingdom himself. It is important to note, however, that he is also known for the role he played in furthering French absolutism through his prime minister, Cardinal Richelieu.

Louis XIV, who was also known as the Sun King, was the King of France during the mid seventeenth to early eighteenth centuries. He is primarily known for weakening the nobles of France and establishing himself as the ultimate, unquestionable authority in France. In fact, Louis XIV is known for the French phrase L'état, c'est moi, which literally means "The state, that's me," though it can also be translated as "I am the state."

Conflicts in France

The people of France were originally divided into a series of social classes. These classes, which are known as the estates, include the First Estate, the Second Estate, and the Third Estate. The First Estate included anyone who was a priest, monk, nun, or another member of the clergy. It is important to note, however, that the higher-ranking members of the Church had more power in the First Estate than the lower-ranking members of the Church. It is also important to note that the First Estate was the smallest of the three estates. The Second Estate included the noblemen and noblewomen of France. This estate was bigger than the First Estate, but significantly smaller than the Third Estate. The Third Estate included the peasants, the merchants, and anyone else that was not a member of the First or Second Estate. This estate, as a result, was the biggest of the three estates, and it had over 95 percent of the French population included within it. Maximilien de Béthune, who is also known as the Duke of Sully, was the French Finance Minister during the late sixteenth to early seventeenth centuries. He is primarily known for the tax practices he implemented in France, which were designed to make sure that the nation's money was appropriately collected, appropriately recorded, and appropriately used.

Annates is a term used to refer to the amount that a church official earned over the amount that he paid in expenses (in other words, the profit that he made) in his first year in office. In most cases, a church official was required to give the annates he earned to a bishop or another high-ranking member of the Church. Francis I attempted to change this, however, when he began to place additional taxes on the profits of the Church. The pope, as a result, tried to convince Francis to allow the Church to collect the annates to which he believed the Church was entitled. This eventually led to an agreement known as the Concordat of Bologna in which the Church agreed to grant the King of France more control over the officials within the French Church, and the king agreed to allow the Church to collect annates from the church officials.

By the mid-sixteenth century, France had a strong Calvinist minority referred to as Hugenots. This caused a lot of friction in France since Catholicism was the official relgion. To try to keep the peace, the French monarchy issued the Edict of Saint-Germain in 1562, which was a French edict that guaranteed the right of the Huguenots to worship in France. An edict of toleration refers to a formal decree in which the leaders of a country guarantee that the members of a specific religion will have the right to worship in their country. It is important to note that an edict of toleration only suggests that the leader(s) of a country will tolerate the religious activities of individuals who belong to a specific religion. It does not guarantee that the country will support or protect the members of a religion.

However the Edict of Saint-Germain was soon broken by the Massacre of Vassy in which Catholic soldiers attacked and killed a group of Hugenots during a church service, prompting open warfare to break out later than year between the two sides. This began the French Wars of Religion which were a series of eight bloody civil wars between the French Hugenots and French Catholics separated by short intervals of peace which lasted from 1562 until 1598.

One of the most famous events during this time period was the Massacre of St. Bartholomew's Day. The Massacre of St. Bartholomew's Day refers to an event that began on August 24, 1572, in which the soldiers of the French Army were ordered to kill the leaders of the Huguenots. A member of the nobility (who is believed to be Catherine de Medici, but there is insufficient evidence to prove it) ordered the French Army to assassinate Admiral Gaspard de Coligny on August 22, 1572, to eliminate the leader of the Huguenots while he was still in Paris. The assassination attempt ultimately failed, however, and the Huguenots, after hearing of the attempt on their leader's life, began to assemble and move toward the castle. Catherine de Medici become more and more concerned with the Huguenot forces that were beginning to descend on Paris. As a result, she ordered the French Army to begin killing the Huguenot leaders. This caused a mob of soldiers and citizens to go on a rampage through the city, killing every Huguenot that the mob came across.

The French Wars of Religion came to an end in 1598 with the Edict of Nantes. The Edict of Nantes was an edict of toleration issued by Henry IV that expanded the rights the Huguenots received from the Edict of Saint-Germain. This edict granted the Huguenots the right to assemble, the right to worship in public, the right to hold public office, and a number of other similar rights. However while Hugenots' religious freedoms were secured by the Edict, they had lost much of their military and political strength during the wars. Thus the French monarchy was able to revoke the Edict of Nantes in 1685 and make Protestantism illegal in France.

Jules Mazarin, who is also known as Cardinal Mazarin, was the Prime Minister of France during the mid to late seventeenth century. He is primarily known for the role he played in the Fronde. The Fronde (a French word that literally means "sling"), which is also known as the War of the Fronde, refers to a civil war that occurred in France during the mid seventeenth century. This war started as the result of a disagreement between the nobles of France and the French Prime Minister Cardinal Mazarin in which the nobles disagreed with Mazarin on the methods that the government should use to raise money. Mazarin needed to raise money to pay for the enormous costs that the French government had sustained during the Thirty Years' War. The nobles, however, refused to pay taxes, which meant that Mazarin was forced to raise the taxes of every peasant and every merchant. The money Mazarin received from the peasants and merchants, however, was still not enough to pay all the expenses that France had incurred, so Mazarin placed a tax on some of the nobles who were part of the French Parliament. This tax infuriated the nobles and ultimately caused the nobles to revolt. The nobles had some initial successes, but enventually the king prevailed after the population, weary from years of war, rallied behind him as on the side of peace and order.

Reformation in England

The War of the Roses refers to a civil war that occurred in England during the mid to late fifteenth century. This war started as the result of a disagreement between the nobles of the House of York and the nobles of the House of Lancaster regarding the rightful heir to the throne of England. The House of York believed that the Duke of York Richard Plantagenet was not only the rightful heir to the throne, but also a more capable leader than Henry VI because Henry VI suffered from a mental illness. The House of Lancaster, on the other hand, believed that Henry VI, who was the King of England at the time of the dispute, was the rightful holder of the throne. This eventually led the House of York and the House of Lancaster to enter into an ongoing conflict in which the House of York fought to seize the throne and the House of Lancaster fought to protect it. Eventually the House of Lancaster pervailed, thus beginning the Tudor dynasty.

Henry VII was the King of England during the late fifteenth to early sixteenth centuries. He is primarily known for the fact that he seized control of the English throne from Richard III after the War of the Roses. He made a number of reforms to the English government and the English tax system. These reforms were designed to increase the amount of control that the king could exercise over the nobles of England and increase the amount that the government was receiving from taxes.

Henry VIII was the King of England during the early to mid sixteenth century. He is primarily known for the unusual methods that he used to separate himself from the four wives (he had six in total) who did not die of natural causes. These methods included the creation of the Anglican Church so that he could get his marriages annulled and the execution of his wives on the grounds of adultery (although it is unlikely that any of his wives actually committed adultery).

The Act of Supremacy was a law passed by the English Parliament in 1534 that recognized the King or Queen of England, who at the time was King Henry VIII, as the head of the Church of England. This gave the king or queen the right to establish laws that the Church of England and its priests would be required to follow. It also allowed the king or queen to effectively control the religion of the people of England, and King Henry VIII demonstrated this power by creating the Anglican Church. It is important to note, however, that the English Parliament passed the Act of Supremacy primarily at the urging of King Henry VIII. He urged the English Parliament to pass the act because he wanted to annul his marriage to his first wife, Catherine of Aragon, but the Roman Catholic Church refused to carry out the annulment.

The Statute of the Six Articles, which is also known simply as the Six Articles, was a law passed by the English Parliament in 1539 that identified the English Church's position on the doctrines of the Roman Catholic Church during the Reformation. The Six Articles were primarily designed to declare that the English Church agreed with the views of the Catholic Church and not the views of the Protestants. In fact, the Six Articles specifically stated that there were seven sacraments, that priests must be celibate (another view that the Protestants did not share), that private Masses were acceptable, and that a number of other similar Catholic beliefs were the only truths that the English Church would teach. The Six Articles also stated that an individual would be punished if he failed to demonstrate the beliefs identified in the Six Articles..

Mary I of England, who is also known as Mary Tudor, was the Queen of England during the mid sixteenth century. She was the daughter of Henry VIII and a strong supporter of the Catholic Church and is primarily known for the actions that she took to reestablish the Catholic Church as the true Church of England. Mary's most well-known action, however, is an event known as the Marian Persecutions in which Mary ordered the execution of approximately 300 Protestants who disagreed with her religious reforms. These executions led the Protestants to call Mary by her now infamous nickname "Bloody Mary."

Elizabeth I was younger daughter of Henry VIII and became the Queen of England after Mary I during the mid sixteenth to early seventeenth centuries. She is primarily known for the actions she took to protect the Protestants, which included the restoration of a number of laws that Mary I had eliminated. Elizabeth I, however, is also known for the skill that she demonstrated in her foreign policy and her support of the arts. Her nickname was the "Virgin Queen" because she never actually took a husband.

The Thirty-Nine Articles, which is also known as the Thirty-Nine Articles of Religion, was a law passed by the English Parliament under Elizabeth I in 1563 that identified the English Church's position on the doctrines of the Roman Catholicism, Lutheranism, and Calvinism. These articles were primarily designed to declare that the English Church agreed with the views of the Lutherans, not the views of the Catholic Church or the Calvinists. In fact, the Thirty-Nine Articles were, in effect, the complete opposite of the Six Articles that the English Parliament had passed in 1539, as they specifically stated that the English Church believed in justification by faith, that the clergy should be allowed to marry, that there are only two sacraments, that indulgences and holy relics are unacceptable, that the Bible is the only source of religious doctrine, and a variety of other similar Lutheran beliefs. It is important to note, however, that the Thirty-Nine Articles were carefully written to leave enough room for interpretation that virtually every Catholic or Protestant would be allowed to practice his faith.

Sir Francis Drake was a sailor who sailed from England during the mid to late sixteenth century. He was a privateer, or a pirate, who had permission from Queen Elizabeth I to attack and seize Spanish ships. It is important to note, however, that Drake was not only a pirate, but also an able captain who truly demonstrated his skill as a leader when he helped the English Navy defeat the Spanish Armada. The Spanish Armada, which was known as the Grande y Felicísima Armada (which literally means "Great and Most Fortunate Navy"), was smaller than the English fleet, but it had a number of large vessels with powerful, short-range guns. The English fleet, on the other hand, primarily consisted of small vessels with cannons that weren't quite as powerful as the Spanish ships, though they had a longer range. This allowed Drake to order the English ships to continually move out of the range of the Spanish ships while they continued to fire.

Post-1648

Political Struggle in England

The English Civil War occurred as the result of a series of disagreements between the Stuart Kings and the English Parliament. These disagreements were primarily related to the rights that the members of the English Parliament possessed, but there were a number of religious issues involved as well. King James I and King Charles I, who were both members of the House of Stuart, believed that they had the divine right to rule England in whatever way they deemed fit. This meant that they not only believed that they had the right to force the people to worship in the way that they believed appropriate, but they also believed that they had the right to ignore the English Parliament whenever the Parliament's decisions were inconvenient. As a result, both James I and Charles I attempted to greatly limit the power of the Parliament through a number of different actions, which included issuing taxes without the Parliament's approval, arresting individuals that disagreed with the king (specifically members of Parliament), and eventually dissolving the Parliament.

The English Civil War began in 1642 when King Charles I ordered the arrest of John Pym, John Hampden, and several other members of the English Parliament. This led the Parliament to pass an act known as the Militia Ordinance, which gave the English Parliament the right to command the militias of England. Charles I, as a result, was forced to flee to northern England and assemble an army of his own because the act, in effect, gave the Parliament complete control over all the English military forces that were already established. (Militias were the only defense England had against an enemy at the time unless the king declared war.) This ultimately caused the individuals who were willing to fight for the Parliament, who were known as the Roundheads, to attack the forces of the king, who were known as the Cavaliers. In the end, the Parliament defeated the king's forces and executed Charles I after almost ten years of fighting, and the leader of the Parliament's forces, Oliver Cromwell, became the Lord Protector of England (in effect, the King of England).

The English Restoration refers to a political and religious movement that took place after the death of Oliver Cromwell in which a number of individuals, specifically individuals who had supported King Charles I during the English Civil War, attempted to restore England to the way that it was before the war. The movement ultimately succeeded in restoring the power of the Stuart Kings, as Charles II was made not only the King of England, but also the King of Scotland and Ireland as well. The movement also succeeded in restoring the power of the Anglican Church, as the Parliament at the time (which was known as the Cavalier Parliament because of its support of the king) required every English citizen to be a member of the Anglican Church. It is important to note, however, that most of the English Restoration's political and religious successes were eliminated by the Parliament that existed during the Glorious Revolution.

The two English political parties that formed during the English Restoration were the Tories and the Whigs. The Tories were the conservative party, which primarily consisted of individuals who supported Charles I during the English Civil War (in other words, the Cavaliers). They ultimately believed that the power to govern should reside primarily with the king or queen and not the Parliament. The Whigs, on the other hand, were the liberal party, which primarily consisted of individuals who had supported the Parliament during the English Civil War (in other words, the Roundheads). They believed that the power to govern should reside with the Parliament and that the people of England should be allowed to worship in whatever way they deemed fit. The ideas that the Whigs had regarding religious freedom were not only a major shift in the ideas of the time, but also a major issue on which the two parties disagreed.

The Glorious Revolution refers to a political and religious movement that took place after the English Restoration in which a number of individuals, including both individuals who had supported the Parliament and individuals who had supported King Charles I during the English Civil War, attempted to remove James II from the English throne. The movement ultimately succeeded in removing James II from the throne, and William III of Orange became the new King of England. This allowed the Parliament to pass a series of acts that limited the power of the King or Queen of England, defined the powers and rights of the Parliament, and guaranteed certain rights to the people. These acts included the English Bill of Rights, the Tolerance Act, and the Habeas Corpus Act.

John Locke was a philosopher who lived in England during the mid seventeenth to early eighteenth centuries. He is primarily known for his philosophical works in which he discussed the role that people play in their own government and their own religion. In fact, one of Locke's most famous works was his Two Treatises on Civil Government in which he states that a government only has the authority to govern if it has the consent of the governed, or in other words, the permission of the people to rule. In fact, Locke believed that the government could only remain in power if the people agreed. In addition, he believed that the people had a right to revolt against the government if the government acted against the best interests of the people. It is important to note that Locke also believed that there was no way for an individual or a group to determine whether the beliefs of a specific religion were true or not, and it was, therefore, unacceptable for the government to judge an individual's religious beliefs.

Scientific Revolution

The Scientific Revolution refers to the period immediately before the Enlightenment (specifically during the early sixteenth to late seventeenth centuries) in which a number of astronomers, physicists, physicians, and other men of science made a wide range of important scientific discoveries. These discoveries not only introduced new scientific techniques and theories to the world, but also changed the way the Europeans looked at the world around them. These discoveries ultimately allowed the scientists of the Scientific Revolution to form the logical foundation on which the philosophers of the Enlightenment based their view of the world. Some of the most famous individuals of the Scientific Revolution include Nicolaus Copernicus, Johannes Kepler, Galileo Galilei, Sir Isaac Newton, Francis Bacon, René Descartes, and William Harvey.

Johannes Kepler was an astronomer who lived in Germany during the late sixteenth to mid seventeenth centuries. He is primarily known for the discoveries that he made regarding to the way the planets move. These discoveries are typically described in terms of three laws, which are known as the laws of planetary motion. Kepler's first law states that the orbit of a planet as it travels around the sun is always an ellipse. In other words, the path that a planet takes as it travels around the sun will always resemble a stretched circle and not a round one. Kepler's second law states that the speed at which a planet travels around the sun will increase as the planet approaches the sun and decrease as it moves farther away from the sun. Kepler's third law states that an individual can calculate the length of time it takes a planet to travel around the sun if the individual knows the diameter of the planet's elliptical orbit.

Galileo Galilei, who is more commonly known simply as Galileo, was an astronomer and a physicist who lived in Italy during the late sixteenth to mid seventeenth centuries. He is primarily known for the discoveries that he made regarding the way that objects move, the position of the Earth within the solar system, and the position and orbits of the other celestial bodies of the solar system. In fact, Galileo actually discovered four of Jupiter's moons, Saturn's rings, the black spots that appear on the surface of the sun (which are known as sunspots), the basic concepts that eventually formed Newton's first law of motion, and a variety of other similar celestial bodies and concepts. However, one of Galileo's most important discoveries was that the moons of Jupiter actually moved around Jupiter and not the Earth. This was significant because most of the people at the time still believed that all the objects in the universe revolved around the Earth, but Galileo's discovery proved that there were objects that did not orbit the Earth.

Sir Isaac Newton was a mathematician, a philosopher, and a physicist who lived in England during the mid seventeenth to early eighteenth centuries. He is primarily known for the discoveries he made regarding the way that objects move. These discoveries are typically described in the terms of three laws, which are known as the universal laws of motion. Newton's first law states that an object in motion will stay in motion, and an object at rest will stay at rest unless an outside force acts upon it. This law also states that an object in motion will continue to travel at the same speed unless an outside force acts upon it. Newton's second law states that the force that an object exerts is equal to the mass of the object times the object's acceleration. Newton's third law states that for every action, there is an equal and opposite reaction.

According to Newton's law of universal gravitation, a large celestial body will exert a force on the objects around it that will draw objects toward it. This law also states that an individual can calculate the amount of force that a celestial body will exert on the objects around the body if the individual knows the mass of the celestial body, the mass of the object that the celestial body is attracting, and the distance between the celestial body and the object. In other words, a large object (such as a planet or a star) will exert a force that pulls objects (such as planets, stars, or people) toward the planet, and this force can be calculated with the appropriate information. This law was extremely important to the Enlightenment because the very idea that an individual could use science to explain the movement of the planets encouraged individuals to look at the world in terms of what they observed rather than in terms of what they believed.

Philosophiae Naturalis Principia Mathematica (which is a Latin phrase that literally means "Mathematical Principles of Natural Philosophy"), was a collection of three books written by Sir Isaac Newton. These books, which are also known simply as Principia Mathematica, explained the basic concepts of physics that would later be known as the universal law of motion and Newton's law of gravitation. Principia Mathematica, as a result, not only played an important role in expanding the realm of science, but also an important role in changing the way that the average person viewed the world.

Enlightenment

The Enlightenment refers to a philosophical movement that occurred during the late seventeenth to late eighteenth centuries. This movement was based on the idea that an individual's ability to reason was all that an individual needed to understand the world around him. It is important to note that this concept demonstrated a major shift in the beliefs of the time because most people, up until the Enlightenment, believed that an individual had to understand the religious doctrines of the Church to truly understand the world. The philosophers of the Enlightenment, however, disagreed; they believed that an individual's religious beliefs were not necessary for the individual to understand the world at all.

 The French term philosophe literally means "philosopher." The term is typically used to describe the philosophers and writers of the Enlightenment period because most of the philosophers and writers of the Enlightenment were French.

Conversations on the Plurality of Worlds was a book written by Bernard le Bovier de Fontenelle in which Fontenelle attempted to explain Nicolaus Copernicus's concepts of the universe in a way that the average person could understand. This book, as a result, was an extremely important part of the Enlightenment because it was one of the first written works to encourage individuals outside the scientific community to learn about the world around them.

The Enlightenment produced new, and often competing, theories in many fields including economics, religion, medicine, and philosophy. Mercantilism refers to an economic system in which a country's government attempts to increase the number of products that the country exports and decrease the number of products that the country imports. This system is primarily designed to ensure that the government has the maximum amount of capital (such as gold or silver) possible and that the country has the minimum amount of excess goods possible. This economic system originally used a series of high tariffs, taxes, and subsidies to discourage imports, but the system is rarely used in the world today. Laissez-faire, which literally means "let make" or "let do," refers to an economic system in which the government allows the businesses within the country to control the amount that the country imports and exports. The Greek term physiocrat literally means "supporter of the natural government." The term is typically used to describe the philosophers of the Enlightenment who supported the laissez-faire system.

Adam Smith was a philosopher and an economist who lived in Scotland during the early to late eighteenth century, and he played an extremely important role in the laissez-faire movement. Smith wrote a book entitled An Inquiry into the Nature and Causes of the Wealth of Nations in which he discussed his views on the laissez-faire system and the mercantile system. This book allowed Smith to describe his belief that the economy of a nation would be stronger if it was left to its own devices or, in other words, if the country allowed the economy to function with as little government interference as possible. Smith also described his belief that the wealth of a nation could not be measured in gold or silver, but it instead should be measured in terms of the number of goods that a nation produces. This book, as a result, was extremely important to the laissez-faire movement because it defined the major economic concepts on which the movement was founded.

Deism refers to a religious belief system which enjoyed some popularity during the Enlightenment in which an individual believes that he can use his own ability to reason to explore and understand the world. Typically, this belief system is based on the idea that there is a God, but there is no reason for God to interfere in the affairs of the average person. In fact, deists typically see the average person as a part of a master plan that was placed into the world that God established, so that God didn't have to do anything other than observe. This master plan is usually described in terms of a master clock that God, as the Divine Watchmaker, designed with a series of parts to achieve a specific purpose. The deists, therefore, believe that an individual may not be able to understand the true purpose of God's design, but an individual can determine how each part of God's world works without divine intervention.

Andreas Vesalius was a physician who lived in Belgium during the early to mid sixteenth century. He is primarily known for his book De Humani Corporius Fabrica Libri Septum (which is a Latin phrase that literally means Seven Books on the Fabric of the Human Body) in which he used pictures and descriptions to depict the anatomy of the human body in great detail.

William Harvey was a physician who lived in England during the late sixteenth to mid seventeenth centuries. He is primarily known for his book Exercitatio Anatomico de Motu Cordis et Sanguinis in Animalibus (which is a Latin phrase that literally means An Anatomical Exercise on the Movement of the Heart and Blood in Animals). Harvey's book, which is sometimes known simply as De Motu Cordus (or Movement of the Heart), was the first book to provide an accurate explanation of the inner workings of the circulatory system.

Francis Bacon was a philosopher and a writer who lived in England during the mid sixteenth to early seventeenth centuries. He is primarily known for his work, the Novum Organum (which is a Latin phrase that literally means "New Instrument"), in which he described the basic concepts that later formed the foundation for the scientific method. These concepts formed a set of procedures known as the inductive method (which was also known as the Baconian method or the experimental method) that an individual could use to gather information about the world and draw accurate conclusions based on that information. These procedures included making observations, recording information about each observation, identifying the potential causes of an observed result, testing each potential cause through experimentation, and making conclusions based on the results of the individual's observations and experiments.

René Descartes was a philosopher and a physicist who lived in France during the late sixteenth to mid seventeenth centuries. He is primarily known for his work, a Discourse on Method, in which he described his belief that an individual should not assume something is true unless he can prove it. Descartes described this idea through a series of basic concepts known as the Cartesian Method, which were designed to help an individual draw a conclusion even if the individual could not conduct an experiment to gather the information that he needed. This method was based on a concept known as Cartesian Dualism, which stated that every aspect of the world could be identified as a part of the material world or a part of the mental world. Descartes used this idea to explain his belief that the material world could be analyzed through experimentation, but it was actually better for an individual to deduce the truth of both the material and the mental world from the information that an individual already had available.

François-Marie Arouet, who is more commonly known as Voltaire, was a philosopher who lived in France during the late seventeenth to late eighteenth centuries. He is primarily known for the poems, letters, and stories that he wrote in which he discussed the need for religious and political reforms. These poems, letters, and stories specifically addressed issues such as the abuse of power, the basic human rights to which every individual is entitled, censorship, civil rights, the need to eliminate government corruption, the dangers of religious dogma, the need for religious tolerance, the importance of science, the dangers of superstition, the dangers of ignoring the evils of humanity and the fate that those evils may bring, and other similar issues. Voltaire's most famous works include Letters on the English, Micromégas, Candide, and The Maid of Orleans. Voltaire was also known for the catchphrase écrasez l'infâme (which is a French phrase that literally means "crush the infamous") that he used to encourage individuals to take action against religious and political corruption.

Jean Jacques Rousseau was a philosopher who lived in France during the early to late eighteenth century. He is primarily known for the books and essays that he wrote in which he discussed his views on civilization, education, the role of the government, the role of the individual, and the importance of nature in an individual's life. It is important to note, however, that he is also known for the plays, operas, and romantic novels that he wrote. In fact, Rousseau's romantic novels played an extremely important role in the Enlightenment because they helped establish the stage for the literary movement known as Romanticism, which encouraged authors to describe a wide array of human emotions. Some of Rousseau's most famous works include Emile, The Social Contract, and Julie.

Rousseau addressed a number of different issues, but there are two major issues on which Rousseau focused. The first issue Rousseau focused on was related to the role that civilization played in an individual's education. Rousseau believed an individual's experiences with nature and the world would be more useful than the lessons that the individual would learn from the formal education that he received from society. In other words, Rousseau believed that society was corrupt and that the education an individual receives from society is, therefore, corrupt as well. As a result, an individual must learn in an environment that allows the individual to be a "noble savage," or, in other words, allows the individual to be closer to nature. The second issue Rousseau focused on was the role that an individual plays within society. Rousseau believed than an individual was not simply a follower of society, but was instead a part of a larger societal group that could use its "general will" to influence the government.

Charles-Louis de Secondat, baron de Montesquieu, was a philosopher who lived in France during the late seventeenth to mid eighteenth centuries. He is primarily known for the essays and books that he wrote in which he discussed his views on different types of government. Montesquieu's greatest achievement, however, was his work entitled The Spirit of the Laws in which he described a system of checks and balances that a government could use to ensure that a single individual or a group of individuals could not control the entire government. This concept was based on Montesquieu's belief that it was impossible for an individual or a group of individuals to make a perfect government, but an individual or a group could establish a government in which the powers of any single group would be limited. In fact, Montesquieu believed that a government's powers should be separated into three branches (the executive branch, the legislative branch, and the judicial branch) to make it difficult for any single individual or group to seize control.

Denis Diderot was a philosopher and an editor who lived in France during the early to late eighteenth century. He is primarily known for the collection of philosophical ideas and facts, known as the Encyclopédie, that he edited and published. The Encyclopédie included information about history, religion, science, literature, music, and a variety of other similar topics. However, the Encyclopédie's primary focus was philosophy and the way that the philosophes viewed the world around them. In fact, Jean-Jacques Rousseau; Voltaire; François Quesnay; Charles-Louis de Secondat, baron de Montesquieu; and a large number of other prominent philosophers and writers discussed a wide range of different issues within the Encyclopédie.

François Quesnay was a physician, an economist, and a writer who lived in France during the late seventeenth to late eighteenth centuries. He is primarily known for the books and essays that he wrote in which he discussed the laissez-faire system. In fact, Quesnay established some of the basic concepts on which the laissez-faire system was founded in his Tableau économique and his Encyclopédie articles entitled "On Farmers" and "On Grains."

Marie Thérèse Rodet Geoffrin was a salonnière (a French term that literally means "owner of a living room") who lived in France during the late seventeenth to late eighteenth centuries. She is primarily known for the dinners that she held in which a number of prominent artists, philosophers, and writers met in her living room to discuss a variety of issues. These meetings, which were known as salons (a French term that literally means "living room"), ultimately gave philosophers such as Charles Louis-de Secondat, baron de Montesquieu; Adam Smith; and Denis Diderot a location in which they could refine their philosophical ideas.

Mary Wollstonecraft was a philosopher and a writer who lived in England during the mid to late eighteenth century. She is primarily known for the books that she wrote in which she addressed women's rights and the equality of the sexes. Wollstonecraft's most famous works include Thoughts on the Education of Daughters, A Vindication on the Rights of Men, and A Vindication on the Rights of Women.

French Revolution

Despite the growth of towns and the middle class, much of France still maintained the Feudal system prior to the French Revolution. Feudalism refers to a type of government in which a king or queen ruled a country through a network of nobles that each controlled a specific section of the country. These nobles were typically responsible for both the defense and the law enforcement of the region that they controlled. It is important to note that feudalism was common throughout the Middle Ages, but it began to decline after the Renaissance and was virtually nonexistent by the time of the French Revolution. Manorialism refers to a system that typically existed as part of a feudal government in which the peasants of a specific area were required to pay taxes to and work for the noble who controlled that area. This system was still in use in France at the beginning of the French Revolution, and it played an important role in encouraging the peasants to revolt.

In this system, the taxes fell almost entirely upon the peasants and middle class. The term corvée refers to a requirement of the manor system in which a peasant was required to work for the noble who controlled the area in which the peasant lived, but the noble was not required to pay the peasant for his work. The term gabelle (which comes from the Latin word for tax) refers to a salt tax that the peasants of France were required to pay to the nobles who controlled the area in which the peasant lived. The term taille refers to a property tax that the peasants of France were required to pay on the land that they owned (specifically the land on which their homes were located). A tithe refers to a religious tax that the people of France were required to pay to the church. The tithe (which actually comes from the Old English word for tenth) was equal to one tenth of the amount that a peasant or noble earned from his lands.

The Old Regime in France had several different problems immediately prior to the French Revolution, but there were two major problems that greatly contributed to the fall of the Old Regime. The first problem that contributed to the fall of the Old Regime was that the Old Regime had a desperate need for additional funds. The Old Regime incurred many expenses from the Seven Years' War, the American Revolution, and a variety of other conflicts. The Old Regime, as a result, needed to find a way to pay the incredible amount of debt that it had acquired, and the only way that the Old Regime could find to pay this debt was to increase taxes. The second problem that contributed to the fall of the Old Regime was the fact that the government of France was poorly organized at the time. This is because the Old Regime had numerous government offices and bureaucrats, and no one knew exactly what each office was supposed to do.

The Estates General was a meeting in which the three estates of France met to discuss the issues that the French government had to address. This meeting rarely took place, but King Louis XVI called the Estates General to order in 1789 to discuss the issue of taxes. This occurred because Louis XVI desperately needed to increase the tax revenue the government was receiving to pay all the debts that the government had incurred, but the courts ruled that the king did not have the authority to increase taxes without the consent of the Estates General. As a result, Louis XVI was forced to call the Estates General to order, so he could receive the approval that he needed to raise taxes. The estates, however, were more interested in reforming the government than they were in passing a new tax.

The estates were not pleased with the king or the conditions of France at the time, and there was very little interest in passing the taxes that Louis XVI requested. The king, as a result, decided to order each of the estates to discuss the issue of taxes in separate sessions, so they could cast a single vote for the entire estate. This meant that the Third Estate, which comprised nearly 95 percent of the population, would only receive a single vote. On the other hand, the First and Second Estates, who were not typically required to pay taxes, would have a combined voting power of two votes. The individuals that would not be required to pay the tax would therefore have a sufficient number of votes to pass the tax without the vote of the individuals who would actually have to pay the tax.

This led the Third Estate, which primarily consisted of the peasants of France, to leave the Estates-General and form a new body known as the National Assembly. The Assembly was designed to help the people seize control of the French government, so they could reform it. The king, however, was not ready to allow the peasants to take control of the government, and he ordered his soldiers to lock and guard the doors of the hall in which the Assembly met. This forced the Assembly to find a new place to meet, which actually ended up being at a tennis court. There they swore an oath that they would continue to meet until there was a French constitution.

The king's attempts to prevent the National Assembly from meeting ultimately failed, and the king was forced to begin gathering an army to protect the throne. This army, which primarily consisted of mercenaries that the king hired from Germany and Switzerland, began to move toward Paris and Versailles to help protect the government in the case of a revolt. The sudden increase in the number of troops around Paris and Versailles only increased the fears of the people, however, as many people believed that the army's movements were designed to force the National Assembly to disband. This eventually led the people of Paris to riot, and on July 14, 1789, a mob of angry Parisian citizens attacked and successfully stormed the French prison known as the Bastille.

The Great Fear refers to an event that took place throughout France from the middle of July to the beginning of August in 1789. The people of France feared that the king would put an end to the revolutionary movement that had developed in France, and these fears caused the people to riot. The people's fears, however, were only strengthened as the rioting continued, and rumors began to spread throughout France that the king and the nobles were plotting against the peasants. In fact, it was a common belief at the time that the nobles were actually paying thieves to steal food from the peasants so that the nobles could add it to their own stockpiles and starve the peasants who were taking part in the revolutionary movement. These rumors eventually caused the peasants to panic, and they began to attack the homes of prominent nobles to seize their food and destroy tax records.

The Decree of August 4, 1789 was one of the first documents issued by the National Assembly of France. This document described a series of reforms that the newly forming government planned to implement immediately to eliminate the feudal system and the manor system that had existed in France for centuries. These reforms abolished the corvée, the tithes, the annates, the regional court system that was in place in France at the time, the sale of public offices, and a variety of other similar elements of the French government. The Decree of August 4, 1789 also declared that every person would be entitled to the same rights as everyone else, that each person would be taxed in the same way, and that the nobles would no longer have any rights that the average citizens did not have.

The Declaration of the Rights of Man and of the Citizen, which is also known simply as the Declaration of the Rights of Man, was one of the first documents issued by the National Assembly of France. This document, which was issued in late August 1789, described the basic rights to which every male citizen of France was entitled according to the National Assembly. These rights included freedom of speech, freedom of religion, freedom of the press, the right to assemble, the right to petition the government, the right to due process, the right to equal treatment, and a variety of other similar rights. The Declaration of the Rights of Man also declared that the government of France could only rule over the people as long as it had the people's consent and that the people had the right to change the government if it did not act in the people's interests.

Far from being a uniform movement, the French reformers were composed on multiple factions. The Cordelier Club, which is also known as the Society of the Friends of the Rights of Man and of the Citizen, was a group of political reformers that formed during the French Revolution. This group primarily believed that the French government should be a republic; as a result, they called for the removal of King Louis XVI. The Feuillant Club was a group of political reformers that formed during the French Revolution. This group believed that the French government should be a constitutional monarchy and that the powers of King Louis XVI and other future kings should be limited. The Jacobin Club was a group of political reformers that formed during the French Revolution. This group originally believed that the French government should be a constitutional monarchy, but the opinions of the group changed as its key members changed, and the group eventually began to support the idea of a French republic.

The National Assembly of France had already begun to institute a series of reforms by the end of 1789 to eliminate the injustices that existed in France under the Old Regime. These reforms, however, did very little to improve the financial situation of the French government, which was nearly bankrupt. The National Assembly, as a result, decided to take the land that belonged to the churches of France so that the government could use the value of each parcel of land to secure (or, in other words, guarantee the value of) the currency that the nation needed to print. This allowed the National Assembly to print paper bills called assignats that they could use to pay off some of the nation's debt. The churches, however, could not function without the land that the Assembly took, and the Assembly, as a result, took control of the churches to ensure that the churches could continue to function.

The Flight to Varennes refers to an event that took place on June 20, 1791, in which King Louis XVI attempted to flee France. This occurred because the National Assembly was attempting to develop a constitution for a new French government at the time, and King Louis XVI was concerned that this constitution was not only a threat to his power, but a threat to his life as well. Consequently, King Louis XVI gathered his wife, sister, and children and disguised them as servants. This allowed the royal family, with the aid of the Marquise de Tourzel, to sneak out of Paris in the middle of the night and make their way toward the royal fortress at Montmédy. The royal family, however, never actually made it to Montmédy, as they were captured in the town of Varennes and forced to return to Paris.

The Civil Constitution of the Clergy was a document issued by the National Assembly of France in July 1790. This document described a series of reforms that the newly forming government planned to implement in the churches of France. These reforms required priests and bishops to be elected; required priests and bishops to live in the area in which they preached; eliminated convents and other similar religious orders; prohibited priests and bishops from requiring any fee other than what the government paid them; prohibited priests and bishops from following the orders of any foreign power, including the pope; required every member of the clergy within the nation of France to swear their loyalty to the nation; and required every member of the clergy to swear that they supported the Civil Constitution of the Clergy. It is important to note, however, that there were many bishops and priests within France who did not support the Civil Constitution of the Clergy, and approximately half the priests within France refused to swear the oath.

The French Constitution of 1791 was a document issued by the National Assembly of France in September 1791. This document established the basic system of government that the Assembly intended to implement in France, which, at the time, was a constitutional monarchy with a system of checks and balances. This constitutional monarchy was divided into three government branches that each held a different set of powers. These branches included an executive branch with the king as the head of the branch, a judicial branch in which the judges were elected by the populace, and a legislative branch with a group of officials known as the Legislative Assembly who were elected by the general populace. The French Constitution of 1791 also reaffirmed the rights that the Declaration of the Rights of Man and of the Citizen granted to the citizens of France and added additional rights such as the right to a trial by jury.

War of the First Coalition

King Louis XVI attempted to flee France while the National Assembly was drafting the French Constitution of 1791 because he feared that the constitution would not only limit his power, but also reduce the likelihood that the revolutionaries would allow him to live. The king's attempt to flee, however, only strengthened the revolutionary cause, as more and more people began to see the king as an obstacle to a new government rather than as a part of it. In fact, the people of France began to doubt the king's willingness to be a part of any reform at all, and they feared that he might derail their attempts at forming a new government. As a result, the people made the king a prisoner in his own palace, so he couldn't interfere. The fact that the king was a prisoner in his own palace caused the kings of other countries to become concerned; they feared that the actions of the revolutionaries might inspire similar actions in their own countries.

The Declaration of Pillnitz was a decree that the King of Austria Leopold II (who was also the Emperor of the Holy Roman Empire) and the King of Prussia Frederick William II made on August 27, 1791. This decree stated that the kingdoms of Austria and Prussia were willing to use all the military forces at their disposal to crush the rebellion in France if the revolutionaries made any further threat to the life of King Louis XVI or if the revolutionaries failed to surrender control of the country to the king. The kings of Austria and Prussia were concerned that the actions of the revolutionaries in France might put Louis XVI's life at risk and inspire similar actions in their own countries. The kings, as a result, issued the Declaration of Pillnitz in the hope that the very threat of force would be enough to discourage the revolutionaries in France. The declaration, however, actually had the opposite effect because the revolutionaries saw the decree not as a threat, but as a declaration of war on France.

This view of the Declaration as a declaration of war was only further solidified when Prussia and Austria officially formed an alliance at the beginning of 1792. The revolutionaries, as a result, declared war on Austria and its allies on April 20, 1792, to protect their newly forming nation. This led Prussia and Austria to send forces into France to put an end to the rebellion, but the French Army was eventually able to repel the invasion, and the Prussian and Austrian armies were forced to retreat. This then led the French Army to begin invading other countries that were allied with Austria, including Germany, Italy, and Belgium. In fact, the French Army continued to move throughout Europe until almost every European country was involved in the conflict, including Spain, Portugal, England, the Netherlands, and several other countries.

The War of the First Coalition occurred as the result of the belief that the Declaration of Pillnitz was, in effect, a declaration of war on France. This belief led the more radical groups within France to seize control of the revolutionary movement taking place at the time as they called for war, encouraged the people to unite against the invaders, and shouted the phrase Liberté, égalité, fraternité (a French phrase that literally means "Liberty, equality, fraternity"). The radical groups were not the only groups to influence the politics of France, however, as the groups that were once more conservative, such as the Jacobins, began to become more radical as well. This eventually caused the political interests of the revolution to shift from that of a constitutional monarchy to that of a republic, and the Legislative Assembly, as a result, formed a National Convention to create a new constitution that would make France a republic.

Reign of Terror and End of the Revolution

Far from being a uniform body, the French revolutionaries are divided into a number of different factions. Sans-culotte is a French term that literally means "without knee breeches." The term is typically used to describe the peasants and other members of the Third Estate who supported the more radical actions taken during the French Revolution. These peasants earned the name sans-culotte from the pants that they typically wore. Enragé is a French term that literally means "enraged." The term is typically used to describe a group of individuals from the Third Estate that existed at the time of the French Revolution. This group is primarily known for attacking anyone who, in their belief, opposed the movement toward a republic. The Girondins, who were also known as the Brissotins or the Girondists, were political reformers who supported the constitutional monarchy that the revolutionaries formed at the beginning of the French Revolution and not the republic that the radicals proposed. It is important to note that many prominent Girondins were arrested and put on trial by the Enragés during the Reign of Terror.

Georges Jacques Danton was a political reformer who lived in France during the mid to late eighteenth century. He was the leader of the Cordelier Club and later a chief member of the Committee of Public Safety. It is important to note that the groups Danton headed were two of the most radical organizations that existed during the French Revolution, and they ultimately allowed Danton to exercise a great deal of influence over the political actions that took place during the revolution. Jean Paul Marat was a doctor, writer, and political reformer who lived in France during the mid to late eighteenth century. He is primarily known for the pamphlets that he wrote in which he encouraged the peasants of France to take control of their country and remove the Old Regime. Maximilien Robespierre was a political reformer who lived in France during the mid to late eighteenth century. He is primarily known for the role that he played in the execution of Louis XVI and the Reign of Terror.

The Storming of the Tuileries Palace took place on August 10, 1792, in which the sans-culottes (or, in other words, a group of French peasants who supported the revolution) attacked the Tuileries Palace. This occurred because the king had supported the Austrians in their attempt to crush the rebellion, and the sans-culottes became increasingly upset with the king's decision to support the enemies of the revolution. This eventually led the sans-culottes to attack the palace, murder the members of the Swiss Guard who were protecting it, and ransack it in an attempt to find the king. The king, however, had already escaped by the time the sans-culottes made their way in, and the sans-culottes proceeded to sweep through the city killing anyone who supported the king.

King Louis XVI was forced to flee the Tuileries Palace when the sans-culottes, or the French peasants who supported the revolution, attacked. The king, however, could not escape the city because there were too many radical revolutionaries patrolling the streets of Paris at the time, so the king took the only course of action that he had available and begged the Legislative Assembly for help. The Legislative Assembly had very little interest in helping the king, however, as the

Assembly was not pleased with the role that the king had played in encouraging the Austrians to interfere in France's internal affairs. Consequently, the Assembly arrested King Louis XVI on the charge of treason and eventually placed him on trial. In the end, King Louis XVI was declared guilty and executed by guillotine on January 21, 1793.

The Committee of Public Safety was a government agency formed by the National Convention of France in April 1793. The committee was originally designed to end the conflicts both within and outside France that were threatening the safety and security of the French people. The committee, however, quickly lost sight of its intended purpose, and it became a way for the more radical members of the revolution to exert their power over France. In fact, Maximilien Robespierre, who had previously called for the execution of King Louis XVI, effectively seized control of the committee when he encouraged the Enragés (violent supporters of the revolution) to remove the Girodins from the committee. This allowed Robespierre to use the committee's power to hunt down and execute anyone who opposed the new government as he envisioned it. The vicious tactics that Robespierre and the Committee of Public Safety used to eliminate anyone they perceived as a threat to the new republic eventually caused the period of the committee's reign to be known as the Reign of Terror.

The Thermidorian Reaction took place throughout the summer of 1794 in which the leaders of the Committee of Public Safety were executed. This occurred because the committee was using its power to arrest and execute anyone the committee perceived as a threat to the new republic, including George Jacques Danton who was originally a member of the committee. These actions quickly led the people of France to view the committee as nothing more than a tyrannical force designed to spread terror throughout the nation without any regard for the lives or rights of the people. The growing fear that the committee would kill anyone for any reason ultimately forced the National Convention to order the arrest and execution of Maximilien Robespierre and his supporters within the committee for their role in the Reign of Terror. In the end, Robespierre was executed by guillotine on July 27, 1794, and the National Convention began to design a new government as they continued to remove the radicals from power.

The Directory was the government that existed in France at the end of the French Revolution after the National Convention was dissolved. The National Convention, which was originally designed to create a new constitution to make France a republic, was, in effect, the government of France for a large portion of the French Revolution. However, the National Convention ceased to exist as soon as the constitution for the new republic, known as the Constitution of 1795, was finished. The new government, known as the Directory, took its place. The Directory, as stated in the Constitution of 1795, was split into an executive branch, a judicial branch, and a legislative branch. The executive branch consisted of five individuals, known as Directors, who were appointed by the legislative branch of the new government. The judicial branch was primarily the same as it had been in the Constitution of 1791, as the judges were elected by the general populace. Finally, the legislative branch included two political bodies, which were the Council of Ancients and the Council of 500.

By the end of the French Revolution, there was a new government, known as the Directory, in power in France. This government was designed to restore order and stability to not only the political aspects of the nation, but to the country as a whole as well. The Directory, however, was faced with many of the same problems that Louis XVI originally tried to address before the French Revolution, as the French government was still bankrupt and the people were still starving. The Directory tried to address these problems as best it could, but it could not secure the food that it needed to feed the starving masses without additional resources. The Directory attempted to obtain the financial resources that it needed by collecting taxes, but the peasants and other citizens of France didn't actually have enough to pay all the government's debts. This caused the situation in France to become more and more chaotic as the people demanded food, but the Directory had no way to give it to them.

Napoleon Bonaparte

The Directory, as the acting government of France, was forced to address the problems that King Louis XVI had attempted to address before the French Revolution. The Directory, however, had inherited the debts of the Old Regime, and there was no way for the government to obtain the food that it needed to feed the starving masses. The people became increasingly hostile toward the Directory as they continued to demand the food and internal stability that the country desperately needed. This eventually led the people to riot, and the Directory was forced to use the army to quell the riots. The decision to call in the army, however, only made the situation worse because both the general citizens and the members of the army began to doubt the ability of the Directory to lead. The tensions between the people and the Directory continued to escalate until an artillery lieutenant, Napoleon Bonaparte, used his contacts within the government to stage a coup d'état and take control of the government on November 9, 1799.

While the Directory was attempting to address the situation in France, the French Army continued to move throughout Europe, expanding the new republic's influence into every country it invaded. The alliances that Austria and Prussia had formed during the War of the First Coalition had been crushed by the French forces, and the countries of Europe desperately sought a new way to halt the French advance. This eventually led Great Britain to form an alliance with Austria, Portugal, Russia, and several other countries to create a Second Coalition that was designed to eliminate the French threat. The Second Coalition, however, met a similar fate to the First Coalition because Napoleon Bonaparte led the French Army to defeat the Austrians, the Russians, and every other member of the alliance except the British. This allowed Napoleon Bonaparte, as the new leader of France, to negotiate peace treaties with each of the former alliance members.

The Constitution of 1799 was one of the first documents issued by the French government after Napoleon Bonaparte took control of France. This document was designed to create a new government with Napoleon as the head of it, and this government, which was known as the Consulate, was split into two major branches. The first branch was an executive branch that consisted of three consuls, or officials, who ruled over the country as a committee with one of the consuls as the head consul, or First Consul. It is important to note that the consuls were supposed to be elected, but Napoleon was declared to be First Consul (and later Emperor) for life several years after the Constitution of 1799 was passed. The second branch was a legislative branch that consisted of three political bodies, which included the Conservative Senate, the Legislative Body, and the Tribunate. The legislative branch's powers, however, were severely limited, and it was actually the First Consul who was given the power to make most of the decisions related to the government.

The Concordat of 1801 was an agreement between Napoleon Bonaparte, acting as the first consul of France, and Pope Pius VII. This agreement stated that the French government agreed to acknowledge the Catholic religion as the religion of most French citizens and to allow the pope to confer religious offices to the bishops that the government nominated. In return, Pope Pius VII agreed to officially relinquish the Church's claim to the lands within France, which the French government had already seized from the Church. The Concordat of 1801 also stated that the Catholic Church would be allowed to establish convents and other religious orders within France, that bishops would be allowed to appoint priests, and that the French government would continue to provide financial support to the clergy within France. It is important to note that the Concordat of 1801 was primarily designed to improve the relationship that existed between the French government and the Roman Catholic Church and that the Concordat of 1801 removed several regulations instituted by the Constitution of the Civil Clergy with which the Catholic Church disagreed.

The Napoleonic Code, which is also known as the Code Napoleon or the French Civil Code, refers to a series of regulations that the First Consul of France Napoleon Bonaparte passed in 1804. These regulations were designed to establish a new legal system for the French government that was based heavily on the ideas of the reformers of the French Revolution. This system guaranteed the people the right to worship as they deemed fit, the right to equal treatment under the law, equal employment opportunities regardless of their social status, the right to seek a divorce under certain circumstances, and other similar rights. Among other things, the Napoleonic Code also established that the laws of the government would only be enforced after they were published and that the laws of the state would not be retroactive (or, in other words, would not punish an individual for an action that he took before that action was considered illegal).

At the end of the War of the Second Coalition, the French negotiated a peace treaty with the British known as the Treaty of Amiens. This treaty allowed the French to keep all the lands that France conquered even though the French never actually defeated the British Army. The British, as a result, were not pleased with the terms of the treaty, and they eventually declared war on France to take back the lands that the French had taken from them. This led the countries of Austria, Naples, Portugal, Sweden, and Russia to ally themselves with Great Britain to form a Third Coalition that was designed to end the French threat. The Third Coalition, however, ended in much the same way as the First and Second Coalitions that came before it. Napoleon Bonaparte led the French Army to defeat every member of the alliance except Great Britain and Russia.

By the end of the War of the Third Coalition, Great Britain had consistently proven itself to be a threat to France that the French Army simply could not eliminate. Consequently, Napoleon Bonaparte decided to institute and enforce a boycott of British goods (known as the Continental System) throughout Europe. This boycott was designed to cut off the supplies that Great Britain typically received from its European allies, but the British ships continued to enter ports throughout Europe despite the boycott. In fact, British ships regularly traded with the ports of Portugal, and it became increasingly difficult for the French to block the British ships sailing to Portuguese ports. This led Napoleon to order the invasion of Portugal and Spain (because the French Army had to move through Spain to invade Portugal) to protect the boycott. This invasion allowed the French Army to seize control of Spain and allowed Napoleon to claim the Spanish throne for his brother, Joseph Bonaparte, but the people of Spain revolted as soon as Joseph Bonaparte claimed the throne.

The Continental System was a series of decrees that were issued by Napoleon Bonaparte, which were designed to weaken Great Britain. These decrees were issued because the British had consistently proven themselves to be a threat to France that the French Army simply could not eliminate. In fact, the British were one of the only forces at the time that consistently defeated the French, and they were responsible for most of the major conflicts that the French Army had been involved in since the French Revolution. Napoleon, as a result, decided to eliminate the threat of Great Britain through economic sanctions rather than military force. To achieve this, he issued the Berlin Decree in which he compelled the holdings and allies of France to boycott every British ship. He then issued the Milan Decree in which he ordered the French Navy to attack any ship that provided supplies to a British port.

Napoleon Bonaparte ordered the French Army to invade Portugal and Spain to protect the Continental System, or the boycott, that Napoleon had established against Great Britain. Portugal, however, was not the only threat to the Continental System that Napoleon had to address, as Russia quickly became a threat as well. This occurred because Russia was beginning to find it increasingly difficult to acquire the financial resources it needed without British merchants. As a result, the Russians began to allow British ships to enter Russian ports in 1812 to acquire the money that Russia needed. This action led Napoleon to amass an army of over 600,000 men, which he used to invade Russia. The Russian Army, however, was able to use a series of tactics, including destroying their own cities, to prevent the French from gaining any tactical advantage from the land the French captured, eventually forcing the French to retreat. This allowed the Russian Army to use the terrain and the weather to its advantage, as the Russians continued to attack the French Army as it fled. The French Army was able to escape, but nearly 400,000 French soldiers were killed. Another 100,000 French soldiers were taken prisoner before the French made it to the Russian border. Russia, as a result, decided to form an alliance with Prussia and Austria to destroy the weakened French Army. This new alliance launched an attack against the French forces stationed in Leipzig, Germany. After several days of fighting, the alliance defeated the French in what came to be known as the Battle of Leipzig or the Battle of Nations.

Napoleon Bonaparte was eventually forced to abdicate, or resign from, his position as the Emperor of France on April 11, 1814, after the armies of Austria, Prussia, Russia, and several other nations marched into Paris. This occurred because the French Army could no longer mount any serious resistance to the invaders after the French defeat in Russia, the French defeat at the Battle of Leipzig, and the revolution against the French in Spain (which Great Britain supported). The European nations wanted not only to remove Napoleon from the throne of France, but also to restore Europe to the way it had been before the French Revolution. The nations of Europe, as a result, agreed to hold a meeting to discuss the best way to restore the balance of power in Europe. This meeting, which became known as the Congress of Vienna, eventually led to an agreement in which the boundaries of each nation were altered and the families that formerly ruled each nation were restored.

Napoleon Bonaparte was not only forced to resign his position as Emperor of France, but he was also forced to move to the island of Elba where he was supposed to remain in exile. Napoleon, however, left the island of Elba in late February 1815 and arrived in France in early March. Upon Napoleon's arrival, the new King of France King Louis XVIII dispatched a force to arrest Napoleon and the small group of supporters who had helped Napoleon reach France. Napoleon managed to convince the soldiers to join his cause, and he led the soldiers into Paris to reclaim the throne on March 20, 1815. The Hundred Days refers to the period from March 20, 1815, to June 18, 1815, in which Napoleon Bonaparte reclaimed the French throne. Napoleon's actions greatly alarmed the nations of Europe, as they feared that Napoleon would be able to reestablish his army and once again expand the French Empire's influence throughout Europe. These fears led the nations of Austria, Prussia, Russia, and Great Britain to form an alliance that was designed to force Napoleon back into exile. Napoleon, in response, ordered his troops to march into Belgium to destroy the alliance. Napoleon's forces managed to win a series of battles throughout Belgium, but they were eventually defeated by a combined British and Prussian force that was nearly twice the size of Napoleon's army at the town of Waterloo. As a result, Napoleon was exiled to the island of Saint Helena where he eventually died.

The Concert of Europe, which is also known as the Congress System or the Quadruple Alliance (which later became the Quintuple Alliance when France joined the Quadruple Alliance in 1818), was a military alliance formed by Austria, Great Britain, Prussia, and Russia in 1815. This alliance was created to enforce the decisions that the European nations made during the Congress of Vienna and to ensure that there was no way for Napoleon Bonaparte and other revolutionaries like him to cause any further harm to the monarchies of Europe. In fact, the Concert of Europe met several times during the early nineteenth century to discuss and take action against the revolutions that developed in Italy and Spain. It is important to note, however, that the Concert of Europe eventually fell apart in 1822 after the British refused to intervene in the affairs of other countries.

Technological and Social Advancements

The mid-sixteenth century to late nineteenth centuries saw the Commercial, Agricultural, and then Industrial Revolutions take place in Europe. These sucessive revolutions saw increasingly rapid advancements in technology and society.

An open-field system refers to a type of farming in which a farmer is allowed to use a specific portion of a public field. In other words, in an open-field system, the farmers of a specific area identify the land that is suitable for farming and then divide the land so that each farmer receives an equal portion of the land. This system was commonly used during the Middle Ages, but it is rarely used today. An enclosure system refers to a type of farming in which a farmer is only allowed to use the farmland that he owns. This system is named for the fact that most farmers use fences to enclose the land that they own, so they have more control over the crops and the land. Farmers began to move toward the enclosure system in the late seventeenth century, and it is still the primary system that farms use today.

The Enclosure Acts (or Inclosure Acts as they were originally spelled) were a group of laws passed by the British Parliament throughout the eighteenth and nineteenth centuries. These laws allowed the landowners of England to install fences or other barriers around the common lands that farmers had previously been allowed to use to grow crops and graze cattle. This led to numerous changes in the agricultural industry within Great Britain. Most notably, the Enclosure Acts allowed wealthy landowners to expand their farms drastically and made it more difficult for peasant farmers to continue farming. Each farmer was supposed to receive a certain portion of the common lands that were distributed to private owners, but the wealthy landowners typically took more land than they were legitimately entitled to. As a result, the peasant farmers were forced to find urban jobs while the wealthy farmers were able to acquire more land, produce more food, and ultimately acquire more wealth.

The Commercial Revolution refers to the period immediately before the Agricultural Revolution (specifically during the mid sixteenth to early eighteenth centuries) in which the nations of Europe used the mercantile system to amass large amounts of gold and silver. This gold and silver was primarily acquired from the lands that the European nations conquered in North and South America, but the European nations used the mercantile system to keep the gold and silver in Europe after they acquired it.

The Agricultural Revolution refers to a farming movement that occurred immediately before the Industrial Revolution (specifically during the late eighteenth to late nineteenth centuries) in which European farmers began to acquire their own lands and use new farming techniques. These new techniques included the cultivation of crops that had not previously been cultivated such as potatoes and peas, the use of new inventions such as the seed drill and the mechanical reaper, and the implementation of new breeding techniques for farm animals.

The Industrial Revolution refers to a manufacturing movement that occurred during the late eighteenth to late nineteenth centuries in which a series of inventions were created to improve goods or increase the speed at which goods could be produced. This movement led to inventions such as the cotton gin, the steam engine, the steamship, and the internal combustion engine.

Capitalism refers to an economic system in which the individuals participating in the economy are allowed to invest their money or use their money to purchase land or goods for their own benefit even if those investments or purchases may not benefit the nation as a whole. Capitalism, which is primarily based on the laissez-faire system, typically allows the businesses within the economy to exercise a considerable amount of control over the economy.

71

Capital refers to any financial resource that an individual or an organization can invest or use to purchase other resources. The term capital, as a result, typically refers to money, and the term capitalism is actually derived from this term.

Inflation refers to an economic process in which the value of a nation's currency decreases and the prices of the goods that can be purchased with that currency increase. In other words, inflation refers to an economic change in which the money of a nation cannot be used to purchase as much as it could before the change occurred. It is important to note that inflation can occur in any economic system, but it is much more common in the mercantile system than in other economic systems because the mercantile system encourages an increase in the amount of currency that the nation produces and a simultaneous decrease in the amount of goods that the nation retains.

Chartered companies were businesses that received permission from the government of a particular nation (typically in the form of a legal document known as a charter) to be the only business or one of the only businesses to perform a specific function in a specific industry. Chartered companies were responsible for banking, defending outposts, establishing outposts, exploring, mining, transporting goods, and other similar activities. It is important to note that chartered companies were typically funded by the investments of a small group of wealthy merchants, and they were similar in some ways to modern-day partnerships.

Joint-stock companies were businesses owned by a large group of individuals who were each allowed to purchase a small portion of the company. Each portion of the company was represented by a stock certificate that an individual could buy or sell, and the company's shareholders were granted many of the same rights as the shareholders of a modern-day corporation.

The flying shuttle was a loom part invented by John Kay in 1733 that made the loom easier to use. This device was a major advance in the textile industry because it allowed a single individual to weave fabric faster that he would have previously been able to weave with someone else's assistance. The spinning jenny was a spinning wheel invented by James Hargreaves in 1764 that allowed an individual to spin more than one thread at a time. This device was another major advance in the textile industry because it allowed a single individual to spin the same amount of yarn that eight to ten individuals could spin on a standard spinning wheel in the same amount of time. The water frame was a spinning wheel invented by Richard Arkwright in 1769 that allowed an individual to spin stronger threads than he could spin on other spinning wheels. The cotton gin was a farming device invented by Eli Whitney in 1793 that automatically separated the fibers in cotton from the seeds.

The steam pump was a device invented by Thomas Savery in 1702 that allowed an individual to move water from one location to another. Savery's steam pump was used primarily to regulate the flow of water to the households of a few wealthy families, but some individuals tried, unsuccessfully, to use the steam pump to drain water from coalmines. The Newcomen steam engine was a device invented by Thomas Newcomen in 1712 that allowed an individual to power a machine. The Newcomen steam engine powered steam pumps that were used to drain water from coalmines, but it required a large amount of coal to operate. The Watt steam engine, which is also known as the condensing chamber steam engine, was a device invented by James Watt in 1769 that allowed an individual to power a machine with a much smaller amount of coal than the Newcomen steam engine.

The steamship, which is also known as the steamboat or the steamer, was a ship brought into commercial use by Robert Fulton in 1807 that used a steam engine to power a paddlewheel, which propelled the ship. Steamships allowed individuals to transport goods across canals, rivers, and even the ocean at much faster speeds than most ships were able to achieve previously. The steam locomotive, which is also known as the steam-powered locomotive or the railroad steam engine, was a train brought into commercial use by George Stephenson in 1829 that used a steam engine to power the train. Steam locomotives not only increased the speed at which goods could be transported, but they also created an entirely new industry that employed thousands of workers. The internal combustion engine was a device brought into commercial use by Nikolaus Otto and Gottlieb Daimler during the late nineteenth century. This device allowed an individual to use gasoline rather than coal to power a vehicle.

The telegraph was a device invented by Samuel F.B. Morse in 1836 and patented in 1837 that allowed an individual to send a message to another location via a wire. This device allowed individuals to communicate quickly over long distances. The telephone was a device invented by Alexander Graham Bell in 1876 that allowed an individual to actually speak to an individual (rather than just sending a message to an individual) in another location via a wire. This device drastically increased the speed at which individuals could communicate over long distances because it eliminated the need for an individual to wait for a response. The radio was a device invented by Guglielmo Marconi in 1897 that allowed an individual to transmit a signal to a single location or to multiple locations without a wire. This device drastically increased the speed at which an individual or an organization could communicate with a large group of individuals.

A number of new artistic movements were taking during this time period was well. Romanticism was an artistic movement that took place during the late eighteenth century in which individuals attempted to describe or depict human emotion. The literary, musical, and artistic works created as a result of this movement were typically designed to invoke a strong emotional response such as fear or awe. Realism was a literary movement that took place during the mid nineteenth century in which a series of writers attempted to describe the events occurring in the world around them as accurately as possible. Impressionism refers to an artistic movement that took place during the late nineteenth century in which artists attempted to paint what they felt rather than what they saw. The artwork created as part of this movement typically depicted a real person, place, or thing in an unusual way to create a certain effect rather than an accurate portrayal of the subject.

Industrial Economics

The Sadler Committee on Child Labor was a committee formed by the British Parliament in 1832 to investigate the working conditions that children and women experienced in the factories of Great Britain. The British Parliament formed the Sadler Committee in response to a bill that Michael Thomas Sadler had introduced to address some of the labor issues associated with the factories at the time. This bill led the committee, under the leadership of Sadler, to conduct a series of interviews with the young male and female factory workers to evaluate the validity of the bill. The information gathered in these interviews was eventually compiled into a report known as the Sadler Report in which the committee described the horrific conditions under which the average factory worker was expected to work. Even though the information the committee collected about factory conditions convinced both the Parliament and the public that they needed to act, it did not ultimately convince the Parliament to pass Sadler's bill.

The Sadler Report provided information about the horrific conditions under which the average factory worker was expected to work. This information eventually led the British Parliament to pass a series of laws known as the Factory Acts, which were each designed to improve the conditions under which children and women were expected to work. Some of the major Factory Acts included the Labor of Children in Factories Act of 1833, the Factories Act of 1844, and the Factory Act of 1850. The most influential of the Factory Acts, however, was the Factory Act of 1878, which expanded all the laws that had previously been passed. The Factory Act of 1878 limited the hours that a child under fourteen could work in a single day to four hours, limited the hours that a child over fourteen (but under eighteen) could work in a single day to ten hours, made it illegal for children under ten to work, made it illegal for children over ten (but under eighteen) to work overnight, and required employers to provide lunch breaks for children.

Thomas Malthus was an economist who lived in England during the late eighteenth to mid nineteenth centuries. He is primarily known for writing An Essay on the Principle of Population in which he discussed the effects of population growth. Malthus believed that the population of the world would continue to grow at a much faster rate than the world's food supply and that most people, as a result, would eventually starve.

David Ricardo was an economist who lived in England during the late eighteenth to mid nineteenth centuries. He is primarily known for his book, The Principles of Political Economy and Taxation, in which he discussed the relationship between wages and the labor force. Ricardo believed that an individual's earnings would increase as the number of workers available in a particular industry decreased and that an individual's earnings would decrease as the number of workers available in a particular industry increased. Ricardo also believed that an increase in wages would lead an individual to have more children, which, in turn, would increase the size of the labor force.

Jeremy Bentham was a philosopher and economist that lived in England during the mid eighteenth to mid nineteenth centuries. He is primarily known for the works he wrote in which he discussed the concept of utilitarianism and the government's role in the laissez-faire system. Bentham believed that every action should be judged based on the number of people that the action would make happy. He also believed that it was the government's responsibility to ensure that the actions of an individual or an organization would encourage "the greatest good for the greatest number."

John Stuart Mill was a philosopher and an economist who lived in England during the early to late nineteenth century. He is primarily known for the works that he wrote in which he discussed worker's rights and the government's role in the laissez-faire system. Mill believed that the government had a responsibility to ensure the safety and personal well-being of the individuals who worked within the nation and that employers should not be allowed to expand their wealth beyond reasonable limits.

More commonly known as the Count of Saint-Simon, Henri de Saint-Simon was an economist who lived in France during the mid eighteenth to early nineteenth centuries. He is primarily known for the works he wrote in which he discussed the basic concepts of socialism and the role that the government should play in the economy. Saint-Simon believed that the government should control the industries within the economy to ensure that each business is actually working toward the benefit of the entire nation.

Karl Marx was a philosopher and an economist who lived in Germany, and later in France and England, during the early to late nineteenth century. He is known for his written works, especially The Communist Manifesto, concerning the validity of capitalism and establishing the basic concepts of communism. Marx believed that the economy of a nation would continue to evolve, changing from one economic system to another until everything is owned by the community and nothing is owned by private individuals or the government.

Industrial Politics

The turmoil from the French Revolution and all the social and demograpghic changes of the period led to a widening of particpation in the political process and new political ideologies taking hold.

Utilitarianism refers to a moral concept that states that the validity of an action should be evaluated based on its utility, or the number of people that the action would make happy and the degree to which it makes each individual happy. For example, the concept of utilitarianism suggests that an individual should take an action that makes one hundred people happy over an action that would only make ten people happy. Determinism refers to a philosophical concept that states that the events currently taking place in the world are always caused by the events that took place before them.

Socialism refers to an economic system in which a nation's government owns or controls most or all the industries within the nation. It is important to note that socialism may allow the private ownership of a business in some cases. Communism refers to an economic system in which the community owns or controls all the industries within a nation, so the community can ensure that each industry operates in a fashion that is beneficial to the community as a whole. It is important to note that communism does not allow private ownership because everything belongs to the community.

The dialectic refers to a cycle, originally proposed by Georg Wilhelm Friedrich Hegel, in which society is defined by its conflicts. This cycle is based on the idea that a thesis (the current viewpoint of society) will eventually be altered by an antithesis (a differing viewpoint), which will lead to a synthesis (a new viewpoint). Originally proposed by Karl Marx, dialectic materialism refers to the evolution of an economy in which the economy is defined by its conflicts. This evolution is based on the idea that the current economy will be altered by the economic beliefs of the lower class, which will continually lead to a new economy until the economy reaches communism and there are no classes.

The French term bourgeoisie roughly translates to "city-dweller," "inhabitant of a market town," or "middle class." The term is typically used to describe the middle class of a society, or the individuals who are not considered to be the poorest or the richest individuals within a particular area. The term is frequently used to describe merchants or other groups who are not considered to be part of the peasant class or the noble class. The Latin term proletariat literally means "a citizen of the lowest rank." The term is used to describe members of the working class of a society who are typically the poorest individuals within a society.

The class struggle refers to the idea that a society with more than one social class will always encourage a conflict between the upper classes and the lower classes and that this conflict will eventually lead to a new social order. The inevitable socialist revolution refers to the Marxist idea that a capitalist economy will eventually force the proletariat, or the working classes, to revolt against their employers because the proletariat will not be able to afford the basic necessities needed for survival with the amount of income their employers are willing to pay them. The utopian society under communism refers to the Marxist idea that the revolt of the proletariat will lead to a communist economy in which there are no classes, everything is owned by the community, and everyone will receive everything they need to survive.

Liberalism refers to a political movement that is based on the philosophical idea that every individual is entitled to certain liberties, or rights. It is important to note that this movement, which originally began during the eighteenth century, gained significant strength during the American and French Revolutions, and it was ultimately responsible for numerous revolutions that occurred during the late eighteenth to mid nineteenth centuries. Some of the rights that the liberal movement fought to obtain included basic human rights, the right to free trade, the right to participate in any religion, the right to free speech, the right to equal representation, and the right to assemble. Nationalism refers to the philosophical belief that an individual is defined by the nation in which he lives. In other words, an individual's nation is responsible for an individual's language and culture. As a result, the individual is not simply an individual, but he is also a part of the nation as a whole.

The German term Burschenschaft literally means "fraternity." The term is typically used to describe any of a group of student organizations that were formed during the early 1800s to promote the unification of Germany. The Carlsbad Diet was a meeting in which the representatives of the German Confederation (Austria, Prussia, and several other nations) met in Carlsbad, Bohemia, to discuss the actions of the Burschenschaft in 1819. The Burschenschaft was a group of students who assassinated a writer named August von Kotezubue in March 1819 because he had written a series of articles in which he strongly opposed the liberal movement that the students were attempting to start. The fact that the students took violent action to further their liberal agenda concerned the kings of the German Confederation. Under the leadership of Prince Klemens von Metternich, the Carlsbad Diet decided to take action. The Diet issued a series of decrees known as the Carlsbad Decrees in which the Diet made it illegal for students to form organizations without the government's consent, made it illegal for individuals to convey any information that might encourage a liberal or revolutionary agenda, and prohibited several other similar activities.

The Chartist Movement was a political movement that took place in Great Britain during the mid nineteenth century in which numerous individuals attempted to bring about a series of voting reforms. This movement ultimately hoped to expand the reforms that were implemented in the British Parliament by the Reform Bill of 1832, and it was largely based on a document known as the People's Charter in which the leaders of the movement identified the six reforms that the movement hoped to achieve. These six reforms included the right for every adult man to vote, the right to vote with a secret ballot, the right for an individual to seek public office regardless of personal wealth or social status, the right of a representative to be paid a set amount, the right to representation by population size rather than borough, and the right to elect new representatives each year.

The Reform Bill of 1832, which is also known as the Great Reform Bill or the First Reform Act, was a law passed by the British Parliament in June 1832 that was designed to address issues related to an individual's voting rights and the way that individuals were represented within the British Parliament. This bill was passed because the British Parliament was dominated by wealthy landowners and noblemen even though it was split into two houses, one specifically for the commoners (The House of Commons) and one specifically for the noblemen (The House of Lords). The wealthy landowners and noblemen were able to use their money to buy the votes of the voters in small boroughs (or districts) and could, in effect, buy a seat in the House of Commons for the representative of their choice. The Reform Bill of 1832 changed this, however, by restructuring the borough system so that more individuals could vote and so that each community was represented within the Parliament.

Prince Klemens von Metternich was the Foreign Minister of Austria during the early to mid nineteenth century. He is primarily known for the role he played in the Congress of Vienna. Not only was he the Austrian representative to the Congress, but he was also the driving force behind the conservative decisions that were reached by the Congress. In fact, the period immediately after the Congress of Vienna is sometimes known as the Age of Metternich because most of the European nations attempted to ensure that Metternich's conservative ideas were actually put into practice. Metternich played an important role in the politics of the European nations because he encouraged the suppression of revolutionary ideas such as liberalism, democracy, and nationalism. It is important to note, however, that Metternich's desire to eliminate revolutionary ideas before they could spawn full-fledged revolutionary movements contributed to the revolutions of 1848.

The revolutions of 1848 were a series of riots that occurred in Austria, Bohemia, France, Germany, Hungary, and Italy from the end of February 1848 to the summer of 1849. These riots began in France on February 22, 1848, when the Prime Minister of France François Guizot ordered a group of liberal political reformers to disband and stop meeting. This led the citizens of Paris who supported the government reforms that the liberal reformers proposed to revolt against King Louis Philippe and the rest of the French government. It is important to note, however, that the Parisian citizens' decision to revolt not only affected France; it also affected the other European nations, as liberal reformers in each country began to use the revolution in France to encourage similar movements within their own countries. This eventually led to revolutions in almost every part of Europe, as liberal reformers demanded additional rights and attempted to implement government reforms.

The revolutions of 1848 affected almost every nation in Europe, including the nations that belonged to the German Confederation. King Frederick William IV of Prussia, however, attempted to form an assembly to bring the revolution in Prussia to an end. This assembly was designed to create a constitution for Prussia, but several individuals throughout the German Confederation began to wonder if a similar assembly could be used to create a constitution for a unified Germany. This led the supporters of the unification movement to form a second assembly known as the Frankfurt Assembly in which they discussed the different ways that a unified Germany could be structured (specifically regarding whether Austria or Prussia should rule Germany and which nations should be included in the new country). The Frankfurt Assembly eventually created a plan for a unified German government, but the plan was never actually put into effect.

Benjamin Disraeli was the Prime Minister of Great Britain during the mid nineteenth century. He is primarily known for encouraging the British Parliament to pass the Reform Bill of 1867, which is also known as the Second Reform Bill, to ensure that the Tory Party would remain in control of the British Parliament. Disraeli's plan ultimately failed, however, as the Whig Party took over the Parliament during the 1868 election, but the Reform Bill of 1867 greatly increased the number of individuals who were allowed to vote.

William E. Gladstone was the Prime Minister of Great Britain during the mid to late nineteenth century. He is known for the educational, government, and labor reforms that he encouraged the British Parliament to implement. These reforms included a law that allowed workers to form unions, a law that allowed the government to fund public schools, and a law that allowed an individual to vote for his representative to Parliament via a secret ballot.

Louis-Philippe was the King of France during the mid nineteenth century. He willingly abdicated, or resigned from, his position as the King of France during the revolutions of 1848 to end the revolution in France. It is important to note, however, that Louis-Philippe also played an important role in beginning the revolutions of 1848, as he implemented several policies with which the liberal reformers disagreed. (Most of these policies specifically concerned the amount of control that the wealthy citizens of France had over the French government.)

Louis-Napoleon Bonaparte was the President of the Second Republic in France, and later the Emperor of France, during the mid to late nineteenth century. He is known for the conservative reforms that he implemented to limit the power of the revolutionary movement after the revolutions of 1848. It is important to note, however, that he also implemented a series of liberal reforms to eliminate some of the problems that originally led to the revolutions of 1848.

The Crimean War refers to a series of battles that started in the Ottoman Empire (the area that is now known as Turkey) in October 1853. These battles occurred as the result of a disagreement between Russia, France, and Great Britain regarding the rightful ruler of the lands of the Ottoman Empire. Russia believed that it had the right to control the Ottoman Empire because of a treaty between the Ottoman Empire and Russia known as the Treaty of Kuchuk Kainarji. This treaty granted Russia the right to protect Christians within the Ottoman Empire; as a result, Russia believed that it had the right to intervene in the Ottoman Empire's affairs. The French and British governments, however, feared that the Russians would gain too much power if they were allowed to control the lands of the Ottoman Empire, so they also made a claim to the land. This led the Russians to send forces into the Ottoman Empire to protect its claim, and France and Great Britain consequently sent troops to stop Russia.

The Dreyfus Affair refers to a series of events that took place in France from 1894 to 1906 in relation to the arrest, trial, and conviction of Captain Alfred Dreyfus. Dreyfus was a captain of a French artillery unit who was accused of selling information about the weapons, structure, and movements of the artillery units of the French Army to Germany. These accusations occurred after a French Intelligence Department agent discovered a letter in the German Embassy that described a series of important details about the French Army. This letter provided no evidence of any connection to Dreyfus other than the fact that it was signed with a D, but the single initial and a series of rumors were enough for the French government to order his arrest. Dreyfus was then put on trial and ultimately convicted because he was Jewish, which led to a major dispute in France between the individuals who believed Dreyfus was innocent and the anti-Semitic individuals who supported the verdict.

The Austro-Hungarian Empire was a historically German state ruled by a German family, however the majority of the citizens of the Empire were Slavs. This led to increasing problems as the wave of nationalism swept across Europe. The term dual monarchy refers to a type of government in which two different countries are ruled by the same government, but each country has some control over its own actions. For example, the Austrian-Hungarian Empire was actually a dual monarchy that came into existence after the Compromise of 1867. Austroslavism was a political movement that took place in the Austrian Empire during the mid nineteenth century in which a group of liberal reformers attempted to establish a series of regional governments within the Austrian Empire. This movement was designed to allow the Slavic individuals living within the Austrian Empire to have some control over their own government, but the movement ultimately failed. Pan-Slavism was a political movement that took place throughout Europe during the mid nineteenth century in which a group of Slavic nationalists attempted to form a single unified Slavic nation independent of the other European nations.

The area known as Italy had not been unified since the fall of the Roman Empire over a thousand years prior. Constantly divided and redivided between Italian city-states and foreign empires, it was during this time period that the unification of the pensulina and the creation of a specifically Italian state was seriously attempted and eventually suceeded.

Giuseppe Mazzini was a political reformer who moved throughout the area that is now Italy during the early to late nineteenth century. He is primarily known for the organizations that he created to further the unification movement by force, which included groups such as Young Italy and Young Europe. It is important to note, however, that he is also known for his book, The Duties of Man, in which he discussed the concept of nationalism and explained his belief that unification should be achieved by any means necessary.

Count Camillo di Cavour was the Prime Minister of Sardinia-Piedmont, which later became part of Italy, during the mid nineteenth century. He is known for the reforms he implemented to address some of the issues that had angered the liberal reformers and led to the liberal movement in the Italian states. He also negotiated a series of agreements with other countries to obtain the outside aid that the Italian states needed to create a unified Italy.

Giuseppe Garibaldi was a political reformer who moved throughout the area that is now Italy during the early to late nineteenth century. He created a revolutionary army known as the Red Shirts, which he used to seize the throne of the Kingdom of the Two Sicilies, so that the Kingdom of the Two Sicilies could be joined with the rest of the Italian states. It is important to note that Garibaldi was a strong supporter of the unification movement, and he believed, like Giuseppe Mazzini, that unification should be achieved by any means necessary.

Victor Emmanuel II was the King of Sardinia-Piedmont and later the King of Italy during the late nineteenth century. He led and supported most of the forces that seized the thrones of the Italian states for the unification movement, and he was the first king to rule over Italy after the Italian states were united.

German Unification

Much like Italy, Germany at this time was a fragmented collection of states ranging in size from the large Kingdom of Prussia to small single city sized political entities only loosely held together in the German Confederation. However in the wake of the Napoleonic Wars, there was a growing German nationalist movement aimed at the unification of all the German states into a single country. Unification refers to the process by which a group of nations joins together to form a single nation. For example, the individual states of the German Confederation eventually joined to form the nation of Germany.

One of the results of this movement was he Zollverein, which is also known as the German Customs Union, was an organization formed by some of the nations within the German Confederation to control the import and export of goods into and out of the German states. This organization addressed issues related to the tariffs that each nation was required to pay and the regulations that each nation was required to follow to import goods. These tariffs and regulations were designed to make it easier for the German states to trade with one another and harder for each state to trade with countries outside of the union.

Wilhelm I was the King of Prussia and later the King of Germany during the late nineteenth century. He allowed Otto Von Bismarck, the prime minister of Prussia, to establish his own agenda and, in effect, control Prussia. It is important to note that Wilhelm I was the first king to rule over Germany after the German states were united.

Otto Von Bismarck was the Prime Minister of Prussia and later the Chancellor of Germany during the late nineteenth century. He is primarily known for a speech he made in which he stated the only way that the German states were going to be united was through "blood and iron" (in other words, the use of military force). This is an example of the German term realpolitik literally means "practical politics." It is typically used to describe a political agenda that is designed to achieve power by any means. It is important to note that Bismarck also instituted several reforms within the government without the consent of the Landtag (Prussian Parliament) to create a powerful Prussian Army that he could use to create a unified Germany. Kulturkampf is a German term that literally means "culture struggle" or "culture war." The term is typically used to describe a series of laws that Otto Von Bismarck passed to limit the power that the Catholic Church exerted over the people of Germany.

The Second Schleswig War, which is also known as the War Against Denmark, was a war that occurred in Germany and Denmark from February 1, 1864, to October 30, 1864. This war occurred as the result of a disagreement between Denmark and the German Confederation regarding the rightful ruler of Denmark and the rightful ruler of the Schleswig region. Christian IX, the king of Denmark during the war, assumed the throne of Denmark after his caretaker Frederick VII, the former King of Denmark, died without any children. This allowed Christian IX to also claim the Schleswig region for Denmark, as Frederick VII was the former Duke of the Duchy of Schleswig. The German Confederation, however, did not recognize Christian IX as the rightful heir to the throne because he was not actually Frederick VII's son. This led the German Confederation to send troops into Denmark to force Christian IX to relinquish his claim to the Duchy of Schleswig (which was primarily inhabited by Germans), and the Danish were eventually forced to surrender the region after the nine-month war ended.

The Seven Weeks' War, which is also known as the Austro-Prussian War, was a conflict that occurred primarily in Bohemia (but also occurred throughout modern-day Germany and Italy) from the middle of June to the middle of August 1866. This war occurred as the result of a disagreement between Austria and Prussia regarding the rightful ruler of the Schleswig region. Austria and Prussia were able to claim the Duchy of Schleswig and the Duchy of Holstein during the Second Schleswig War, and the two nations agreed to control the duchies under a joint government. Otto Von Bismarck, the prime minister of Prussia, however, was looking for a reason to seize some of the lands that Austria controlled, so he began to create a disagreement between the two nations regarding which nation had the right to actually make decisions for the duchies. Austria, as a result, called for a Diet to discuss the issue, and Prussia attacked and defeated Austria because Austria was supposedly using the Diet to take control of both duchies.

The Franco-Prussian War, which is also known as the Franco-German War, was a war that occurred in France and Prussia from July 19, 1870, to May 10, 1871. This war occurred as the result of a disagreement between Prussia and France regarding the new ruler of Spain. This disagreement was related to the fact that the former Queen of Spain, Isabella II, was forced to surrender the throne and leave Spain after her own troops revolted in 1868. The new Spanish government, however, was not prepared to place a specific individual on the Spanish throne, and other nations began to identify potential candidates. The Prussian government nominated Prince Leopold of Hohenzollern-Sigmaringen as a potential candidate for the Spanish throne. The French, however, feared that Leopold's connections to Prussia could pose a problem for the French if he was allowed to form an alliance between Spain and Prussia, so they demanded that the Prussian king issue a formal decree protesting Leopold's candidacy. Because the Prussians refused to do so, France attacked Prussia, and Prussia ultimately defeated France.

Bismarck used the victory in the Franco-Prussian War to officially unify the German states and create the German Empire. New governmental houses were established for the new German state. The Bundesrat is a German term that literally means "Federal Council." The term is typically used to describe the house within the German legislature that was originally designed for the nobles and princes of Germany. (It is similar in some ways to the British House of Lords.) The term is still used to this day, but the Bundesrat now consists of appointed officials rather than royal representatives. Reichstag is a German term that literally means "Imperial Diet." The term is typically used to describe the house within the German legislature that was originally designed for the peasants and merchants of Germany (It is similar in some ways to the British House of Commons.)

Age of Imperialism

Imperialism refers to a political tactic in which a country attempts to use the resources of another nation to expand its own power. It is important to note that imperialism may refer to a situation in which a country uses military force to seize the land, materials, or other resources of another nation, but imperialism does not necessarily have to involve the use of force. In fact, imperialism may refer to any process in which a country is able to use a set of diplomatic, economic, military, or cultural tactics to control the resources of another nation. Colonialism refers to a political tactic in which a country attempts to claim more land so that it can expand its own power. It is important to note that colonialism typically refers to a situation in which a country has established a colony in another part of the world.

There were several different reasons why some nations of the world decided to expand their power throughout the mid to late nineteenth century. Two major reasons for the rise in imperialism were related to the philosophical and religious beliefs of the imperialist nations. The first reason that is important to note is that the general philosophy of Europe at the time was greatly affected by the concept of Social Darwinism. This is because Social Darwinism encouraged the European nations to believe that they would not survive unless they could prove their strength and expand. The second reason that is noteworthy is that there was a drastic increase in the number of missionaries who were traveling from Europe to other nations to promote Christianity during the mid to late nineteenth century. This meant that the European nations had to find new ways to protect their citizens as more and more people traveled overseas, and many nations began to establish outposts to accomplish this goal.

Charles Darwin was a scientist who lived in England during the early to late nineteenth century. He is primarily known for his book, On the Origin of Species, in which he formally established the theory of evolution and the theory of natural selection. Darwin believed that every creature on Earth was actually the evolved form of the creatures that came before it. He also believed that each creature would continue to evolve as the weaker members of a species died out and the stronger members of a species adapted to their environment.

Herbert Spencer was a philosopher and scientist who lived in England during the early nineteenth to early twentieth centuries. He is primarily known for his book, Synthetic Philosophy, in which he established the concept of Social Darwinism. Social Darwinism states that human society evolves through the process of natural selection and that society ultimately promotes "the survival of the fittest." In other words, according to Social Darwinism, an individual is more likely to survive if he is better educated, more powerful, and wealthier than other individuals.

There were several different reasons why some nations of the world decided to expand their power throughout the mid to late nineteenth century. Two major reasons for the rise in imperialism were related to the economic and political concerns of the imperialist nations. The first reason that is important to note is that there was a common belief at the time that a nation would not be able to compete with the other nations of the world unless they established military bases, naval bases, and trading outposts throughout the world. As a result, many nations began to seek out areas where they could establish ports and bases in strategic locations. The second reason that is noteworthy is that the Industrial Revolution increased the speed at which goods could be produced, which meant that the European nations needed to seek out more resources to produce those goods.

The British East India Company was a company owned and operated by a large group of British merchants who each owned a small portion of the company (in other words, a joint-stock company). The company was designed to establish trade agreements with India, China, and other countries throughout Eastern and Southern Asia. The British East India Company had a great deal of power in both Asia and Great Britain because the agreements it established typically gave it absolute control over the areas in which it operated and made it difficult for any merchant or merchant organization outside the company to trade with Asia. The Dutch East India Company was a company that received permission from the Netherlands to be the only company allowed to establish and defend Dutch colonies within Asia (in other words, a chartered company for colonial expansion). The Dutch East India Company established outposts in India, China, South Africa, and a variety of other countries.

The Opium Wars were two separate but related wars that occurred in China from 1841 to 1842 and from 1856 to 1860 in which the Chinese government attempted to eliminate the opium trade in China. Opium, which was known to be an addictive substance at the time, was legal in Great Britain but not in China. This became a problem when British merchants realized they could make a large profit by selling opium to individuals who were not typically able to acquire it. Some British merchants began smuggling large quantities of opium into China so that they could sell it to the Chinese. The Chinese government began to seize the opium that was coming into the country or even approaching Chinese waters to stop the trade. The British government was not willing to allow the Chinese to attack its merchants, and it eventually declared war on China to protect its ships and cargo.

The Open Door Policy refers to a trade agreement that the United States attempted to implement between the nations of Europe regarding China. This policy stated that the European nations, Japan, and the United States agreed to allow the other nations involved in the agreement to trade in China, that each nation involved in the agreement agreed to refrain from any action that would restrict the ability of another nation to enter or trade in a Chinese port, and that each nation involved in the agreement agreed to refrain from any action that would allow a nation to seize land from China. Significantly, this agreement was not originally designed to protect China or grant China any control over its own trade; it was instead designed to protect the ability of the United States and the European nations to trade with China.

The Sepoy Mutiny, which is also known as the Sepoy Rebellion or the Great Rebellion, refers to a series of events that took place in India from the end of January 1857 to the middle of June 1858 in which the people of India revolted against the British East India Company. At the time, the British East India Company was responsible for managing Great Britain's activities in India, and it controlled a large army of Indian troops, which the company used to protect its outposts in India and other countries. However, these troops were not happy about the arrangement the company had in India, and a series of rumors began to spread. One of these rumors was that the rifle ammunition the company issued was actually covered by an outer wrapper coated with fat from cows and pigs. Eventually some of the soldiers revolted because the rumor, if it were true, would have meant that the soldiers had to violate their religious beliefs to remove the ammunition wrapper.

The Suez Canal is a man-made waterway that the French opened in Egypt in 1869. This waterway was built by a French company known as the Suez Canal Company to connect the Red Sea (via the Gulf of Suez) to the Mediterranean Sea so that the nations of Europe could sail straight through Egypt. The Suez Canal, as a result, played an extremely important role in the imperialism movement because it drastically decreased the amount of time it took the Europeans to reach Asia. In fact, up until this point, the nations of Europe had to sail around the Cape of Good Hope to reach Asia, which made it difficult for the European nations to resupply and reinforce their outposts. The canal, however, made it easier for the Europeans to establish and protect their outposts because the Europeans could now transport their goods, settlers, and soldiers straight to India and the other parts of Asia.

Cecil John Rhodes was an entrepreneur and a politician who was born in England and later lived in South Africa during the mid nineteenth to early twentieth century. He is primarily known for the diamond mines that he helped establish in Kimberley, South Africa, and the surrounding area, as some of these mines were actually used to establish the De Beers Diamond Company. (In fact, Rhodes helped establish the company.) It is important to note that Rhodes was also a politician who eventually earned a seat in the Cape Parliament (the government that the British established in South Africa). This allowed Rhodes to promote the expansion of the British holdings in South Africa through taxes designed to raise funds for expansion. He also encouraged passage of laws that allowed British troops to remove the native Africans from their land so that British entrepreneurs could take the land even through military action, such as in the Jameson Raid in which a small British force unsuccessfully attempted to seize the Transvaal region.

The Berlin Conference refers to a trade agreement that the Chancellor of Germany Otto Von Bismarck helped establish in 1885. This agreement stated that the European nations would each claim a specific area within Africa and that each nation would recognize the boundaries of the areas claimed by other nations as long as the nations continued to use and protect those areas. Further, the Berlin Conference stipulated that all the nations involved in the agreement would be allowed to trade in Africa, that all the nations involved in the agreement would be allowed to use the rivers of Africa, and that all the nations involved in the agreement would halt the acquisition and sale of slaves. It is important to note that this agreement was not designed to protect Africa or give Africa any control over its own trade; it was instead designed to protect the ability of Germany and other European nations to establish colonies in Africa so that they could trade in Africa.

The Russo-Japanese War refers to a war that occurred in China from February 10, 1904, to September 5, 1905, in which the Japanese attempted to remove a Russian force from Manchuria. Although an official agreement was never signed, Russia and Japan had previously agreed to refrain from any action that would allow them to seize land from China as part of the Open Door Policy established by the United States. Russia, however, wanted to establish a series of bases and ports in both China and Korea, and a rebellion known as the Boxer Rebellion that occurred in China in 1898 gave Russia an excuse to do this. In fact, the rebellion encouraged Russia to send forces into Manchuria under the promise that it would withdraw them as soon as the rebellion was over, but Russia never withdrew its forces. This eventually led the Japanese to attack the Russians, and the Russians were eventually forced to sign a treaty in which Russia was granted control of northern Manchuria and Japan was granted control of southern Manchuria.

The Bismarck Alliance System, which is also known as the Bismarckian Alliance System, refers to a series of alliances that the Chancellor of Germany Otto Von Bismarck established to ensure that it would be nearly impossible for any nation to aid France. Bismarck based his system of alliances on the idea that a nation would not risk war with another country if that country was in a large alliance because the war would simply cost too many men and too many resources.

The Three Emperor's League was an alliance that Austria, Germany, and Russia formed in 1873. This alliance was designed to help preserve the balance of power in Europe, but the alliance was eventually dissolved when the Russians attempted to help the Serbians defeat the Ottoman Empire during the First Balkan Crisis. The Dual Alliance was an alliance that Austria and Germany formed in 1879 after the Three Emperor's League was dissolved. This alliance, which actually lasted until the end of World War I in 1918, was primarily designed to help protect Austria and Germany if Russia decided to attack either country. The Triple Alliance was an alliance that Austria, Germany, and Italy formed in 1882. This alliance was originally designed to prevent the French from expanding their influence into the territories of the Triple Alliance members, but it was later used to form the basis for the Central powers of World War I (Austria, Bulgaria, Germany, Italy, and the Ottoman Empire).

Other alliances were created in response to the German alliance network. The Franco-Russian Alliance was an alliance that France and Russia formed in 1894. This alliance was primarily designed to protect France and Russia if the Triple Alliance (Austria, Germany, and Italy) decided to attack either country. In fact, the terms of the Franco-Russian Alliance actually stated that the Franco-Russian Alliance would remain in effect until the Triple Alliance was dissolved. The Anglo-Japanese Alliance was an alliance that Great Britain and Japan formed in 1902. This alliance was primarily designed to protect Great Britain and Japan if the members of the Franco-Russian Alliance or the members of the Triple Alliance decided to attack either country. The Triple Entente was an alliance that France, Great Britain, and Russia formed in 1907. This alliance was primarily designed to protect the members of the Triple Entente in the event of an attack by the Triple Alliance, but it was later used to form the basis for the Allied powers of World War I (France, Great Britain, the United States, and Russia).

The First Moroccan Crisis, which is also known as the Tangier Crisis or the Moroccan Crisis of 1905, refers to a disagreement between France and Germany regarding which nation had the right to control Morocco. France believed that it had the right to control Morocco because it had established a series of outposts throughout the area. Also, its merchants and colonists had been living and trading in and around Morocco for over seventy years. In fact, France had already begun to form agreements and alliances with other nations to make Morocco a protectorate of France long before the dispute with Germany began. Germany, however, was concerned about the alliances that France was forming as well as the strategic resources that France might be able to obtain from Morocco. These concerns led Germany to declare that it also had the right to establish outposts within Morocco and that France could not declare Morocco to be a protectorate.

The Algeciras Conference was a meeting in which Austria, France, Germany, Great Britain, Italy, Russia, and Spain met in Algeciras, Spain, to discuss the dispute that had arisen between France and Germany during the First Moroccan Crisis. The Emperor of Germany William II called for the conference in 1906 to gather support to backup Germany's claim to Morocco. William II hoped that the other nations of Europe would support Germany's claim or that they would at least be too concerned with their own affairs to support France's claim. France, however, had already formed a series of strong alliances with the nations of Europe to establish Morocco as a protectorate, and William II quickly realized that his plans were not going to succeed. Consequently, William II became more and more frustrated, and he eventually attempted to turn the other delegates on one another. This ultimately backfired, however, as William II's actions not only encouraged the nations of Europe to vote in favor of a French protectorate, but also encouraged the other nations of Europe to shun Germany.

The Second Moroccan Crisis, which is also known as the Agadir Crisis or the Moroccan Crisis of 1911, refers to a disagreement between France and Germany regarding which nation had the right to control Morocco. This disagreement occurred because the citizens of the Moroccan city of Fez rebelled in an attempt to overthrow Sultan Abdelhafid, a supporter of the French government. France, who had already received the permission of the nations of Europe (with the exception of Austria and Germany) to make Morocco a protectorate, sent forces to Fez to protect Sultan Abelhafid and end the rebellion. Still not pleased with the idea that France would be able to establish bases and obtain other strategic resources throughout Morocco, Germany dispatched a gunboat known as the Panther to Agadir, Morocco, to make it clear that it did not approve of the protectorate. This action greatly angered the French, but it really had no effect on Morocco, as the French were eventually able to form the protectorate anyway.

The First Balkan War was a conflict that occurred across the Balkan Peninsula (located in southeastern Europe) from October 8, 1912, to May 30, 1913, in which Bulgaria, Greece, Montenegro, and Serbia attempted to seize land from the Ottoman Empire. By this time, the Ottoman Empire had suffered a series of costly defeats in which it lost large portions of land and resources as well as a considerable number of men. These defeats ultimately weakened the Ottoman Empire to the point that the smaller nations of Europe could actually defeat the empire's forces and potentially claim its land. As a result, the nations of Bulgaria, Greece, Montenegro, and Serbia formed the Balkan League and launched a massive attack in an attempt to claim Macedonia, Thrace, and several other areas held by the Ottoman Empire. In the end, the Balkan League was able to defeat the Ottoman Empire and capture most of the empire's land, but the nations of the Balkan League could not agree on how to divide the land.

The Second Balkan War was a conflict that occurred across the Balkan Peninsula (located in southeastern Europe) from June 16, 1913, to July 18, 1913, in which Bulgaria attempted to seize some of the land that Greece, Montenegro, and Serbia had acquired from the Ottoman Empire during the First Balkan War. The nations of the Balkan League (Bulgaria, Greece, Montenegro, and Serbia) had seized a large amount of land from the Ottoman Empire during the First Balkan War, but the nations could not agree on how to divide the land. In fact, the nations of the Balkan League eventually came to an agreement, but Bulgaria and Serbia both believed that they had received less than their fair share of land. Consequently, both Serbia and Bulgaria demanded a larger portion of the land within Macedonia, and Bulgaria eventually attacked the Serbian troops in Macedonia to take the land by force. Bulgaria, however, was ultimately defeated and forced to surrender a large portion of its land by the combined forces of Greece, Montenegro, the Ottoman Empire, Romania, and Serbia.

World War I

The assassination of Archduke Francis Ferdinand refers to an event that took place in Sarajevo, Bosnia, on June 28, 1914. Francis Ferdinand and his wife, the Duchess Sophie, were in Sarajevo, Bosnia, to inspect the Austrian troops stationed there. A Serbian terrorist group known as the Black Hand was extremely upset that Austria had supported Bulgaria's position during the negotiations that followed the First and Second Balkan Wars, and the group's members decided to use this opportunity to assassinate Archduke Ferdinand as a means of demonstrating their discontent. The Black Hand's plan ultimately succeeded, as the group shot and killed both Francis Ferdinand and his wife, Sophie. The Austrian government quickly discovered that the Serbian government actually had information about the assassinations prior to the terrorist attack. Austria then declared war on Serbia, Russia pledged all its resources to Serbia, and Germany pledged all its resources to Austria. (It is important to note that the German and Russian resource pledges were known as "the blank checks.")

The Schlieffen Plan was the military strategy that the Central powers (Austria, Bulgaria, Germany, Italy, and later the Ottoman Empire) used in World War I. This plan was designed to allow the Central powers to march straight through Belgium into France so that the Central powers could defeat France before its allies could mobilize and send reinforcements. The strategy used in the Schlieffen Plan was based on the belief that the Central powers would never be able to outlast the combined resources of the Allied powers (France, Great Britain, Russia, and later the United States) unless they could divide and conquer the military resources of the Allied powers before they had to fight a war on multiple fronts. Not only did the Schlieffen Plan underestimate the speed at which France's allies could mobilize, but it also underestimated the determination of the Belgians and the French to keep the Central powers out of Belgium and France.

The western front of World War I refers to the battles that took place in Belgium and France from 1914 to 1918. The German Army marched into Belgium on August 4, 1914, to make its way to France. The Belgians, however, were not willing to allow the Germans to march through Belgium unhindered, and they launched a series of attacks against the Germans that weakened and slowed down the German forces. This cost the Germans a large amount of time that was vital to the Schlieffen Plan, but the Germans continued their advance and made it to the edge of France by the beginning of September 1914. When the Germans reached France, a series of battles ensued between the French and the British forces that had arrived in France by the time Germany made its way through Belgium. These battles ultimately resulted in the deaths of hundreds of thousands of men on both sides, but they did very little to improve the position of either side throughout most of the war.

The eastern front of World War I refers to the battles that took place in Austria, Germany, Hungary, Poland, Prussia, and Russia from 1914 to 1917. The First and Second Russian armies marched into East Prussia and Poland in mid August 1914 to make their way to Austria and eventually Germany. The German forces stationed in East Prussia were able to force the First Russian Army to retreat, but the Second Russian Army was able to move into Poland and destroy the Austrian forces stationed there. The German forces, as a result, moved into Poland to force the Second Russian Army to retreat, and after a series of battles, the Germans eventually forced the Russians back into Russia. This allowed the Germans to advance farther and farther into Russia until the people of Russia finally revolted against the Russian government to end the chaos, famine, and death that the war was causing in Russia. This forced the Russian government to sue for peace and exit the war.

The Gallipoli Campaign refers to a military offensive that the British and French forces started on February 19, 1915, to seize control of the Ottoman Empire. This offensive occurred because the Ottoman Empire controlled the Dardanelles Strait, which was the only sea route that the Allied powers could use to quickly transport troops and supplies to Russia. The Ottoman Empire, which had already joined the Central powers by the end of 1914, was not about to allow the Allies to use its straits and waterways. France and Great Britain sent a fleet of ships to attack the Gallipoli Peninsula so that the Allies could land troops near the Dardanelles Strait. These troops were then supposed to move north to capture the capital of the Ottoman Empire, Constantinople, but the Turkish troops of the Ottoman Empire forced the Allied forces to retreat before they were ever able to reach the capital.

The Lusitania was a British ocean liner that was attacked and sunk by a German submarine on May 7, 1915. This attack occurred because the Germans believed that the Lusitania was carrying weapons and ammunition from New York to Great Britain. (In fact, the ship's manifest actually stated that it was carrying ammunition.) This led the Germans to order a U-boat (short for undersea boat; in other words, a submarine) to intercept the Lusitania and sink it. The Lusitania, however, was not only carrying supplies for the war effort, but it was also carrying over 1,900 passengers, including numerous American civilians. The attack on the ship caused the deaths of nearly 1,200 of the ship's passengers, which included 139 Americans. Because American civilians were killed, the American people quickly demanded immediate action against Germany, and these demands eventually contributed to the United States' decision to enter the First World War in 1917.

Wilson's Fourteen Points refers to a speech that President Thomas Woodrow Wilson made in 1918 to describe the plan that he hoped to use to establish an extended peace in Europe. This plan consisted of fourteen concepts that President Wilson believed would allow the nations of Europe to create and preserve peaceful relations. These fourteeen concepts included the elimination of covert diplomacy of any kind (in other words, the elimination of any alliances or treaties that were not publically discussed or known); the right of all nations to use the seas outside of a country's coastal waters without interference; free and equal trading rights for all nations; a significant decrease in the numbers of weapons that each country controlled; a series of fair and reasonable decisions to settle the colonial claims of each nation; the removal of all troops belonging to the Central powers from the nations that they attacked during the war; the right of the Central powers to have some degree of self-determination; and the creation of an organization to discuss the issues that arise between nations.

The Treaty of Versailles was a treaty that France, Germany, Great Britain, Italy, Japan, and the United States signed to end World War I. This treaty was specifically designed to establish the terms under which Germany surrendered, and it identified several concessions that the Germans had to make. The terms of the treaty specifically required Germany to surrender a large portion of land it acquired both before and during the war, required Germany to pay reparations for the damage that it caused in each of the Allied nations, required Emperor Wilhelm II of Germany and other members of the German Army to be tried as war criminals, required Germany to reduce the size of its army and navy, required Germany to allow the Allied powers to establish a demilitarized zone in the Rhineland, and required Germany to make many other similar concessions.

Early 20th Century Russian Politics

Alexander Alexandrovich, who is also known as Alexander III, was the Tsar of Russia during the late nineteenth century. He used a series of brutal tactics to eliminate anyone who was not a member of the Russian Orthodox Church. It is important to note that Alexander III is also known for a series of laws, regulations, and police orders that he issued to suppress the liberal movement in Russia.

Nikolay Alexandrovich Romanov, who is also known as Nicholas II, was the Tsar of Russia from the late nineteenth century to the end of World War I. He was forced to abdicate, or resign from, his position as the Tsar of Russia after the March Revolution. Like his father, Alexander III, Nicholas II is also known for a series of laws, regulations, and police orders that he issued to suppress the liberal movement in Russia. Alexandra Feodorovna Romanova was the Tsaritsa of Russia (in other words, the Russian Queen) from the late nineteenth century to the end of World War I. She is primarily known for allowing the mystic, Grigori Rasputin, to exercise an unusual amount of control over the Russian government. It is also important to note that she ruled Russia in Tsar Nicholas II's place after he left the capital to lead the Russian Army in 1915. Grigori Rasputin, who is also known as the "Black Monk" or the "Mad Monk," was a mystic who lived in Russia during the late nineteenth to early twentieth century. He manipulated the Tsar or Russia Nicholas II and his wife, the Tsaritsa Alexandra, by convincing them that he could heal their son and rid him of his blood illness (hemophilia). It is important to note that Rasputin was eventually murdered by a group of Russian nobles.

The Revolution of 1905 refers to a series of riots that occurred throughout Russia from mid January to mid December 1905. The industrial workers of Russia, who were suffering under the harsh working conditions that existed in the Russian factories, petitioned the Tsar of Russia Nicholas II to implement a series of reforms that would grant the workers additional rights. These rights included freedom of speech, freedom of religion, freedom of the press, the right to insurance for health and injury costs, the right to create a Russian constitution, and the right to create a new legislature in which the people of Russia could elect representatives. Tsar Nicholas II was not willing to allow the people to form a constitutional government that would limit his own power. The tsar, as a result, agreed to guarantee the workers some rights, but he refused to guarantee them the right to create a constitution or the right to create a new legislature.

Bloody Sunday refers to an event that took place in St. Petersburg, Russia, on January 22, 1905. The industrial workers of Russia, who were suffering under the harsh working conditions in the Russian factories and the harsh rule of Tsar Nicholas II, asked the tsar to implement a series of reforms to help the workers. The tsar, however, was not willing to grant all the reforms that the workers requested. The workers, as a result, refused to work. This caused all the major industries within St. Petersburg to grind to a halt as the workers continued to strike for several weeks. A priest known as Father Gabon eventually formed a protest march to hand-deliver a petition from the city's workers to the Winter Palace to end the strike. This protest march was supposed to be nonviolent, but the soldiers stationed near the Winter Palace fired on the group, and the workers rioted in response.

The October Manifesto, which is also known as the Manifesto on the Improvement of the State Order, refers to a decree that the Tsar of Russia Nicholas II made on October 30, 1905. This decree described a series of reforms that the tsar planned to implement immediately to end some of the major problems that had led to the Revolution of 1905. These reforms guaranteed the citizens of Russia the right to assemble, freedom of speech, freedom of religion, the right for every adult man to vote, the right to form unions, and the right to due process. The October Manifesto also declared that the Russian government would create a constitution outlining its powers and a new legislature known as the Duma in which the male citizens of Russia, regardless of social class, would be allowed to elect representatives. It is important to note, however, that Nicholas II actually passed a series of laws to prevent the Duma from passing any regulations he disagreed with.

Alexander Kerensky was a political reformer who lived in Russia during the late nineteenth to late twentieth centuries. He helped the liberal movement in Russia establish a new government, known as the Provisional Government, after Tsar Nicholas II was forced to step down. It is also important to note that Alexander Kerensky later served as the Prime Minister of the Provisional Government.

There were a number different groups of liberal reformers in Russia in the late nineteenth and early twentieth centuries. The Constitutional Democrats, also known as the Cadets, was a group of political reformers that first appeared in Russia during the late nineteenth century. These reformers believed that the Russian government should be a constitutional monarchy and that the people of Russia should be allowed to elect the officials within their government (with the exception of the tsar). The Social Democrats was a group of political reformers that first appeared in Russia during the late nineteenth century. These reformers believed that the people of Russia should overthrow the Russian government and establish a communist system as envisioned by Karl Marx. The Social Revolutionaries was a group of political reformers that first appeared in Russia during the late nineteenth century. These reformers believed that the Russian government should implement a series of reforms to establish a socialist system that would protect the farmers of Russia.

Vladimir Lenin was a political reformer who lived in Russia during the late nineteenth to early twentieth century. He is primarily known for the role that he played in establishing the Russian movement to implement a government based on Karl Marx's idea of communism. (The movement is actually known as the Marxist movement.) Lenin's Marxist movement ultimately led to the formation of the communist government known as the Union of Soviet Socialist Republics (U.S.S.R.)

The Bolsheviks were political reformers who originally belonged to the Russian Social Democratic Labor Party (or the Social Democrats). They believed that the people of Russia would only be able to overthrow the Russian government if they established a full-time force devoted to starting a revolution. The Bolsheviks, as a result, split from the main party to form the Bolshevik Party, which was designed to start the revolution. It is important to note that the Russian term Bolshevik literally means "majority," but the Bolsheviks were actually in the minority until after the March Revolution. The Mensheviks were political reformers who originally belonged to the Russian Social Democratic Labor Party and who believed that the people of Russia would be able to establish a new Russian government if they continued to actively encourage their fellow citizens to pursue it. As a result, the Mensheviks split from the main party to form the Menshevik Party, which was designed to promote government reform.

The March Revolution, which is also sometimes known as the February Revolution (because Russia used a different calendar system at that time), refers to a series of riots that occurred throughout Russia from March 8 to March 15, 1917. The people of Russia, who were beginning to find it more and more difficult to obtain food as the Germans continued their advance, began to demand an immediate end to the war. The Tsar of Russia Nicholas II, however, refused to surrender and instead left the capital to personally lead the Russian Army. This led to further unrest, as the Germans continued to advance in spite of the Tsar's efforts, and the people eventually began to riot. The tsar, in response, ordered his troops to end the riots by any means necessary, but the troops refused. This allowed the peasants to work with the Duma (the Russian Parliament) to form a new government and force the tsar to step down.

The Provisional Government was the interim government (or, in other words, the temporary government) that the Duma (the Russian Parliament) and the people of Russia formed during the March Revolution of 1917. This government was designed primarily to run the country until the people could elect a group of representatives to create a constitution for a new Democratic Russian Republic. It is important to note, however, that the Provisional Government was dissolved before a constitution was created because it ultimately failed to solve the problems that existed prior to the March Revolution. (In fact, Russia was still in World War I after the Provisional Government dissolved.) The Dictatorship of the Proletariat was the government that the Bolsheviks (the Russian supporters of Karl Marx's concept of communism) formed after the Provisional Government dissolved to establish Russia as a communist state. The actions of the Dictatorship of the Proletariat ultimately led to the creation of the communist government known as the Union of Soviet Socialist Republics (U.S.S.R.).

Farm collectivization, which is also known as collective farming, refers to a process in which a group of small, privately owned farms are joined to form a single large farm that the farmers can farm as a group. Farm collectivization was originally implemented in Russia by Joseph Stalin, the general secretary of the Communist Party of the Soviet Union after Vladimir Lenin's death in 1924, in an effort to increase food production. The collective farming arrangement implemented by Stalin actually had the opposite effect, however, as it nearly cut Russia's food production in half. Communes, which are also known as collective farms or kolkhoz (the Russian term for "collective farm"), are large farms that a group of farmers farm together. These farms were originally established in Russia by farmers who volunteered to take part in Joseph Stalin's farm collectivization campaign, but it is important to note that the Soviets eventually forced all the Russian farmers to surrender their land to the communes.

The Soviet Five-Year Plans, which were also known as the Five-Year Plans for the National Economy of the Soviet Union, refer to a group of documents that were originally issued by Joseph Stalin and were later issued by other officials within the Soviet government. These documents described the goals that the Union of Soviet Socialist Republics (U.S.S.R.) hoped to achieve over the next five years and the methods that the U.S.S.R planned to use to achieve those goals. These plans played an extremely important role in the Soviet government because they described the basic actions that the Soviets were expected to take in the near future. Stalin's first

Five-Year Plan established the farming communes within Russia, established state farms, increased coal and electricity production, improved transportation, and ultimately established the groundwork for the industrialization of Russia to occur in future plans (specifically the second Five-Year Plan). The U.S.S.R. ultimately issued 12 Five-Year Plans before it dissolved.

The Great Purge refers to a series of events that occurred throughout Russia from 1936 to 1938 in which Joseph Stalin attempted to eliminate his political enemies. Stalin, who had been the General Secretary of the Communist Party of the Soviet Union for nearly ten years by the time of the Purge, was concerned that some of the individuals within the government might try to replace him because they disagreed with his policies. This belief led Stalin to arrange the assassination of one of his most vocal enemies, Sergei M. Kirov. The assassination, however, was not traced back to Stalin; it was instead traced back to another of Stalin's enemies, Leon Trotsky, and his supporters. (In fact, there is evidence to indicate that Stalin may have planned the assassination so that this occurred.) As a result, Stalin ordered the NKVD (Russian secret police) to arrest anyone who might have been involved in the assassination, and the NKVD imprisoned or executed nearly 8 million Russians before the Purge finally ended in 1938.

Interwar Years

There were a number of artistic movements in the early twentieth century. Expressionism refers to an artistic movement that took place during the early twentieth century in which individuals attempted to depict the world around them as they perceived it or as they imagined it. Expressionism is very similar to impressionism. (In fact, expressionism is in some ways an evolution of impressionism.) However, the artwork created as the result of expressionism is typically designed to depict a real person, place, or thing in an even more unusual way than the artwork created as the result of impressionism. Cubism refers to an artistic movement that took place during the early twentieth century in which individuals attempted to create a certain mood. Surrealism refers to an artistic movement that took place during the early twentieth century in which individuals attempted to convey a philosophical concept, an idea, or something they imagined. Surrealistic artwork is not typically designed to depict a real person, place, or thing.

Friedrich Nietzsche was a philosopher who lived in Germany from the mid nineteenth century to the turn of the twentieth century. He is primarily known for the books that he wrote in which he discussed his views on Christianity and the effects that religion had on morality and society. Some of his most famous works include Daybreak, The Gay Science, Beyond Good and Evil, and The Will to Power.

Sigmund Freud was a psychologist who lived in Germany from the mid nineteenth to mid twentieth centuries. He is primarily known for the books he wrote in which he attempted to describe the way that a human's subconscious works by separating the subconscious mind into three parts. These three parts include the id (what a person instinctually desires), the superego (what a person knows is morally right), and the ego (the part that attempts to balance a person's desires with his morality).

The Weimar Constitution was a document issued in 1919 by the National Assembly of Germany, which was a government body the German people formed to create a new government after World War I. This document established the basic system of government that the Assembly intended to implement in Germany, which was a democratic republic at the time. This democratic republic was divided into two main government branches: an executive branch and a legislative branch. (Notably, the Weimar Constitution also established a judicial system that functioned separately from the rest of the government.) The executive branch consisted of a president, who was elected by the people every seven years, and his advisors. The legislative branch consisted of two political bodies, the Reichstag and the Reichsrat. The Reichstag (a lower house with elected officials) was primarily the same as it was before Germany became a republic, but the Reichsrat (an upper house with appointed officials) replaced the Bundesrat (an upper house with nobles) that had existed prior to the new government.

The Ruhr Crisis, which is also known as the Ruhr Occupation, refers to an event that took place in Germany in 1922. The Treaty of Versailles, which the Germans were forced to sign at the end of World War I, required the Germans to pay reparations for the damage that Germany caused to the Allied nations. The total amount that Germany was required to pay was supposed to be divided into a series of payments so that each Allied country would receive a portion of the total amount based on the amount of damage that each country sustained during the war. Germany, as a result, was required to pay close to $33 billion, with France receiving approximately half of that amount, or $17 billion. Germany didn't actually have the money to pay the reparations that it was supposed to pay, and it quickly began to miss payments. This eventually led Belgium and France, who desperately needed the money, to invade the Ruhr Valley to take the resources that they needed by force.

The Dawes Plan was an agreement that Belgium, France, Germany, Great Britain, Russia, and the United States announced in 1924 to help Germany pay the reparations it owed and ultimately end the Ruhr Crisis. This agreement stated that Belgium and France would return the Ruhr Valley to Germany; that Germany would be required to continue making payments, but that it could adjust those payments based on the state of the German economy; and that Germany could receive a loan from the United States to pay for some of the infrastructure repairs that the country needed to continue functioning. The Young Plan was an agreement that Belgium, France, Germany, Great Britain, Russia, and the United States announced in 1929 to ensure that Germany could continue to pay the reparations it owed without bankrupting the country. According to this agreement, Germany would only be required to pay a small portion of the total amount it originally agreed to pay and would have more time to make each payment.

Great Britain experienced numerous problems immediately after World War I. First, the British economy, like the French and German economies at the time, began to decline rapidly as a result of the war. This decline occurred because Great Britain owed a large amount of money to other countries for the supplies it had purchased during the war as well as a large amount of money to its own people for the repairs and programs the country needed to conduct (unemployment, war relief, etc.). Great Britain didn't have the money to pay its debts, and it no longer had the capability to earn the money it needed without the merchants and ships that the country had lost during the war. Another major problem that arose was that Ireland was continually attempting to gain its independence from Great Britain, which meant that Great Britain had to address the question (known as the Irish Question) of whether to free Ireland or fight to keep it.

The Great Depression refers to a period from the late 1920s to the early 1940s in which the economy of almost every major nation began to decline rapidly. The beginning of this period is typically associated with the date that the stock market crashed (October 29, 1929), but the Great Depression actually resulted from a series of different problems in different nations at different times. In fact, the Great Depression was actually caused by so many different problems (industry changes, inadequate stock regulation, war relief costs, etc.) that it ultimately affected each nation in a different way. France, Germany, and Great Britain began to feel the effects of an economic decline in the early 1920s, but the conditions of the economies of each of these nations deteriorated almost immediately after the stock market crash. This led to the widespread closure of businesses throughout Europe, and the unemployment rate increased drastically in each of these nations as a result. Russia, on the other hand, was virtually unaffected because of its communist economy.

The New Deal refers to an economic plan that the President of the United States Franklin D. Roosevelt announced in 1933 to address some of the problems that had arisen in the United States as a result of the Great Depression. This plan consisted of a series of reforms that were designed to establish stronger regulations for banks and corporations, to create a support system for the elderly and disabled, to provide financial support to farmers, to protect the rights of workers, and to accomplish a variety of other similar goals.

The Popular Front Reforms, which are also sometimes known as the French New Deal, refer to a series of reforms that the Prime Minister of France Leon Blum implemented in 1936 to address some of the problems that had arisen in France as a result of the Great Depression. These reforms were primarily designed to establish stronger regulations for banks, to provide financial support to farmers and business owners, and to protect the rights of workers.

The Fascists were a group of radical political reformers who wanted to create a nation in which all the people in the nation were not treated as individuals but instead as parts of a greater whole who were each expected to respect the absolute authority of the government and work toward the ultimate glory of the nation. It is important to note, however, that fascism (in other words, a fascist government) doesn't typically allow an individual to have any rights at all.

Benito Mussolini was the leader of the National Fascist Party and later the Prime Minister of Italy during the mid twentieth century. He is known for establishing the Fascist Party, helping the Fascist Party take control of Italy, and ultimately attempting to expand Italy's influence across Europe during World War II.

The Nazis, who were also known as the National Socialist German Workers' Party, were radical political reformers who wanted to create a nation in which the government was not only allowed to restrict the actions of its people without question, but a nation in which the government was actually expected to restrict the actions of its people (in other words, a totalitarian government). Adolf Hitler was the führer (a German term that literally means "leader") of the Nazi Party and later the führer of all Germany during the mid twentieth century. He is known for establishing the Nazi Party, helping the Nazi Party take control of Germany, and ultimately being responsible for the actions that Germany took during World War II (including the Holocaust). He is also known for his book, Mein Kampf, in which he discussed his belief that Germany's problems could be traced back to the Jewish population.

Lebensraum is a German term that literally means "living space" or "habitat." The term is typically used to refer to Adolf Hitler's belief that Germany needed to expand eastward to obtain more living space (in other words, more land). The concept of Lebensraum played an extremely important role in World War II because the Nazis ultimately entered the war to expand Germany and fulfill their perceived need for Lebensraum.

The Schutzstaffel, which is more commonly known as the SS, was a paramilitary force (in other words, a civilian militia) that the Nazis established in 1934 to "protect" Germany from the individuals the Nazis believed to be unfit or undesirable. The SS was ultimately responsible for most of the actions the Nazis took against the Jewish community during the Holocaust. Not only were they responsible for imprisoning Jewish individuals, but they were also responsible for operating the concentration camps. The Gestapo was a secret police force that the Nazis established in 1934 to hunt down and eliminate the enemies of the Nazi Party. This police force, which was actually a division of the SS, was originally designed to hunt down Adolf Hitler's political enemies and anyone who spoke out against the Nazis. The Gestapo was later used to locate and capture Jewish individuals who had been able to escape or avoid the concentration camps.

The Nuremburg Laws were a series of regulations that the Nazi Party passed in 1935 to promote the party's anti-Semitic (or anti-Jewish) agenda. These regulations identified the specific criteria that the Nazis planned to use to determine whether an individual was Jewish or not and established the basic rights that Jewish individuals were no longer allowed to exercise. The Nuremburg laws prevented Jewish individuals from marrying individuals who were not Jewish, from having intercourse outside of marriage with individuals who were not Jewish, from employing women who were not Jewish unless they were over a certain age, and from exercising other similar rights. Ghettos, as they relate to the Holocaust, were small, overcrowded, and poorly maintained communities that the Nazi Party forced Jewish citizens to live in during the late 1930s to the early 1940s.

Kristallnacht, which is also known as the Crystal Night (the English translation of the German term Kristallnacht) or the Night of the Broken Glass, refers to an event that occurred in Germany from November 9 to November 10, 1938, in which members of the Nazi Party attacked Jewish homes, cemeteries, stores, and synagogues throughout the country. The Nazis organized these riots because a German official named Ernst vom Rath was assassinated by a young Jewish man. Kristallnacht ultimately led to the imprisonment or death of over 30,000 Jewish individuals and over $4 million in damage.

The invasion of Poland in 1939 is often considered to be the official beginning of World War II. It is important to note, however, that the Axis powers (Germany, Italy, and Japan) were involved in several military actions immediately prior to the invasion of Poland. In fact, Japan, had sent forces to seize control of Manchuria in 1931 and then later sent troops to seize control of the rest of China in 1937. Japan was actually engaged in a series of battles with the Chinese throughout most of the 1930s. (These battles actually lasted until the end of World War II.) Italy, like Japan, attempted to expand its influence by sending forces into Ethiopia in 1935 and by later sending troops to seize control of Albania in 1939. Finally, Germany, who left the League of Nations in 1933 so that it could begin its massive expansion campaign, had sent forces to reclaim the Rhineland in 1936 and then later sent forces to claim Austria in 1938 and Czechoslovakia in 1939.

Isolationism refers to the political belief that a country shouldn't interfere in the affairs of other nations and that a country should avoid any activity that would involve the country in the activities of another nation whenever possible. The United States and the nations of Europe began to move away from isolationism after World War I, but many nations still had a strong desire to avoid a conflict. Appeasement refers to a political tactic in which a country seeks to avoid a conflict by simply allowing another nation to conduct whatever activities it wants. Both tactics were used by countries prior to World War II and allowed Hitler to operate uncontested until his attack on Poland in 1939.

The Anti-Comintern Pact was an agreement that Germany and Japan formed in 1937, which Italy later joined, to establish an alliance against the Soviet movement. This pact was designed to allow Germany, Italy, and Japan to discuss the best course of action against the Soviets if the Soviets attacked any of the nations that agreed to the pact. Notably, the Anti-Comintern Pact was not only used to form an alliance against the Soviets, but it was also later used to form the basis for the Axis powers of World War II. The German-Soviet Nonaggression Pact, which is also known as the Molotov-Ribbentrop Pact or the Hitler-Stalin Pact, was an agreement that Germany and the Union of Soviet Socialist Republics (U.S.S.R.) formed in 1939. This agreement stated that the U.S.S.R. would remain neutral if Germany was involved in a war with another nation, that Germany would remain neutral if the U.S.S.R. was involved in a war with another nation, and that Germany would give the U.S.S.R. part of Poland if Germany invaded Poland.

World War II

The German Army invaded Poland on September 1, 1939, to reclaim the land the Germans had lost in the Treaty of Versailles and to expand Germany's influence eastward. The Polish Army, which was already preparing itself to defend against a German attack, was positioned to defend a series of important factories and cities spread out along the German border. These factories and cities were vital to the Polish war effort, but they were located in positions that were difficult to defend. The Germans, as a result, used a tactic known as the blitzkrieg (a German term that literally means "lightning war") in which they concentrated their forces to push through the Polish forces as quickly as they could. This led the Polish Army to pull its forces back to regroup and hold off the German Army until the British and French forces (who had agreed to help Poland if Germany attacked) were able to mobilize. Germany, however, was ultimately able to seize Poland before the Polish Army could receive reinforcements from the British and the French.

The Luftwaffe (a German term that literally means "air weapon") was the name of the German Air Force during World War II. The Luftwaffe was a key component of the Nazi war machine because the Nazis regularly used the planes of the Luftwaffe to clear the way for their infantry and vehicles. The German Army invaded Belgium on May 10, 1940, to move toward France and continue Germany's expansion eastward. Belgium and its nearby allies (the Netherlands and Luxembourg) attempted to stop the Germans, but the Belgian Army was ultimately no match for the German Army. This allowed the German Army to move into France on June 5, 1940, after Germany seized control of Belgium, Luxembourg, and the Netherlands. The French Army, which was expecting an attack from Germany at the time, was spread out along a long line of defensive structures (artillery stations, ammunition dumps, observation posts, etc.) known as the Maginot Line. These defenses were designed to help the French Army hold the German Army at the German border and keep it away from the French cities until the rest of the French Army could mobilize. The German Army, however, used the same tactic that it used in the invasion of Poland (the blitzkrieg) and focused its infantry, tanks, and planes on specific areas across the French line. This allowed the German Army to ultimately defeat the French.

The Battle of Britain refers to a series of aerial assaults that occurred in Great Britain from the middle of August to the end of September 1940. The Germans, who had already taken control of Belgium, France, Luxembourg, the Netherlands, Poland, and several other countries by this time, wanted to invade Great Britain to eliminate the only major European power that still opposed them. (Russia had agreed to remain neutral, and Italy was allied with Germany.) Germany, however, realized that the only way to invade Great Britain was by air or sea and that there was no way the German Navy could compete with the British Navy. As a result, the Germans, decided to use the Luftwaffe (the German air force) to establish German air superiority (in other words, complete control of the skies) over Great Britain. The Germans initiated a series of fighter-escorted bomber attacks to destroy the major bases and cities of Great Britain, but the British Royal Air Force was able to prevent the Germans from controlling the skies. The Royal Air Force (RAF) was the name of the British Air Force during World War II. The RAF was one of the first forces to effectively use radar, and it regularly used radar to detect and intercept the Luftwaffe before it could attack British bases.

In direct violation of the German-Soviet Nonaggression Pact, which stated that Germany would not attack the U.S.S.R., the German Army invaded the Union of Soviet Socialist Republics on June 22, 1941. This attack was designed to allow the Germans to push through the Soviet forces quickly so that the Germans could capture the major cities and resources (ammunition, food, machinery, oil, etc.) the Soviets needed to supply their troops. The Soviets, however, were not willing to allow the Germans to seize their resources. They proceeded to move their resources or even destroy them, making it difficult for the Germans to acquire the resources they needed to continue their advance. the Germans were eventually forced to stop and wait for additional supplies. The Soviets, in response, used this time to gather reinforcements from Manchuria. They also used the terrain and harsh weather, which was common in the region, to their advantage so that they could mount a counteroffensive and push the German forces back. The Red Army, which was later known as the Soviet Army, was the name of the army that the Union of Soviet Socialist Republics controlled during World War II. The Red Army was not involved in the war until 1941, but it played an important role in weakening the German Army after the U.S.S.R. entered the war.

Franklin D. Roosevelt was the President of the United States from 1933 to 1945 and, as a result, was the Commander-in-Chief of the U.S. Armed Forces during World War II. Roosevelt played an important role in not only encouraging the U.S. to focus its attention on all the Axis powers rather than just Japan (after the Japanese attack on Pearl Harbor), but also in helping Winston Churchill and Joseph Stalin (a group sometimes known as the "Big Three") establish the strategies that the Allied forces used during the war.

Winston Churchill was the Prime Minister of Great Britain and the British Minister of Defense (a position that he established to coordinate the efforts of the British naval, air, and land forces) during World War II. Churchill played an important role in not only encouraging the Allied forces to continue the fight, but also in helping Franklin D. Roosevelt and Joseph Stalin design the battle plans that eventually allowed the Allies to win the war.

Erwin Rommel was a Field Marshal in the German Army (a rank equivalent to a five-star general in the U.S. Army) during World War II. He is primarily known for leading one of the fastest moving German divisions to invade France in 1940. (The division was actually known as the Ghost Division because it moved so quickly that it seemed to disappear and reappear somewhere else.) He also led the German forces in North Africa (known as the Afrika Korps) to continually defeat the British. The battles Rommel fought in the deserts of Africa and Egypt actually earned him the nickname that he is more commonly known by: "The Desert Fox." Bernard Montgomery was a Field Marshal in the British Army during World War II. He was able to ultimately defeat the German forces that "The Desert Fox" (Erwin Rommel) commanded (the Africa Korps) at the Battle of Alamein, a battle that occurred in Egypt between British and German forces.

The tide turned against Hitler once the United States entered the war. The harsh Russian winter halted the German advance into Russia short of Moscow in 1941. The Germans made further gains in the summer of 1942, but were decisively beaten at the battle of Stalingrad and were slowly pushed back out of Russia from then on. American and British troops landed in North Africa in 1942 and used that as a springboard to invade Italy in 1943. In 1944, the Americans and British opened yet another front with a massive invasion of northern France in the D-Day landings.

The D-Day Invasion, which is also known as the Invasion of Normandy or Operation Overlord, refers to an event that began in Normandy, France, on June 6, 1944. The Allied forces, who had already begun to push the Axis forces back by this point in the war, decided to mount a full-scale invasion by air and sea to liberate France from German control. This decision led Canada, Great Britain, and the United States to send nearly 25,000 troops by air to parachute into France and over 150,000 troops by sea to land on the shores of France. These troops met fierce resistance from the German forces stationed in the bunkers and on the cliffs near the shores of Normandy, but they managed to breach the German defenses and advance into France. This ultimately allowed the Allied forces to clear the way for more troops to arrive so that the Allies could liberate the major cities of France (including Paris) and eventually the rest of France as well. Nearly 10,000 Allied soldiers were killed or wounded in taking the beaches. Fighting numerically superior forces on multiple fronts, the Germans steadily lost ground and the Allies pushed into Germany from both East and West in 1945. Surrounded and with the war lost, Hitler commited suicide in his bunker in Berlin in April, 1945 and the remaining German forces surrendered shortly afterwards.

The Teheran Conference was a meeting of the leaders of the Allied forces (Winston Churchill, Franklin D. Roosevelt, and Joseph Stalin) that occurred in Teheran, Iran, in 1943. This meeting played an important role in the politics of World War II because the three leaders not only discussed the terms under which they would accept the surrender of their enemies (they decided that Japan and Germany would have to make an unconditional surrender), but they also discussed the fate of the land that the Soviets had captured during the war (primarily that Stalin desired to keep all of it). The Yalta Conference was a meeting of the leaders of the Allied forces that occurred just outside of Yalta, Crimea, in 1945. This meeting is significant because the Allied leaders agreed to restore the European nations that Germany had seized during the war, to divide Germany into four occupied zones, and to create the United Nations.

The Holocaust, which is also known as the Shoah or the Final Solution, refers to a series of events that occurred in Germany from November 9, 1938, to the end of World War II in which the Nazi Party attempted to kill every individual the Nazis considered to be undesirable throughout the world, including Jews, Poles, Soviets, homosexuals, disabled individuals, and others. These attempts ultimately led to the deaths of well over 10 million people.

Dachau, which is located in the southeastern section of Germany, was the location of the first concentration camp. The Dachau Concentration Camp was first used in 1933 to house, torture, and execute individuals who disagreed with the Nazis. It is important to note, however, that the camp's purpose changed in 1938 when it became the first Nazi camp to house, torture, enslave, and execute Jewish individuals. In fact, over 30,000 people died at this camp as the result of starvation or the result of a firing squad. Auschwitz, which is located in the southwestern section of Poland, was the largest concentration camp that the Nazis used. The Auschwitz Concentration Camp, which is also known as the Auschwitz-Birkenau Concentration Complex, was first used in 1942 to house, torture, enslave, and execute Jewish individuals. Over 1 million Jewish individuals were executed by the Nazis at Auschwitz (typically via the gas chamber) by the time the camp was liberated in 1945.

Cold War

The Cold War refers to the period immediately after World War II in which the Union of Soviet Socialist Republics (U.S.S.R.) and the United States performed several political, economic, and scientific actions to demonstrate their superiority and to ultimately prepare themselves for an American-Soviet War. The Cold War, which lasted until the fall of the U.S.S.R. in 1991, was not a war in the traditional military sense; instead, it was a series of ongoing political actions designed to improve the political and military position of the U.S.S.R. and the U.S. Notably, the Cold War was based on the American fear that the U.S.S.R. was planning to attack the U.S. and on the Soviet fear that the U.S. was planning to attack the U.S.S.R, but the two nations never actually attacked each other. Ultimately, the actions of the two nations were preparation for a war that never occurred.

The Soviet Bloc, which is also known as the Communist Bloc, were the nations throughout Europe that the Union of Soviet Socialist Republics (U.S.S.R.) assumed control of after World War II even though they were not officially part of the U.S.S.R. The nations within the Soviet Bloc included Albania, Bulgaria, Czechoslovakia (although Czechoslovakia was not forced to join the Soviet Bloc), East Germany, Hungary, Poland, Romania, and Yugoslavia. These countries were referred to as "satellites" because they weren't actually part of the U.S.S.R. but were instead in the surrounding area like a series of moons orbiting a planet. The nations of the Soviet Bloc were forced to redesign their governments to create communist systems that the Soviets could control. The term "iron curtain," which was first used by Winston Churchill, refers to the buffer zone that the Soviet Bloc, in effect, created between Eastern and Western Europe and the military defenses the Soviets established to protect that zone.

The Morgenthau Plan was a plan that the United States Secretary of the Treasury Henry Morgenthau created in 1944 to redesign Germany's economy so that it would be impossible for Germany to attack another nation. This plan was designed to not only eliminate Germany's army, but also to eliminate all its factories and machinery so that there would be no way for Germany to produce weapons. The Morgenthau Plan was never implemented, but the decision to create the plan angered the Soviets because they wanted to use Germany's resources to rebuild their own cities.

The Marshall Plan, which is also known as the European Recovery Program (ERP), was a plan that U.S. Secretary of State George C. Marshall announced in 1947 to address the economic problems the European nations faced after World War II. This plan was designed to provide the financial resources that the European nations needed to repair the damage caused by the war and to protect themselves from enemy nations like the U.S.S.R.

The Truman Doctrine was a policy that the President of the United States, Harry S Truman, established in 1947 to address the issue of whether the U.S. should intervene in the affairs of other nations. This policy basically stated that it was the duty of the United States to protect a free nation from any military force that endangered the ability of the people within that nation to remain free regardless of whether that threat came from within the nation or outside it.

The North Atlantic Treaty Organization (NATO) is an alliance that Belgium, Canada, Denmark, France, Great Britain, Iceland, Italy, Luxembourg, the Netherlands, Norway, Portugal, and the United States formed in 1949. This alliance, which still exists today, was originally designed to protect noncommunist nations if the Soviets decided to attack a noncommunist country and force it to establish a communist system. Severalother nations joined NATO after its formation (including Greece, Turkey, and West Germany), but NATO is now designed to protect its member nations from any outside threat.

The Berlin Blockade refers to an event that took place from June 20, 1948, to May 12, 1949, in which the U.S.S.R. attempted to prevent France, Great Britain, and the United States from sending supplies to Berlin. Berlin, which was divided into four zones that were each occupied by one of the four nations included in the agreement made at the Yalta Conference, was located in the section of Germany that the Soviets controlled. As a result, France, Great Britain, and the United States had to use some of the railroads and roads that the Soviets controlled to transport the supplies that the troops and the German people living within their respective zones needed. The Soviets, however, were unhappy that their former allies had decided to combine the three sections of Germany that they controlled into a new republic. Consequently, the Soviets began to stop the supplies entering or leaving Berlin. This ultimately led Great Britain and the United States to implement an air operation known as the Berlin airlift to drop supplies into Berlin.

The Korean War was a war that occurred in North and South Korea from June 25, 1950, to July 27, 1953. This war occurred because the Soviets established a communist government in North Korea after the Allied forces defeated the Japanese in World War II. (Korea was actually part of the Japanese Empire until the end of World War II.) At the same time, the United States established a democratic government in South Korea. North and South Korea, as a result, had two very different governments with opposing views. After the Soviets and the Americans left the areas of Korea that they had occupied, North Korea invaded South Korea to combine both nations into a unified communist state. In response, the United Nations authorized the United States to form a force to stop the invasion, which in turn caused the Soviets and the Chinese to offer their aid to North Korea. This war, which lasted three years, ultimately ended in a stalemate.

The Warsaw Pact was an alliance that Albania, Bulgaria, Czechoslovakia, East Germany, Hungary, Poland, Romania, and the U.S.S.R. formed in 1955. This alliance, which lasted until 1991, was originally designed to protect communist nations in the event that NATO or another noncommunist force decided to attack a communist state.

The Geneva Summit was a meeting that occurred in Geneva, Switzerland in 1955 in which the leaders of France, Great Britain, the United States, and the U.S.S.R. met to discuss various issues. This meeting was significant because it was the first time that the Soviets demonstrated any interest in negotiating with the Western world after World War II. It is important to note, however, that the summit ultimately failed to achieve any real change, and it merely created a sense that the Soviets were now willing to negotiate.

The Paris Summit was a meeting that was supposed to occur in Paris, France, in 1960 in which the leaders of France, Great Britain, the United States, and the U.S.S.R. were supposed to discuss various issues. The Soviets, however, refused to attend the summit after a Soviet surface-to-air missile (SAM) battery shot down a U.S. spy plane just outside of Degtyarsk, Russia.

The Berlin Wall refers to a wall that the Soviets constructed in Berlin in 1961 to separate East Germany from West Germany. Berlin, which was divided into four zones that were each occupied by one of the four nations included in the agreement made at the Yalta Conference, was located in the German Democratic Republic that the Soviets established in East Germany while they occupied it. (Both Germany and Berlin had originally been separated into four separate occupied zones, but all the forces outside Berlin had already been removed by this point.) The people of East Germany, as a result, began to use the city of Berlin to escape the Soviet-controlled state by fleeing from the Soviet zone of the city into one of the other occupied zones. (This exodus became known as "the brain drain" because it was primarily professionals leaving.) The Soviets then constructed the Berlin Wall to separate the Soviet-controlled zone of the city (East Berlin) from the other zones of the city (West Berlin).

The Bay of Pigs Invasion refers to an event that took place from April 17 to April 19, 1961, in which a group of Cuban exiles (in other words, individuals who had fled Cuba to seek political asylum or to simply escape Fidel Castro) attempted to remove Fidel Castro from power under the direction of the United States. Castro, who seized control of the Cuban government during the Cuban Revolution of 1959, began to move the Cuban economy toward a communist system shortly after he took power. The United States was not pleased at the rapid changes occurring in Cuba, so it began to organize and train a group of Cuban exiles for a Cuban invasion by sea. This group was specifically trained by the U.S. Central Intelligence Agency (CIA). However, the invasion was not as successful as the United States had hoped it would be, as the approximately 1,500-man invasion force was quickly captured by a Cuban force of over 200,000 militiamen.

The Cuban Missile Crisis refers to an event that occurred from October 22 to October 28, 1962, in which the United States threatened to take military action against Cuba and the U.S.S.R. unless the Soviets removed the missile platforms that they had already begun building in Cuba. After the Bay of Pigs Invasion, Fidel Castro pledged his support to the communist cause and asked the U.S.S.R. to help protect Cuba from future invasions by the U.S. or U.S.-supported forces. This led the U.S.S.R. to move weapons (guns, tanks, planes, and nuclear missiles) into Cuba to help Cuba build an armament that it could use to defend itself in case of another invasion. U.S. President John F. Kennedy, however, was not willing to allow the Soviets to establish a missile platform that could easily be used to fire a nuclear missile at the United States, and he declared that any nuclear missile fired from Cuba would be considered an attack by the U.S.S.R. on the United States. Ultimately, the U.S.S.R. decided to remove the missiles.

Mohandas Karamchand Gandhi, who is more commonly known as Mahatma Ghandi, was a lawyer and a politician who lived in India during the late nineteenth to mid twentieth centuries. He is primarily known for encouraging the people of India to obtain their independence from Great Britain without the use of force. Notably, Ghandi also played an important role in establishing the foundation for the civil rights movement, as he regularly demonstrated his support for religious tolerance as well as equality for all races and genders.

Ho Chi Minh was a political reformer who lived in Vietnam during the late nineteenth to late twentieth centuries. He is primarily known for leading a liberation army called the Viet Minh to free North Vietnam from French control. It is important to note, however, that he also helped establish the communist government that took shape in North Vietnam. In fact, he later became the President of North Vietnam.

The Algerian War, which is also known as the French-Algerian War or the War for Algerian Independence, was a war that occurred in Algeria from 1954 to 1962 in which Algeria eventually obtained its independence from France. This war occurred because France had originally taken control of Algeria in 1830, but the French government did very little to address the problems of the Algerian people. In fact, French settlers were regularly allowed to seize the land of the native Algerians, and the conditions under which the average Algerian was forced to live began to decline rapidly as more and more Algerians were forced into smaller areas. After over a hundred years of French occupation, the Algerians eventually formed a liberation army known as the National Liberation Front, which began to attack key targets throughout Algeria. These attacks eventually weakened the French Army to the point that the President of France Charles de Gaulle had no choice but to recognize Algeria's independence.

The Brezhnev Doctrine was a policy that the General Secretary of the Communist Party of the Soviet Union Leonid Brezhnev established in 1968 to address the issue of whether the U.S.S.R. should intervene in the affairs of other nations. This policy basically stated that it was the duty of the U.S.S.R. to protect a communist nation from any force, military or otherwise, that might interfere with the ability of a nation to remain a communist state.

Mikhail Gorbachev was the General Secretary of the Communist Party of the Soviet Union and later the President of the Soviet Union during the late 1980s to the early 1990s. He is known primarily for encouraging the reforms that ultimately brought about the fall of the Soviet Union in 1991 through the policies he established. The two most important reform policies that Gorbachev established were known as the glasnost policy and the perestroika policy. Glasnost, which is a Russian term that literally means "publicity" or "openness," refers to a series of reforms Gorbachev implemented to eliminate some of the censorship and communication barriers that had prevented the people of the Soviet Union from receiving and discussing new ideas and information. Perestroika, which is a Russian term that literally means "rebuilding" or "restructuring," refers to a series of reforms Gorbachev implemented to decrease the amount of control that the government of the Soviet Union had over the economy and the actions of the local Soviet governments.

Globalization

The European Community, which is also known as the Common Market, was a trade organization that Belgium, France, West Germany, Italy, Luxembourg, and the Netherlands formed in 1958 to create and maintain a joint market that would be favorable to all the nations involved. This organization, which is now part of the European Union, was originally designed to eliminate some of the trade barriers that existed by reducing the tariffs businesses were required to pay to move goods from one member nation to another and by creating a uniform code of trade regulations. This eventually led to the formation of the European Union (EU) which is an international organization that the European Community formed in 1993 to expand the European Community to include over twenty other countries (including Austria, Belgium, Ireland, Poland, Spain, the United Kingdom, and several other nations). This new, larger form of the European Community was designed not only to maintain a joint economic market, but also to create a coalition to improve the environment, infrastructure, and other components of each of its member nations.

The 9/11 Attacks were a series of terrorist attacks that occurred in the United States on September 11, 2001. A group of radical Islamists known as al-Qaeda wanted the United States to stay out of the Middle East and to refrain from any activity that would interfere with the affairs of the Muslim world. Consequently, al-Qaeda sent a group of nineteen extremists into the United States to learn how to fly a plane. These individuals then used their newfound knowledge to hijack four planes and crash two of the planes into the World Trade Center, one plane into the Pentagon, and one plane into a field in Pennsylvania. There is strong evidence to suggest that the last plane's intended target was the White House or the U.S. Capitol, but the passengers of the plane managed to stop the attack. Nearly 3,000 civilians were killed in the attacks. In response, the United States and the United Kingdom invaded Afghanistan to find the leaders of the terrorist organization responsible for the 9/11 Attacks, and the nations of the world began to look for new ways to stop the spread of terrorism.

Practice Test

1. Sociologist Gerhard Lenski classifies societies into five types. Of these five, which has the least hierarchical social structure?
    a. An advanced agricultural society
    b. A simple agricultural society
    c. A hunter-gatherer society
    d. An industrial society
    e. A special society

2. The Neolithic Revolution enabled all except which of the following to develop?
    a. Economies based on trade
    b. Diversification of labor
    c. Architecture and art
    d. Written languages
    e. Lower death rates

3. Which of the following occurred the most recently in time?
    a. The use of writing in China
    b. The building of wood huts
    c. The use of copper tools
    d. The casting of bronze
    e. The casting of steel

4. Chronologically, which of the following occurred first?
    a. The last of the pyramids were built in Egypt.
    b. Andean societies domesticated animals.
    c. The Shang Dynasty in China saw its ending.
    d. The Minoan civilization in Crete came to a halt.
    e. The Harrapa civilization in India was ended.

5. What is the earliest recorded accomplishment of people in South America?
    a. The development of agricultural villages
    b. The domestication of mountain animals
    c. The cultivation of the staple manioc root
    d. The cultivation of vegetables
    e. The development of fishing for food

6. During the entirety of which of these time periods did the East Roman Empire include Egypt?
    a. 1-100 A.D.
    b. 100-200 A.D.
    c. 250-350 A.D.
    d. 400-500 A.D.
    e. 1-500 A.D.

7. Of the following, which is not associated with polytheism?
    a. Ancient Greek
    b. Ancient Roman
    c. Judaism
    d. Buddhism
    e. Hinduism

8. Which of these religions is not found in China?
   a. Confucianism
   b. Taoism
   c. Buddhism
   d. Judaism
   e. These all are

9. Which of the following did the Huns not do between the 4th and 5th centuries A.D.?
   a. Drove the Goths from the Black Sea west into regions of the Roman Empire
   b. Broke up the Gupta Empire and disrupted Indian civilization with invasions
   c. Moved from ruling northern China to conquering southern China as well
   d. Settled in Hungary and made raids throughout Europe under Attila
   e. Defeated by Roman and Visigoth forces, still invaded Italy the next year

10. Of the following statements, which is true regarding the transmission of Buddhism via the Silk Road?
   a. The Silk Road in the 4th century A.D. was the first instance of Buddhism coming to China.
   b. Conversion of the Chinese to Buddhism by Central Asian missionaries lasted several centuries.
   c. The earliest known translation of Buddhist scriptures into Chinese was in the 3rd century A.D.
   d. Many Chinese monks made pilgrimages to north India seeking Buddhism from 200 to 300 CE.
   e. None of these statements is correct regarding transmission of Buddhism via the Silk Road.

11. Which Great Khan of the Mongol Empire reigned the earliest chronologically?
   a. Kublai Khan
   b. Genghis Khan
   c. Ögedei Khan
   d. Güyük Khan
   e. Möngke Khan

12. According to historians, which of the following was not a result of the Mongol Empire?
   a. China's population was reduced by half during the 50 years of Mongol rule.
   b. Up to half of Hungary's population was killed by the Mongol invasion.
   c. Approximately 30 million people died during the Mongol Empire years.
   d. About half Russia's people were thought to die in the Mongol invasion.
   e. According to historians, all of these were results of the Mongol empire.

13. After Muhammad's death, four sequential caliphs in a row led the Islamic State before a series of caliphates were established. Who was not one of these first caliphs?
   a. Abu Muslim
   b. Abu Bakr
   c. Uthman
   d. Umar
   e. Ali

14. The Golden Age of Islam, in which Arabic arts, sciences, industry and commerce all flourished, took place during the reign of:
   a. The Umayyads
   b. The Al-Rashidun
   c. The Fatimids
   d. The Abassids
   e. The Mamluks

15. Which of the following statements is true according to the Islamic faith and its holy text?
    a. Islam began with Muslim Prophet Muhammad's birth in Arabia in 570 A.D.
    b. Islam began with Muhammad's first dictations of the Qur'an in the 600s.
    c. Islam began not with Muhammad or the Qur'an but with Adam and Eve.
    d. Islam is properly considered to be only a religion, not a social institution.
    e. Islam is correctly considered to be only a social institution, not a religion.

16. Of the following countries, which did not have cities located along the Silk Roads?
    a. Italy
    b. France
    c. Russia
    d. Pakistan
    e. Afghanistan

17. Which of these Mesoamerican cultures is known for having the only fully developed written language system of the Americas during the Pre-Columbian period?
    a. The Incas
    b. The Mayas
    c. The Aztecs
    d. The Olmecs
    e. The Toltecs

18. What statement is a consequence of the fall of the Roman Empire in the early Middle Ages?
    a. Long-distance trade fell apart as connections were lost without Rome's unification.
    b. Intellectual and cultural developments were damaged by loss of geographical unity.
    c. The Catholic Church was the main source of cultural unity after the Roman collapse.
    d. Europe was divided into a number of decentralized regional kingdoms at that time.
    e. All of these statements are consequences of the fall of the Roman Empire.

19. In the late Middle Ages, nation-states such as the Kingdom of England and the Kingdom of France rose to power. Which of the following kingdoms on the Iberian Peninsula was not one of these emerging nation-states?
    a. Aragon
    b. Castile
    c. Gibraltar
    d. Navarre
    e. Portugal

20. Which of the following is not true about the Black Death pandemic in Europe?
    a. It lasted roughly from 1346 through 1350 and then stopped, never to return.
    b. It consisted of outbreaks of bubonic plague.
    c. It killed between 30% and 60% of Europe's population.
    d. It was exacerbated by the superstitious mass killing of cats.
    e. It was fully 150 years before the population of Europe was able to recover.

21. What event below did not occur between 1450 and 1460?
    a. Johannes Gutenberg made the first movable-type printing press in Mainz, Germany.
    b. The Ottoman Empire under the Sultan Mehmed II conquered the Byzantine Empire.
    c. Ferdinand II and Isabella ruled most of Iberia once Ferdinand II was King of Aragon.
    d. The Wars of the Roses between Lancasters and Yorks began at St. Albans in England.
    e. At the Siege of Belgrade, Hungarians delayed Ottoman advances to Europe for 70 years.

22. Which of these were not introduced to these locations via the Columbian Exchange?
    a. Horses to Native Americans of North America's Great Plains
    b. Manioc (cassava), corn, peanuts, and sweet potatoes to Africa and Asia
    c. Potatoes to Ireland where they became the main staple crop for centuries
    d. Coffee and sugar, becoming main crops on South American plantations
    e. All of them were first introduced to these locations via the Columbian Exchange.

23. Which of the following were not originally brought to these locations by explorers/colonizers during the Columbian Exchange?
    a. Florida oranges
    b. Italian tomatoes
    c. Mexican burros
    d. American turkeys
    e. Hawaiian pineapples

24. What is not an accurate statement about the Songhai Empire?
    a. In the 16th and 17th centuries it was one of the biggest African empires in history.
    b. The Songhai Empire established its main power base on the Congo River's shore.
    c. A small Songhai state had continued in the capital city of Gao since the 11th century.
    d. The Songhai state had obtained its freedom from the Mali Empire by 1340.
    e. The Songhai people established the Dendi Empire after the Songhai Empire fell.

25. Which of the following is false regarding the Mughal Empire?
    a. The Mughal Empire ended in 1805 when England dispersed the Mughal army.
    b. At its peak, c. 1700, the Mughal Empire ruled most of the Indian subcontinent.
    c. The Mughals were responsible for the dissemination of Persian culture to India.
    d. The Mughal emperors descended from Tamerlane and their religion was Islam.
    e. At its height the Mughal Empire extended from Bengal as far north as Kashmir.

26. Of these American colonies, which first legalized slavery in the 17th century?
    a. Virginia
    b. Maryland
    c. Connecticut
    d. Massachusetts
    e. New York and New Jersey

27. Among the following infectious diseases, which were thought to have been brought to the Old World from the New World?
    a. Scarlet fever and yellow fever
    b. Chicken pox and measles
    c. Syphilis and tuberculosis
    d. Cholera and malaria
    e. Leprosy and typhus

28. The Scientific Revolution is often viewed as having begun with the publication of two books in 1543. Which of these choices correctly names both of these works?
    a. De Revolutionibus orbium coelestium by Nicolaus Copernicus and De humani corporis fabrica by Andreas Vesalius
    b. Philosophia Naturalis Principia Mathematica by Sir Isaac Newton and De Revolutionibus orbium coelestium by Nicolaus Copernicus
    c. Philosophia Naturalis Principia Mathematica by Sir Isaac Newton and Sidereus Nuncius by Galileo Galilei
    d. Mysterium cosmographicum by Johannes Kepler and De Revolutionibus orbium coelestium by Nicolaus Copernicus
    e. De humani corporis fabrica by Andreas Vesalius and Sidereus Nuncius by Galileo Galilei

29. Which is false about Freemasonry during the Enlightenment?
    a. Freemasonry was the most popular of all Enlightenment groups.
    b. Freemasonic lodges were found only in western Europe during the Enlightenment.
    c. Freemasons in France were estimated at 100,000 by the Revolution's start in 1789.
    d. The French Revolution's "Liberté, egalité, fraternité" was associated with the guilds.
    e. The 18th century European Freemasons embraced the Enlightenment and referred to it.

30. Which of these religions was not established between 1450 and 1750?
    a. Indian Sikhism
    b. Haitian Voodoo
    c. Protestantism
    d. These all were
    e. Mormonism

31. During the Industrial Revolution, workers trained in new technologies who then changed jobs could carry their knowledge to other companies. Of the following, which was not a manner in which information about new inventions and processes was spread?
    a. By people conducting study tours to learn new information
    b. By informal societies discussing and publishing knowledge
    c. By publishing encyclopedias containing technical methods
    d. By publishing periodical journals on techniques and patents
    e. Information about innovations was shared by in all the above ways.

32. Which of these is false about from the effects of industrialization and urbanization in the 18th to early 20th centuries?
    a. The death rate of young children increased due to urban health problems in this period.
    b. Rates of payment for industrial workers increased significantly from 1813 to 1913.
    c. Britain's population doubled from 1801 to 1851 and almost doubled again by 1901.
    d. Europe's population doubled in the 18th century and again in the 19th.
    e. Tuberculosis infected 70 to 90% of urban populations in Europe and North America.

33. In America, which was the first labor union to organize workers in a variety of occupations?
    a. The Knights of Labor
    b. The National Labor Union
    c. The Mechanics' Union Trade Association
    d. The Grand National Consolidated Trade Union
    e. The Congress of Industrial Organizations (CIO)

34. Which of these lists national revolutions in correct chronological order?
    a. Xinhai Revolution; American Revolution; French Revolution; Mexican Revolution; Haitian Revolution
    b. American Revolution; French Revolution; Haitian Revolution; Mexican Revolution; Xinhai Revolution
    c. Mexican Revolution; Haitian Revolution; Xinhai Revolution; American Revolution; French Revolution
    d. Haitian Revolution; American Revolution; Xinhai Revolution; Mexican Revolution; French Revolution
    e. French Revolution; Mexican Revolution; Haitian Revolution; American Revolution; Xinhai Revolution

35. Of the following countries, which did not gain independence from a larger empire in the 19th century?
    a. Greece
    b. Hungary
    c. Belgium
    d. Poland
    e. Serbia

36. During the rise of nationalism in Europe, which of the following events took place in the 20th century?
    a. Bulgarian independence
    b. Greek independence
    c. Italian unification
    d. German unification
    e. Hungarian autonomy

37. Which of these did not occur in the late 19th to early 20th centuries?
    a. The separation of church and state became official in France.
    b. England kept its isolationist policy toward continental Europe.
    c. England fell behind Germany and the United States in industrial production.
    d. Russia's Pan-Slavic policy caused conflicts between empires.
    e. All of these statements are true.

38. During the world era of New Imperialism from 1870 to1914, Russia and Japan were the two major Eastern powers. Western powers included the United States of America. Which of the following was not one of the other four primary Western powers?
    a. Italy
    b. France
    c. Spain
    d. England
    e. Germany

39. What was not a development in Japanese art and architecture during the Meiji Period?
    a. The Tokyo Train Station and the National Diet Building showed Western influence.
    b. The first Manga, or comic books and print cartoons, were drawn in the Meiji Period.
    c. The Technological Art School opened using Italian teachers for Western techniques.
    d. Two categories of painting styles, Yōga and Nihonga, developed.
    e. The developments in arts and architecture of the Meiji Period included all of these.

40. Of these 19th century Western artists who incorporated Japanese influences in their work, which one actually used Japanese woodblock cutting techniques?
    a. Henri de Toulouse-Lautrec
    b. Vincent van Gogh
    c. Mary Cassatt
    d. Paul Gauguin
    e. James McNeill Whistler

41. Which of these composers reflected Japanese influence in 19th century works?
    a. French composer Camille Saint-Saëns
    b. English partners Gilbert and Sullivan
    c. Italian composer Giacomo Puccini
    d. None of these showed this influence
    e. All three of these showed an influence

42. Which is an accurate statement about the Holocaust?
    a. Laws were passed to move Jews to camps after World War II had begun.
    b. The total number of Holocaust victims was 6 million.
    c. All of the Nazi camps were designed to exterminate victims via gas chambers.
    d. Freemasons and Jehovah's Witnesses were among the Nazis' victims.
    e. All of these statements are accurate regarding the Holocaust.

43. Which of the following is true regarding the League of Nations and the United Nations?
    a. The League of Nations accomplished the mission stated in its covenant.
    b. The League of Nations and the United Nations coexisted between World Wars I and II.
    c. The United Nations succeeded the League of Nations, inheriting some agencies.
    d. The United States proposed the League of Nations, signed its covenant, and joined it.
    e. These statements are all true about the League of Nations and United Nations.

44. Which of the following statements is false about events following the end of World War II?
    a. The Cold War, including the nuclear arms race, lasted for 44 years.
    b. The spread of Fascism in Italy, Spain and Germany was facilitated by the Depression.
    c. Though the United States bombed Japan to end the war, the two later became allies.
    d. Most European holdings in Asia and Africa were decolonized and freed.
    e. None of these statements is correct about events following World War II.

45. The Bretton Woods Conference met to facilitate post-WW II international trade. Which of the following were established to enable and oversee the freeing and globalizing of commerce?
    a. All of the following facilitated and oversaw free international commerce.
    b. The International Bank for Reconstruction and Development (the World Bank)
    c. The International Monetary Fund
    d. The General Agreement on Tariffs and Trade (GATT)
    e. The World Trade Organization (WTO)

46. Which of these proxy wars did not occur during the Cold War period?
    a. Lebanese Civil War
    b. Second Congo War
    c. Greek Civil War
    d. Vietnam War
    e. Korean War

47. Of the following events in first-wave feminism, which took place in America?
    a. Some female voting rights via the Representation of the People Act
    b. Increased female employment via the Sex Disqualification Act
    c. Margaret Fuller's publication Women in the Nineteenth Century
    d. Equalized grounds for divorce via the Matrimonial Causes Act
    e. Virginia Woolf published famous essay, A Room of One's Own

48. Critics of economic globalization cite the 1992 United Nations Development Program Report, which showed the 1989 distribution of world GDP (Gross Domestic Product). According to this report, which of the following is true?
    a. In 1989, the richest .02% of the population controlled 93. 2% of the world's income.
    b. In 1989 the poorest 20% of the population controlled 19. 9% of the world's income.
    c. In 1989, the richest 10% of the population controlled 74. 5% of the world's income.
    d. In 1989 the poorest 20% of the population controlled 2% of the world's income.
    e. In 1989, the richest 25% of the population controlled 82. 1% of the world's income.

49. Of the following 20th century artists, who is best known for incorporating commercial images?
    a. Salvador Dalí
    b. Mark Rothko
    c. Vassily Kandinsky
    d. Roy Lichtenstein
    e. Andy Warhol

50. Which of these environmental groups is not based in the United States?
    a. Greenpeace
    b. The Wilderness Society
    c. The Nature Conservancy
    d. The Environmental Defense Fund
    e. The National Resources Defense Council

Answers and Explanations

1. C: A hunter-gatherer society (c) would have the least hierarchical social structure. Hunter-gatherer bands are nomadic. Mobile societies do not store extra food and all members possess minimal property due to their geographical movements. Some hunter-gatherer groups find sufficient food to store and settle permanently into simple agricultural societies (b) that may eventually develop into advanced agricultural societies (a). Mobile hunter-gatherer societies that do not settle in one area, do not store extra food, and own few things cannot support such roles as leaders, bureaucrats, or artisans. Therefore the roles of members are likely to be more egalitarian. When a community settles in one place and plants, cultivates, and stores food rather than foraging for it, the society becomes more organized and roles with different social levels develop. Industrial societies (d) typically are more hierarchical than agricultural ones. A special society (e), according to Lenski, is one with a specialized means of subsistence, such as fishing, by which that society gets the majority of its food and income.

2. E: The Neolithic Revolution did not enable lower death rates (e) to develop. Compared to nomadic societies, settled communities had higher birth rates, but these balanced out higher death rates. Deaths were likely due to disease which spread more easily in settled communities than traveling ones. Initially this may have resulted from the domestication of animals to whose diseases humans had not yet developed antibodies, and from crowded conditions without adequate sanitation. Staying in one place allowed the storage of food and the ownership of personal property. This in turn resulted in economies based on trade (a). Nomads tended to have children at least four years apart because only one child could be carried at a time when traveling. But settlement allowed societies to produce children more quickly, resulting in greater population densities. This made it possible to diversify labor (b), as well as to create permanent, artfully created buildings and goods (c). Settlement and the development of tools enabled Neolithic peoples to create written symbols for their spoken languages (d), which became both easier to achieve and more necessary in increasingly complex, organized, sedentary societies.

3. A: The most recent development among these choices was written language in China (a), during the Shang Dynasty around 1300 B.C. * The Shang culture also developed the casting of bronze (d), an alloy of copper and (usually) tin, around the same time. The first steel (e) discovered was an alloy cast from iron and (usually) carbon, dating to c. 1400 B.C., or a century before bronze. People of the Paleolithic era built wooden huts (b) for temporary lodging as far back as 380,000 B.C. While the use of naturally occurring copper is believed to go back as early as 800,000 B.C., the use of copper tools (c) had become common in Mesopotamia by 2000 B.C. *(Note: The Egyptian and Sumerian civilizations are believed to have started writing in pictograms even earlier than in China—as early as 3200 to 3300 B.C. The Sumerian pictograms developed into cuneiform writing and the Egyptian pictograms developed into hieroglyphics.)

4. B: The earliest event was (b) the domestication of llamas, alpacas, and vicuñas by early South American civilizations in the Andes Mountains highlands around 3500 B.C. The last of the pyramids had been built in Egypt (a) by around 1814 B.C. The period of the Harrapan or Indus Valley civilization ended (e) in India roughly between 1800 and 1700 B.C. This civilization had its earliest beginnings around 6000 B.C., and reached its maturity around 2300 B.C. While there are theories, it is not known what caused the demise of these people. The Minoan civilization on Crete, estimated to have existed since around 3100 B.C., at the beginning of the Bronze Age, was ended (d) around 1420 B.C., when Crete was conquered by the Mycenaeans. The Shang Dynasty in China ended (c) around 1045 B.C., when the Shang Emperor was conquered by the Zhou.

5. D: The earliest recorded accomplishment of people in South America was (d) the cultivation of vegetables. There is evidence that as early as 6500 B.C., people in the highlands of the Amazon Basin were planting beans, potatoes, and chilies as food sources. Agricultural villages had developed (a) in this area by 2000 B.C. South Americans began to domesticate animals (b) such as llamas and alpacas by around 3500 B.C., for meat, wool, and as pack animals to transport goods, as they were sure-footed in the mountains and could carry weight. The plant known variously as cassava, yuca (Spanish), or manioc root (c), which is still a staple today, was cultivated by around 2000 B.C. During this same time period—around 2000 B.C. —agrarian villages developed (a) in this region, while along the coast, fishing also became common (e) as another source of food.

6. D: Egypt was included in the East Roman or Byzantine Empire between 400 and 500 A.D. (d). (The East Roman Empire was also known in the 300s as the Byzantine Empire. According to some historians, this began in 395 A.D., when the Empire was divided into Eastern and Western parts.) A Roman province was established in Egypt between 1 and 100 A.D. (a), but Egypt was not part of the Roman Empire then. A Christian community was begun in Alexandria, Egypt between 100 and 200 A.D. (b), but Egypt was not yet a part of the East Roman Empire. Between 250 and 350 A.D. (c), St. Antonius founded the Monastic movement and built its first monastery, which still exists in the desert between the Nile River and the Red Sea. The period between 1 and 500 A.D. (e) encompasses the time periods of the other four choices; since (d) is the only correct time period, (e) is incorrect.

7. C: Judaism (c) is the only one of these religions that does not contain multiple deities. Judaism is monotheistic. Ancient Greeks (a) as well as ancient Romans (b) believed in a pantheon of gods. Buddhism (d) does not teach the worship of one or more gods, but believes in the existence of many supernatural beings or devas. Gautama Buddha also resisted being deified by others. He disagreed with the idea of a god as Creator. Nonetheless, Buddhism is associated with polytheism for its acceptance of multiple deities. Hinduism (e) exists in monotheistic, polytheistic, and pantheistic forms; therefore it is associated with polytheism by definition as it has some polytheistic sects.

8. E: These all are (e) religions found in China today. In addition to the majority of Chinese citizens who practice Confucianism (a), Taoism (b), and Buddhism (c)*, there are minorities in China practicing Judaism (d), Hinduism, Christianity (there are millions of Christians in China, but these millions are still a minority of the country's huge population), and Islam, as well as several other sects. *(Note: many Chinese people consider themselves to be both Buddhist and Taoist. Also, note that while majority and minority religions can be broadly defined, specific numbers or percentages of each religion in China are currently impossible to determine accurately due to the country's population of more than a billion people and a lack of reliable statistics.)

9. C: The Huns did not conquer southern China (c) between the 4th and 5th centuries A.D. They did rule northern China during this time, dividing it up into 16 kingdoms. However, the south of China remained under the control of the Six Dynasties while northern and southern China were separated. The Huns originally lived on the steppes of central Asia and were driven west by the central Asian Mongol war confederation known as the Juan-juan. The Huns did attack the area between the Baltic and Black Seas, driving the Gothic inhabitants there west to Roman regions (a). Huns also invaded India, destroying the Gupta Empire (which had ruled the Golden Age of Hindu civilization) and disrupting Indian civilization (b) for a long time. After driving the Goths west, the Huns established their base in Hungary; under Attila they began sacking and plundering cities throughout Europe (d), going through Gaul (modern-day France) until, at the Battle of the Catalaunian Fields in Gaul in 451 A.D., Attila's forces were defeated by the armies of the Roman Flavius Aetius and the Visigoth Theodoric I. Despite this defeat, the following year Attila still managed to invade Italy (e). He died a year after that, and his Hunnish Empire was soon destroyed by a German revolt.

10. B: The only true statement is that (b) the conversion of Chinese people to Buddhism by Central Asian missionaries did go on for several hundred years. While Buddhism arrived in China via the Silk Road in the 4th century, this was not the first instance of it (a). According to recent research, Buddhism had already been long established in China, and was popular before being suppressed by the Emperor in the 3rd century B.C. The earliest known translation of Buddhist scriptures into Chinese was in 148 A.D., or the 2nd century, not the 3rd (c). Many Chinese monks did begin to make pilgrimages to northern India to learn about Buddhism, but this occurred most notably in the 4th century A.D., or the 300s, not the 200s (d) or the 3rd century. As (b) is true, answer (e), none of these, is incorrect.

11. B: Genghis Khan (b) ruled the Mongol Empire from 1206 to 1227 (A.D.). Ögedei Khan (c) ruled from 1229 to 1241, succeeding to the throne after his father Genghis Khan's death. Ögedei Khan greatly expanded the Mongol Empire. Güyük Khan (d), son of Ögedei Khan, ruled from 1246 to 1248. He took the throne only after an impasse lasting over four years, during which the widow Torogene became Empress. She recruited Mongol aristocracy to support her son Güyük as the next ruler. She won over the majority, but Batu Khan, leader of the Golden Horde held out, claiming illness and inability to withstand the Mongolian climate. The lack of leadership until Batu finally agreed to send his brothers and generals to the kurultai (political/military council) caused subsequent events leading to disruption of the unity of the Mongol regimes. Güyük Khan made a number of reforms but died after two years. He suffered from ill health and alcoholism. It is not known if his death during a march west from Karakorum was from natural causes alone or if he was also poisoned. His widow Oghul Ghaimish tried to take over the empire but was not very successful. After several more years of disorder, Möngke Khan (e) succeeded to the throne and ruled from 1251 to 1259. Kublai Khan (a), grandson of Genghis Khan and founder of the Yuan Dynasty, was first appointed by his brother Möngke Khan to rule Persia and the Mongol part of China. Following Möngke Khan's death, he reigned from 1260 to 1294. Under Kublai Khan, the Mongols eventually became the first non-Chinese people to rule all of China after the Song Dynasty surrendered to the Yuan Dynasty in 1276.

12. E: According to historians, all of these were results of the Mongol Empire (e). The census had reports from Chinese dynasties of around 120 million people before the Mongol Invasion. After this invasion was complete in 1279, the census of 1300 reported roughly 60 million people—half their previous numbers (a). Hungary also sustained the loss of about half its people in the Mongol Invasion (b). It is estimated that a total of 30 million people died during the years of the Mongol Empire (c). Some historians estimate that of Russia's total population, about half were also killed in the Mongol Invasion (d). Therefore all of these statements are correct. In addition, the population of the European part of Russia alone lost half a million people in the Mongol Invasion.

13. A: Abu Muslim (a) was not one of the first four caliphs in the early Caliphate period (630 to 660). Abu Muslim was an Abassid revolutionary who instigated resistance to the Umayyad Empire, allowing the Abassid dynasty to take control in 750. The first four caliphs were Abu Bakr [As-Siddiq] (b); Umar (d); Uthman (c); and Ali (e), the last of the four. These first four caliphs were known as the "Al-Rashidun," meaning the "rightly-guided" caliphs in Sunni Islam.

14. D: The Golden Age of Islam took place during the reign of the Abassids (d), from 750 to around 960. Islamic civilization flourished during the rule of this empire. The Abbasids had begun their reign by revolting against the previous regime of the Umayyads (a), who ruled from 660 to 750. The Al-Rashidun (b), meaning the four first "rightly-guided" caliphs, ruled before the Umayyad empire, from 630 to 660. The Fatimids (c) began their dynasty in 909 after conquering the Ikhshidid Dynasty. The Fatimids conquered Egypt and then extended their empire to include Syria, Lebanon, Palestine, Yemen, the Hejaz region of what is now Saudi Arabia, Tunisia, North Africa, Africa's Red Sea coast, Sicily, and South Italy, with Egypt being the center of the empire. The Mamluks (e) were Turks who established a new dynasty in 1250 after conquering Saladin's Ayyubid Dynasty, which had not been in power long. The Mamluks united Egypt and Syria from 1250 to 1517, which was the longest time period of unity between the Abassid Empire and the Ottoman Empire.

15. C: According to the Islamic faith and its holy text, Islam began not with Muhammad or the Qur'an but with Adam and Eve (c), who are considered by Muslims to have been the first prophets of God. Therefore Islam did not begin with Muhammad's birth in 570 (a), or with his first revelations of the Qur'an in the 600s (b), which he dictated over a period of 23 years, beginning in 610 when he was 40 years old, to 632 when he died. Islam is not only a religion (d) or only a social institution (e) but both a religion and a social institution.

16. B: France (b) did not have cities located along the Silk Roads, the enormous transcontinental network of trade routes that connected Asia with the Middle East, North and East Africa, and Europe. They began as overland routes and eventually included sea routes as well. Italy (a) had both Venice and Rome as cities along the maritime Silk Road. Russia (c) had the cities of Astrakhan and Derbent along the maritime Silk Road. Pakistan (d) had cities along both the continental and seafaring Silk Roads, including Peshawar, Debal, Taxila, and Multan, while Afghanistan (e) had the cities of Herat, Bamyan, and Kabul. In addition, there were cities along the Silk Roads in China, Japan, Korea, Sri Lanka, Indonesia, Vietnam and other Southeast Asian countries; India, Oman, Yemen, Aden, Muscat, Egypt, Syria, Iran, Iraq, Turkey, Turkmenistan, Tajikistan, Uzbekistan, and Kazakhstan. The Silk Roads were destabilized by the breakdown of the Mongol Empire, following which political powers became separated culturally and economically. Silk was no longer transported along these routes by around 1400. In recent times the Silk Roads have been revived and many times correspond closely to the ancient paths taken.

17. B: The Maya (b) had the only fully developed written language in the Americas during the Pre-Columbian period. The Maya existed from 2000 B.C. until the Spanish came in the 16th century. The Inca (a) civilization began with a tribe in Cuzco around 1200 A.D., formed the largest empire in Pre-Columbian America, and also ended in the 16th century with Spanish conquests. The Aztec (c) civilization began in Mexico and dominated large parts of Mesoamerica in the 14th, 15th, and 16th centuries. During the Spanish conquests, Hernán Cortés vanquished the city of Tenochtitlan (the site of modern Mexico City), and defeated the Aztec Triple Alliance; this became known as "The Fall of the Aztec Empire." The Olmec (d) civilization resided in what are now Tabasco and Veracruz in south-central Mexico much earlier, from around 1400 to 400 B.C. They are especially remembered for their beautiful artwork, in particular their sculptures of colossal heads. Some historians believe the Toltec (e) existed as a real civilization, while others believe they were a myth invented by the Aztecs or some other group. If they were real, they are thought to have had an empire between the 10th and 12th centuries A.D. The Central Mexican influences seen to have entered Mayan culture during this time period are also often attributed to the Toltecs.

18. E: All of these statements are consequences of the fall of the Roman Empire in the early Middle Ages (e). Without the unifying effects of Roman rule, it was no longer safe to transport goods, and trade connections with other countries were lost (a), resulting in the abrupt cessation of manufactured goods for export. The previous Roman intellectual and cultural accomplishments deteriorated as different states or countries could no longer communicate and interact as before (b). Building and infrastructure maintenance were severely reduced when Roman society collapsed. In the absence of a centralized Roman government, the Catholic Church became the main unifier (c) in Europe. Unlike political governments of the time, the Church was able to maintain a centralized administration via its organization of bishops, whose literacy helped the Church to preserve the arts of reading and writing even as these were widely lost elsewhere during the Middle Ages. In Europe, the vacuum left by the demise of the Roman Empire's centralized government was filled by a number of decentralized regional kingdoms (d) run by local tribes. These included the Angles and the Saxons in Britain; the Franks and the Burgundians in Gaul (now France) and western Germany; the Visigoths (western Goths) in Hispania (now Spain), the Ostrogoths (eastern Goths) in Italy; and the Vandals in northern Africa.

19. C: Gibraltar (c) was the Iberian Peninsula territory that was not a nation-state rising to power during the late Middle Ages. Aragon (a), Castile (b), Navarre (d), and Portugal (e) were all kingdoms of the Iberian Peninsula that became strong nation-states at that time. Gibraltar was run by the Vandals for a short time following the fall of the Roman Empire, after which it became part of the Visigoths' kingdom of Hispania until it was conquered by Muslims in 711. That conquest ushered in the Moorish period of Gibraltar, which lasted 750 years. Re-conquest in 1462 by the Duke of Medina Sidonia began Gibraltar's Spanish period. During the War of the Spanish Succession, England claimed Gibraltar in 1704. It was ceded in perpetuity to the United Kingdom by Spain in the Treaty of Utrecht, signed in 1713. In 2002 the people of Gibraltar rejected joint British-Spanish sovereignty by a nearly 99% majority, choosing British sovereignty. The British government agreed with the Constitution of Gibraltar that it would never give its sovereignty to any other country without its citizens' "freely and democratically expressed wishes." Gibraltar today is still an autonomous British overseas territory.

20. A: The Black Death (a) did not vanish after 1350. Historians believe it began in India or North Africa and migrated to Central Asia, reached the Crimea by 1346 and peaking in Europe between 1348 and 1350. Plague outbreaks continued in Europe until the 19th century. Based upon accounts by writers and artists of the times, the Black Death was probably the bubonic plague (b) Between 30% and 60% of Europe's population succumbed to the plague (c). In the years prior to the infestation, superstitions associating cats with witchcraft caused mass exterminations of cats (d), leaving rats free to multiply. The proliferation of rats provided more hosts for plague-bearing fleas, which contributed to the pandemic proportions of the disease's spread. The Black Death had severe negative impacts on the societies, religions, and economies of medieval Europe, deeply altering European history. It took fully 150 years before the European population recovered (e) from the Black Death.

21. C:Ferdinand II and Isabella ruled most of the Iberian Peninsula once Ferdinand became King of Aragon in 1479 (c), not the 1450s. Ferdinand also ruled Sicily, Naples, Valencia, Sardinia, Navarre, Barcelona, and Castile. Gutenberg built the first printing press with movable type in Mainz, Germany (a) and in 1450. The Sultan Mehmed II led the Ottoman Empire to capture Constantinople, the capital of the Byzantine Empire (b) in 1453. The Ottoman Empire then replaced the Byzantine Empire. In England, the series of civil battles for the throne between the Lancasters and the Yorks, known as the Wars of the Roses, began at the First Battle of St. Albans (d), north of London, in 1455. The Yorks won this battle. At the Siege of Belgrade, John Hunyadi led the Hungarian army to defeat the army of Ottoman Turkish Sultan Mehmed II in 1456. This defeat delayed the advances of the Ottoman Turks to Catholic Europe for 70 years (e).

22. E: All of these animals and plants first came into these countries via the Columbian Exchange (e). European explorers and settlers first brought horses to the New World, transforming the lives of many Native Americans (a) who became nomadic once they could ride horses and hunt bison. Portuguese traders in the 1500s brought manioc, corn, and peanuts from North and South America to West Africa, replacing locally indigenous plants as staple crops for that part of the continent. Spanish colonization introduced corn and sweet potatoes to Southeast Asia (b), increasing population growth there. Potatoes, only grown in South America before the year 1000, were introduced to Ireland during the years of the Columbian Exchange, becoming that country's most important staple crop for hundreds of years (c). The extent of Ireland's dependence on potatoes became evident during the Great Potato Famine of the 1840s when blighted potato crops resulted in a million deaths and the exodus of a million more. Coffee from Africa and sugar cane from Asia were introduced to South America by the Columbian Exchange explorers and quickly became the major crops grown on large plantations in South America (d).

23. D: The Columbian Exchange introduced plants and animals between the Old and New Worlds. However, the Americas did not get turkeys (d) from Europe; they are native to the Americas. Florida, now so famous for its oranges (a), originally got them from Southeast Asia through the Columbian Exchange. Tomatoes originally came to Italy (b), from South America via Spanish conquerors of the Columbian Exchange period. Mexico, (c), originally was introduced to burros from Africa when the conquistadores brought them to the Americas, around the same time as they brought horses. Hawaii, with which the pineapple is now virtually synonymous (e), originally got the trees bearing this fruit from South America when Europeans of the Columbian Exchange introduced them.

24. B: The Songhai Empire did not establish its main power base on the shore of the Congo River (b), but rather on the shore of the Niger River at the river's bend, in what are now Niger and Burkina Faso. The Songhai Empire was one of the biggest African empires in history between the early 16th and late 17th centuries (a). Before the empire's expansion, it had begun as a small state of Songhai people who had lived in the Songhai capital city of Gao since the 11th century (c). Formerly subjects of the Mali Empire, the Songhai achieved freedom from the declining empire around 1340 (d). After the Songhai Empire fell to invasions by the Moroccan Saadi Dynasty in 1591, the Songhai people founded the Dendi Empire (e) in 1592.

25. A: The Mughal Empire did not end in 1805 (a), though the British did disband the previously formidable Mughal army in that year. The Mughal Empire's formal end came in 1858 after the British deposition of the last Mughal Emperor in 1857, following the Indian Rebellion of 1857. The Mughal Empire ruled most of the Indian subcontinent (or the majority of South Asia) at its peak, circa 1700 (b). The Mughals were responsible for bringing Persian culture, including literature, to India (c) during their imperial reign, providing the basis for the Indo-Persian culture. The Mughal Emperors were Muslim and were descended from the 14th century conqueror Timur, known in English as Tamerlane (d), who founded the Timurids, a dynasty of Sunni Muslims from Central Asia whose culture had predominantly Persian influences. At its height the Mughal Empire extended as far north as Kashmir and as far south as the Kaveri Basin in southern India. Its eastern border was Bengal; it extended west as far as Balochistan, which now includes parts of southeast Iran, West Pakistan, and southwest Afghanistan.

26. D: Massachusetts (d) was the first of the American colonies to legalize slavery in 1642. Connecticut (c) was the second, making slavery legal in 1650. Virginia (a) followed, giving slavery official statutory recognition in 1661. In 1662, Virginia passed another statute that children born to slave mothers would "inherit" their slave status. The colonies of New York and New Jersey (e) both legalized the practice of slavery in 1664.

27. C: Syphilis and tuberculosis (c) were brought to the Old World from the New World via the Columbian Exchange. Although it is believed that some strains of syphilis existed in Europe before Columbus and others visited the New World, the first widespread outbreak in Europe is recorded in 1494, two years after Columbus' first voyage to the Americas. Subsequently, it spread throughout Europe in an epidemic; most historians believe a new deadlier form of the disease spread across Europe following Columbus' American trips. Though tuberculosis existed in the Old World, Native American Indian tribes in the New World were also known to have endemic strains of this disease, which were additionally transmitted by explorers to the Old World (c). Scarlet fever and yellow fever (a), chicken pox and measles (b), cholera and malaria (d), and leprosy and typhus (e) were all infectious diseases unknown in the Americas prior to the Columbian colonization voyages, by which Europeans introduced them there. Because the Native Americans had no previous exposure to these diseases, they had never developed antibodies to resist them. This resulted in massive depopulation as their lack of immunity made the diseases much more virulent to them than to their European carriers.

28. A: The two works both published in 1543 and credited with beginning the Scientific Revolution are (a): De Revolutionibus orbium coelestium, or On the Revolutions of the Heavenly Spheres, by Nicolaus Copernicus, and De humani corporis fabrica, or On the Fabric of the Human Body, by Andreas Vesalius. Copernicus' work challenged the long-accepted Ptolemaic idea of a geocentric universe with the astronomer's theory of a heliocentric "universe," since proven correct with respect to our earth's solar system. Vesalius dissected cadavers and made anatomical drawings based on an actual human body, greatly advancing medical knowledge. Sir Isaac Newton published the first edition of his Philosophia Naturalis Principia Mathematica (b), (c), or Mathematical Principles of Natural Philosophy, which presented Newton's Laws of Motion and of Universal Gravitation among other principles, in 1687. This work is considered one of the most important in the history of science. Sidereus Nuncius, or The Starry Messenger (c), (e), published by Galileo Galilei in 1610, was the first scientific work based on observations made through a telescope, including descriptions of the four moons of Jupiter, the quality of the moon's surface, and of stars which could be seen with the telescope but not the naked eye. Mysterium cosmographicum (d), variously called The Cosmographic Mystery, The Cosmic Mystery, The Secret of the World, Sacred History of the Cosmos, was published by Johannes Kepler in 1596 and outlined his theory of cosmology, based on Copernicus' system. None of these important works were published in 1543 or credited with beginning the movement except for the two by Copernicus and Vesalius in choice (a). Choices (b), (d), and (e) each contain one correct and one incorrect answer, while choice (c) contains two incorrect answers.

29. B: Freemasonic lodges were not found only in Western Europe during the Enlightenment (b). They existed throughout Europe. Freemasonry, is demonstrably the most popular of all Enlightenment groups (a); by 1789, there were 100,000 Freemasons in France alone (c). The slogan used during the French Revolution of "Liberty, equality, brotherhood" expressed the same social concepts as the guilds (d) of the time, including the Freemasons. The guilds embraced ideals similar to those of the Enlightenment and the American and French Revolutionary Wars. 18th century Europe's Freemasons made direct references to the Enlightenment and their espousal of it (e). French Freemasonic lodges' initiation rites included the phrase, "As the means to be enlightened I search for the enlightened." And British Freemasonic lodges believed it was their duty "…to enlighten the unenlightened."

30. E: Mormonism (e) was founded by Joseph Smith in the 1840s. He first published the Book of Mormon in 1830. Indian Sikhism (a) was founded in Punjab during the 15th century. Its founder, Nanak, is said in Sikh tradition to have disappeared temporarily at the age of 30, and some time thereafter announced, "There is no Hindu, there is no Muslim." It is said that after this revelation he began to teach the principles which became known as Sikhism. Haitian Voodoo (b) evolved in the 16th century when the slave trade brought African practitioners of Voodoo to the New World. Slave owners forced African slaves to practice Roman Catholicism, but the uprooted Africans tried to preserve their traditional beliefs. As a result, Haitian voodoo incorporates elements of both African Voodoo and Euro-American Christianity. Protestantism (c) grew as a reaction against Roman Catholicism when Martin Luther posted his 95 Theses on the door of the Wittenberg Cathedral in 1517, beginning the Protestant Reformation. Since Mormonism (e) was not newly created between 1450 and 1750, answer (d), these all were, is incorrect.

31. E: The innovations of the Industrial Revolution were shared by all of these (e) means. It was common for people in Europe and America, including industrialists, manufacturers, technicians, and civil servants to make study tours (a) and people making these tours often kept travel journals. Informal societies (b) interested in philosophy and science, such as the Lunar Society of Birmingham in England, would meet to discuss scientific advances and their applications to industry. Also in England, the Royal Society of Arts in London published an illustrated book on new inventions, as well as papers in its annual volume of transactions. During this period, a number of encyclopedias were published that contained large amounts of valuable information on new science and technology with illustrations. Some examples are the Lexicon Technicum (1704) by John Harris; the Cyclopaedia (1802 to 1819) by Dr. Abraham Rees; Description des Arts et

Métiers (1761 to 1788) by the Académie Royale des Sciences in Paris; and Denis Diderot's Encyclopédie (1751 to 1772). In the 1790s, periodical journals (d) were being published about new technologies, often also including notifications of the newest patents granted to inventions and methods. French engineers who made study tours to England to observe new mining procedures there published accounts of these tours in periodicals such as the Annales des Mines (Annals of the Mines).

32. A: The death rate of young children did not increase due to urban health problems in this period (a). While rapid urbanization did cause new health problems in cities due to crowding, poor sanitation, and factory work conditions, death rates among children decreased dramatically as a result of the advances of the Industrial Revolution. For example, children below the age of 5 years in London died at a rate of 74. 5% from 1730 to1749, but their mortality rate was less than half of that—31. 8%—from 1810 to1829. Pay rates rose significantly from the 19th to 20th century (b) as new industries created more work. Britain's population more than doubled from 1801 to1851, going from 8. 3 million to 16. 8 million, and almost doubled again by 1901, to 30. 5 million (c). The population of Europe doubled in the 18th century, from 100 million to nearly 200 million, and again in the 19th century to roughly 400 million (d). between 70% and 90% of the urban populations in Europe and North America had contracted tuberculosis (e) by the late 1800s. Roughly 40% of urban workers died from TB in the late 19th century.

33. C: The first American labor union to recruit members who worked at different trades was (c) the Mechanics' Union Trade Association, formed in 1827. A strike by carpenters in Philadelphia served as the impetus for organization of this union, which realized that regardless of specific trade, all types of labor shared common problems better addressed by unified group efforts. Early labor unions also called for social reforms and political actions to achieve them. After the Mechanics' Union in 1827, the Grand National Consolidated Trade Union (d) was organized in 1834. Its life was cut short by the economic Panic of 1837. The National Labor Union (b), founded in 1866, was a national craft union composed of workers in a variety of crafts. Though this union also did not last long, it established a precedent for future unions. After the NLU deteriorated, the Knights of Labor (a), founded in 1869, became the chief national trade union in America. The CIO (e) was proposed by John L. Lewis in 1932 and organized industrial unions in 1935. The CIO merged with the AFL (American Federation of Labor) in 1955 to form the AFL-CIO.

34. B: Answer (b) lists these revolutions in their correct chronological order. The American Revolution was from 1775 to1783. The French Revolution was from 1789 to 1799. The Haitian Revolution was from 1791 to 1804. The Mexican Revolution began in 1910 and is generally thought to have ended around 1920. (Over time it devolved from a revolt into a multilateral civil war. A Mexican Constitution was produced in 1917 but was not effectively enforced until 1934.) The Xinhai Revolution in China, also known as the Chinese Revolution (though there were other revolutions in China) was from 1911 to 1912.

35. D: Poland (d) did not gain independence in the 19th century. Polish revolts against Russian control from 1830 to 1831, in 1846, 1848, and from 1863 to 1865 were all defeated. Greece (a) declared its independence from the Ottoman Empire in 1821 and achieved this goal in 1829 after an eight-year war. Hungary (b) was granted autonomy in 1867 by the Habsburg Empire. Belgium (c) became independent from the Netherlands in 1831. Serbia (e) was granted independence in 1878, along with Romania and Montenegro, by the Congress of Berlin.

36. A: Bulgarian independence (a) was the only event listed to take place in the 20th century. Bulgaria became independent in 1908. Greece gained independence (b) from the Ottoman Empire in 1829. Italy was unified (c) between 1859 and 1861. Germany was unified (d) between 1866 and 1871. Hungary was granted autonomy (e) in 1867.

37. B: England (b) did not keep its isolationist policy toward continental Europe in the late 19th to early 20th centuries. England had held this policy for almost 100 years, but ended its isolationism by forming the Entente Cordiale with France in 1904. France made the separation of church and state official (a) in 1900. While England maintained its enormous British Empire during this period, it did fall behind Germany and the United States in industrial production rates (c). During the 19th century, the Slavic Orthodox peoples in Eastern Europe revolted several times against the declining Ottoman Empire, creating Slavic Orthodox nations. Russia supported these nations in a policy known as Pan-Slavism. This policy caused conflicts between the Ottoman Empire and the Austro-Hungarian Empire (d). Because (b) is not true, answer (e), all of these were true, is incorrect.

38. C: Spain (c) was not considered one of the major Western powers during the New Imperialism era. During the "Scramble for Africa," Spain occupied a small portion of Morocco and what is now the Western Sahara; otherwise, Spain did not dominate the world in colonization as the other Western powers did. These powers were the nations of Italy (a), France (b), England (d), and Germany (e).

39. E: Meiji Period developments in the arts and architecture included all of these (e). After Emperor Meiji's ascent to the throne ended the 265-year reign of the feudal Tokugawa Shogunate, he began the Meiji Restoration in 1868. Meiji directed a nationwide program of modernization, requiring Japan to follow the example of industrialized nations. His plan succeeded in greatly modernizing Japan. The influence of Western art in the early 20th century can be seen in such architectural works as the Tokyo Train Station and the National Diet Building (a). Influenced by political cartoons from England and France, artists drew the first Manga, Japanese comics or cartoons, during the Meiji Period (b). In 1867 the Technological Art School opened, employing instructors from Italy to teach Japanese students Western techniques (c) in technical arts. A movement headed by Okakura Kakuzo and Ernest Fenolloso, an American, encouraged artists to preserve Japanese traditions and artistic techniques while creating art that appealed to contemporary tastes. This resulted in the development of two categories of painting styles: Yōga, a Westernized style of painting; and Nihonga, a Japanese style of contemporary painting. These two styles continue to be used and are still identified this way today (d). The Meiji Period ended in 1912 with the death of the Emperor Meiji after a reign of 45 years.

40. D: The Western artist who used Japanese techniques to make woodcuts like those by Japanese artists was (d) Paul Gauguin. His fellow Frenchman Toulouse-Lautrec (a) created popular posters that demonstrated Japanese influence. The great Dutch post-Impressionist painter Vincent van Gogh (b) painted a number of canvases that echoed Japanese style. The American Impressionist painter Mary Cassatt (c) created a series of color etchings inspired by Japanese woodcuts she saw at an exhibition in Paris. James McNeill Whistler (e), the American artist who moved to London as a young adult and is best known for his portrait Whistler's Mother, is credited with introducing Japanese art to England as he collected a lot of Japanese artwork while in Paris. He painted a Chinese princess, showing his interest in Asian art, as well as portraits of his mistress with Asian dress and backgrounds. Except for Gauguin, these artists all painted in oils or watercolors, and used printmaking techniques most popular at the time in the West, such as lithography and etching. Other 19th century Western artists who demonstrated Japanese influences included: Edgar Degas, Claude Monet, Pierre-Auguste Renoir, Camille Pissarro, Pierre Bonnard, Gustav Klimt, Edvard Munch, Alphonse Mucha, and the architects Frank Lloyd Wright, Charles Rennie Mackintosh, and Stanford White.

41. E: All three of these showed Japanese influence (e). Saint-Saëns (a) wrote a one-act opera in 1871, setting to music a libretto by French writer Louis Gallet based on a story captured in a Japanese woodblock print. The operetta-writing duo of Gilbert and Sullivan (b) created the popular comic opera The Mikado in 1885 on a Japanese topic, and included a version of a Japanese song ("Ton-yare Bushi") in it. Giacomo Puccini (c) wrote the great tragic opera Madama Butterfly in 1904, about a Japanese courtesan betrayed by her English military lover, and included the same Japanese song in it that Gilbert and Sullivan had used earlier. Since (e), all three of these, is correct, answer (d), none of these, is incorrect.

42. D: Freemasons and Jehovah's Witnesses (d) were killed by the Nazis during the Holocaust, as were Romani (gypsies), ethnic Poles, Soviet prisoners of war, people with disabilities, and homosexuals. Laws allowing the removal of Jews to camps (a) were passed years before World War II began. The total number of victims was far higher than six million (b); this was the number of Jews alone who were killed. In total it is estimated that between 11 million and 17 million people died. Not all Nazi camps were designed for extermination in gas chambers (c). Some camps were work camps. Though many died in work camps due to starvation, disease, being worked to death, and horrific medical "experiments", the camps for forced labor were differentiated from the camps designated for immediate extermination. The death camps existed not to extract forced labor but solely to kill their victims in gas chambers or via mass shootings, as in the infamous Babi Yar massacre. Since none of these statements is accurate except (d), answer (e), all of these statements are accurate, is incorrect.

43. C: The United Nations succeeded the League of Nations, inheriting some of its agencies (c) and continuing their functions. The League of Nations did not accomplish its covenantal purpose (a); to prevent war. The League of Nations was formed pursuant to the Treaty of Versailles (1919 to 1920) after World War I. However, the outbreak of World War II proved that the League of Nations had failed its mission. The League of Nations and the United Nations did not coexist between the two World Wars (b), although they did overlap at another point in time. The League of Nations was officially dissolved in April of 1946, but its headquarters at the Palace of Peace had been vacant for almost six years after the end of WW II. The United Nations was formed in 1945. While it is true that the United States proposed the formation of an organization with the same mission, and that President Wilson signed the covenant, the United States did not join the League of Nations. Since only (c) is true, answer (e), these statements are all true, is incorrect.

44. B: Fascism (b) did spread in Italy, Spain, and Germany, facilitated by the Great Depression of the 1930s, prior to WW II. Post-World War I angst as well as the Depression fostered the rise of Fascism, which came to a head in the Second World War. The Cold War followed WW II, lasting from the mid 1940s until 1991, and included the nuclear arms race (a). Although the United States ended WW II by bombing Hiroshima and Nagasaki in Japan, these two countries later became allies (c). The recent modernization and industrialization of Japan gave it a strong economy, which helped motivate both nations to become allies rather than enemies. Most of the European powers' colonies were decolonized after WW II and gained freedom (d). Since answers (a), (c), and (d) are correct, answer (e), none of these statements is correct, is a wrong answer.

45. A: These were all intended to facilitate and oversee free international commerce (a). The Bretton Woods Conference, the popular name for what was formally called the United Nations Monetary and Financial Conference, met in 1944 to plan for the future post-World War II globalization of trade. The World Bank (b) was one of the institutions founded to oversee efforts to promote free trade among the nations of the world. The International Monetary Fund (c) was another. A series of agreements was negotiated under the aegis of GATT (d) that would eliminate restrictions to free trade. The WTO (e) was founded based on the GATT and implemented a number of initiatives toward this end, such as international recognition of patents, removal of tariffs, creation of free trade zones, increased consistency of intellectual property laws across nations, reduction or elimination of capital controls, reduction of transport costs, and creation of subsidies for multinational corporations.

46. B: So-called proxy wars are those fought outside the countries waging them. The Second Congo War (b) did not occur during the Cold War years (1945 to 1991). The Second Congo War took place from 1998 to 2003, after the Cold War had ended. The Lebanese Civil War (a) took place from 1975 to 1990. The Greek Civil War (c) began right after World War II ended and the Cold War began; it lasted from 1946 to 1949. The Vietnam War (d) was fought from 1959 to 1975, and is considered a proxy war because the Soviet Union supported the North Vietnamese and Viet Minh with training, supplies, and planning, but did not directly fight there as the US did. The Korean War (e) was waged from 1950 to 1953, and is considered a proxy war because the United States led the United Nations forces and the People's Republic of China supported the Communists. Proxy wars also took place in Afghanistan, Latin America, Angola, and the Middle East, and were common during the Cold War because the Cold War's two super-powers, the United States and USSR, avoided direct conflict for fear of a nuclear war.

47. C: The sole event under question that took place in America was (c): Margaret Fuller's Women in the Nineteenth Century appeared. Fuller, an American journalist, editor, and feminist, originally published this piece as an article in The Dial, entitling "The Great Lawsuit. Man versus Men. Woman versus Women" in 1843. She expanded on it and published the expanded piece as a book entitled Women in the Nineteenth Century in 1845. The Representation of the People Act, which permitted female property owners aged 30+ to vote (a), was passed in 1918 in England. The Sex Disqualification Act, allowing women to be employed in the professions and in Civil Service jobs (b) and eliminating marriage as a requirement to working outside the home, was passed in 1919 in England, as was the 1923 Matrimonial Causes Act, giving females the right to the same grounds for divorce as males had (d). Author Virginia Woolf's A Room of One's Own (e), appeared in England in 1929. In it she wrote, "…a woman must have money and a room of her own if she is to write fiction."

48. D: The only statistic that is true is (d): The 1992 UN Development Program Report found that in 1989, the poorest 20% of the population controlled only 0.2% of the world's income. This report showed that in 1989, the richest 20% of the world's population controlled 82.7% of world income; the second 20% controlled 11.7%; the third 20% controlled 2.3%; and the fourth 20% controlled 2.4% while the poorest controlled 0.2%. Therefore answers (a), (b), (c) and (e) all quote false figures and are incorrect.

49. E: Andy Warhol (e) is best known for creating works of art centered on such commercial images as a Campbell's soup can. Probably the most famous member of the Pop Art movement, Warhol was also known for his ideas that Pop Art was not just an artistic style but was, or could be, a lifestyle, and for innovating techniques such as using serigraphs (silk screens), assistants, and mass production to create artworks, downplaying the role of the artist in both importance and personalization. Salvador Dalí (a) was a key figure in the earlier Surrealist movement. The influence of Freudian psychoanalytic theory is seen in his works, which use imagery associated with dreams and the unconscious mind. Mark Rothko (b) was an Abstract Expressionist working away from representation. Early Abstract Expressionists were influenced by Vassily Kandinsky (c) when he made a transition from painting recognizable figures to painting completely abstract works earlier in the 20th century. Roy Lichtenstein (d) was a member of the Pop Art movement along with Andy Warhol. He also incorporated images from pop culture into his works. However, he did not focus on image repetitions as Warhol did; Lichtenstein is best known for creating works that look like comic book art, vastly magnified to show individual tiny dots of ink used in printing comics. Lichtenstein used his art as a gentle parody of popular culture, while Warhol depersonalize his works and did not invest it with humor or satire as many other Pop artists did.

50. A: Greenpeace (a) is not based in the United States. Its headquarters is in the Netherlands, and it has offices in more than 40 other countries. Greenpeace was founded in 1971 in Vancouver, British Columbia in Canada and now has close to three million supporters. The Wilderness Society (b), the Nature Conservancy (c), the Environmental Defense Fund (d), and the National Resources Defense Council (e) are all based in the United States. The Wilderness Society was founded in 1935 and has more than 300,000 supporters and members. The Nature Conservancy was founded in the US in 1951 and now has a presence in over 30 other countries, with more than a million members. With a half million members, the Environmental Defense Fund is based in New York. It has extended offices throughout the US and sends policy experts and scientists all over the world. The National Resources Defense Council (e) founded in 1970, is based in New York City with offices in Washington, D. C., San Francisco, Los Angeles, and Beijing. In America alone the NRDC now has 1. 3 million members and online activists, and employs a staff of more than 300 scientists, lawyers, and other specialists.

Made in the USA
San Bernardino, CA
23 May 2016